# Ringed in Steel

# Ringed in Steel

## Armored Cavalry, Vietnam 1967–68

*Michael D. Mahler*

PRESIDIO

This edition printed 1998

Copyright © 1986 by Presidio Press

Published by Presidio Press
505 B San Marin Drive, Suite 300
Novato, CA 94945-1340

**Library of Congress Cataloging-in-Publication Data**

Mahler, Michael D., 1936–
  Ringed in steel.
  1. Vietnamese Conflict, 1961–1975—Personal narratives,
American. 2. Vietnamese Conflict, 1961–1975—Tank warfare. 3.
Mahler, Michael d., 1936–   . I. Title.
DS559.5.M34  1986  959.704'38  86-8169
ISBN 0-89141-264-6 (hardcover)
ISBN 0-89141-674-9 (paperback)


Printed in the United States of America

*This book is dedicated to my brother professional soldiers who learned their trade in the years of peace that followed the Korean conflict and who took their qualifying exams in Vietnam in the years between 1965 and 1973. Few gained personal glory during the testing, and some failed their exams. Most of those who failed died. Even though most performed their assigned duties in a very professional manner, they came home to be labeled as killers and to bear the guilt by association of My Lai.*

*As a group, they had both failures and successes, but the general public learned most about the failures. In an era that talked grandly of involvement, they were truly involved. During the years when loyalty to self became the highest calling, they remained true to older values. They heeded the call to bear burdens long after it had become far more fashionable to do your own thing. They simply did what had to be done at the time and left the debating to others.*

*I wish that they were all alive today!*

Say neither, in their way,
"It is a deadly magic and accursed,"
Nor "It is blest," but only "It is here."

*John Brown's Body,*
Book Eight, p. 385

# Contents

# Preface

This book is my personal account of one tour of duty in Vietnam with combat elements of the U.S. Army. My perspective is that of a regular army officer—a major of armor, serving in two different infantry divisions in two different capacities. The events recounted in the pages that follow took place between August 1967 and August 1968 in the brigade headquarters of a division located just north of Saigon and in the cavalry squadron of another division that was located all over. I provide these facts at the outset because each rank, combat arm, support service, and technical service has its own story of its own particular tour. Service in Vietnam was very compartmentalized, with each compartment forming a part of the overall mosaic. There are literally thousands of variations on the theme, most untold, that should be woven together to give a true picture of what the media and the protestors and the groups with a cause distorted almost beyond recognition. The goal of this book is to make a beginning at redressing that imbalance.

One thing further: the Vietnamese people do not figure largely in my account because they did not figure largely in my tour. They were merely a background to the action. That fact has been hard for the stay-at-home wizards to accept in the literature on Vietnam—as if that absence somehow proved for them our alleged contempt for the Vietnamese. But the fact is that the Vietnamese people were as irrelevant to an account of American combat in Vietnam as the French inhabitants were to the Battle of Saint-Lo or the Belgians to the Battle of the Bulge or the American farmers to Jackson's Valley Campaign during our Civil War. Search the literature on those events and you will search in vain for lengthy accounts of the inhabitants of the land that served as the settings. They are reflected only in an occasional human-interest vignette. The reason is simple: once the fury of war is released, the main focus is on combatants and the combat. The civilian population—be it cause, beneficiary, or victim—is irrelevant to the course of the combat. So it has always been in war, and so it was in Vietnam for the majority of American combat units.

# I

# Getting There—Phuoc Vinh

Going to Vietnam was different for everyone who went, just as the war we each saw was different from the war that others saw. For me, going to Vietnam was as organized as the nine-year preamble in what has come to be called the pre-Vietnam Army. I had been commissioned and had attended the usual initial officer schools: the basic armor officer course, where I learned about tanks, radios, maintenance, and tactics; the basic Army aviator course, where I learned after three months that I was not cut out to fly (or, rather, to land); and the basic airborne course, where I learned that I could jump out of an airplane despite a fear of heights. I then joined my first platoon, an armored cavalry platoon in an armored cavalry regiment at Fort Knox, Kentucky. The regiment was to deploy to Germany in six months for duty along the interzonal border between East and West Germany, and we trained up for that mission—only to have the deployment cancelled. The following year, by then happily married and with some eleven months' experience in training platoons and basic trainees, I finally went to Germany as an individual replacement to join a tank battalion in an armored division. There, on a two-battalion *kaserne* (post) in a very small town in rural southern Germany, I served as a tank platoon leader, the scout platoon leader, a tank company commander, and, eventually, as an assistant operations officer on the battalion staff. In the course of that three-year progression, I saw a lot of Germany from behind the windshield of a jeep, spent a lot of nights in damp German forests, and learned a lot about my trade that has served me ever since—and which turned out to be all the professional preparation I would need for Vietnam.

I came back from Germany after three years with a new daughter and an assignment to attend an Army school for rising captains. During the nine-month course, I was promoted to captain then spent the next three years teaching English at the U.S. Military Academy at West Point while Vietnam changed from a place to go only if you needed to improve your record to a place to which we all were going.

With the location of my next assignment as firm as if the orders had been issued already, I started preparing to go to my war during my second year of teaching. I attended all the evening lectures that were being given to the cadets to keep them informed as our involvement increased to the point that it was a foregone conclusion as to where most of them would be going too. As my third year of teaching drew to a close, I was promoted to major. By that spring my wife and I had lost enough friends to understand that I was not going on a year-long training exercise; even so, we never discussed the potential dangers. I was going to Vietnam because I was a professional Army officer who had been trained for more than nine years to be a leader in combat and it was now time for me to do what I had been trained for. Beyond that, I wondered only about what it would really be like and how I would perform. After nine years in the Army, I thought that those were the only two unknowns. I had listened to the growing arguments on our involvement in Vietnam, but I had drawn no conclusions and had no strong convictions. I knew that I could be disabled or killed, but I didn't really think about those eventualities. My major concession to the possibility was to make out a will and write final letters to my wife and two daughters.

My transition from suburban America to Vietnam was going to take about forty hours: it would start at my house, and it would end as I walked from the plane to the huge, open shed that served as the passenger terminal in the sweltering humidity of Bien Hoa, South Vietnam. As we descended from our altitude, Vietnam appeared to be soft and green and lush, with narrow white roads and clusters of shacks emerging as we came closer to the ground. Then my eye was caught by a large red scar in the green. The new, ugly, functional lines that mark a temporary U.S. military installation anywhere in the world were unmistakable: neat rows of long low buildings; freshly turned earth, where the Army engineers were working at their eternal digging and grading; and large lined-off plots filled with regular rows of bulky crates. This was Bien Hoa Air Base, close to Saigon, and it looked like any other large, semipermanent troop-training areas that I had been in such as Grafenwoehr in Germany or Fort Drum in New York.

The one ominous sign to my inexperienced eye as we came in to land was the column of thick, black smoke that drifted up from the perimeter of the base. I was sure that there must have been a recent mortar attack and that the base was still smoldering from the hits. There had to be some urgent significance to that smoke. To my chagrin I found out that the smoke represented the routine of Vietnam rather than the dramatic. The smoke was caused by the daily burning off of the "honey pots!" Because of the porous character of the earth, the typical Army field latrines could not be placed over holes dug in the ground as was traditional. Instead, the ends of fifty-five-gallon drums were cut to form circular containers about two feet high. These were slipped under the toilet holes through trap doors at the back of the tin-roofed latrines, which were built of raw wood and screen. Once a day the honey pots were dragged out to a nearby burn area, where they were filled with diesel fuel and burned. That was latrine detail, Vietnam style, and the sight and smell of burning diesel and shit permeated every base camp in Vietnam.

I looked at my watch as our plane touched down. A coincidence of time zones made it unnecessary to adjust the time, even though twenty-four hours had passed since I had boarded the plane in the dim, cool morning hours at McGuire Air Force Base in New Jersey. The three pistol-belted airmen who boarded our plane to orient and welcome this latest batch of replacements, and the machine-gun-mounted jeeps patrolling the taxiway, told me that the change was more than one of time. Soon after, I was walking through the sticky glare of a Vietnamese afternoon toward the huge tin-roofed, open processing shed, with its crowded rows of chairs roped off into plane-load sections and its makeshift official counters, to start my tour in Vietnam.

After a short briefing on the penalties for importing prohibited personal weapons and a cursory customs clearance procedure, I boarded an air-conditioned bus for the short ride to the replacement center, where all incoming officers were processed for final assignment. The buses were air-conditioned, not out of any consideration for us newcomers or our rank, but because it was the least costly way to keep hand grenades from coming through open windows as the buses made their way through the narrow, bustling streets. The Long Binh replacement center was more raw red earth and more low faded wooden buildings with screens instead of windows. There, the next day, my orders were confirmed for an infantry division located nearby.

In midmorning a dusty jeep and trailer pulled up; then two of us were on the way to my division with a major from the personnel section who had been sent to fetch us. The road to Di An, where the division rear area was located, was a main road to Saigon, some ten miles south, and relatively clear of incidents during the day. We moved along freely among scattered military traffic on administrative runs of one kind or another, with the fine dust settling over us in successive layers as each truck or jeep passed.

Di An, five miles west of Long Binh and ten miles north of Saigon, was a sprawling camp that served as the rear base of operations for the division, which was deployed farther north. It contained all the administrative support for personnel and supply, housed in a variety of wood or semiwood structures that ran the gamut from the nicely finished main headquarters complex to canvas and wood shelters set on raised wood floors for troop sleeping accommodations. By that evening I was in the jungle field uniform with proper insignia, sewn on by the local Vietnamese seamstresses. By the next afternoon I was through with all my inprocessing. Then the waiting began.

One reason for the wait had to do with the fact that there had been an 85 percent turnover in division officers during the past two months. The assignment people wanted to be careful to spread out the arriving officers so that everyone in a section or unit would not again leave at the same time the next year. Another reason had to do with jockeying for preferred jobs—there were only about four jobs at battalion level for armor officers because the mass officer influx had already taken place in June and early July when the Army schools let out. A third reason had to do with the commanding general, who insisted on interviewing every new officer of the rank of major or higher before an assignment decision was made. Finally, after two days the major who had driven over from Long Binh with me, and who had served in the same armored division with me in Germany, and I were told that the next morning we would make the thirty-minute helicopter flight to the division forward headquarters at Lai Khe for our ten-minute interviews with the commanding general.

The morning flight to Lai Khe in the doorless helicopter was exciting. I could really feel the land rushing by, and the lush green country that I had seen from up high on the flight into Bien Hoa became a diorama of jungle, rice paddies, narrow roads, rickety buses, and small clusters of shacks. It looked quiet and lovely in the morning sun. Lai Khe, itself, was a place of contrasts: the brown-and-white stucco villas of the French plantation that had been there, with the remnants of the formal gardens, interspersed with the wood-floored tents for the division staff, the bunkered command center, and the bristling, armed perimeter. The commanding general's "social" office was a small hexagonal wall tent on a scrubbed wood floor, with the walls neatly rolled up, set in the center of what had been the plantation's park. It was reached by a thirty-foot raised walk made of whitened wood pallets, which was meant to keep visitors from sinking into the soft ground after rains.

We arrived at about ten in the morning, only to find that the commanding general would not have time to see us until late afternoon. It turned out to be almost five in the afternoon before he was through with his last business, which was entertaining a group of white-shirted congressmen who were making their rounds of the war zone. When it was my turn, I walked up the scrubbed, neatly fitted wood walk, saluted the general, was offered a seat in one of the frail lawn chairs of local manufacture, and heard some bland generalizations about serving in the division, which ended with his remarking that he was glad to welcome an armor officer to the division because it "released an infantry officer for the line." I was not sure that I had heard right! Such a remark is routinely passed in joking between contemporaries from different Army branches, but it was totally unexpected in a conversation with my new commanding general. I saw no trace of humor in the general's face, however, as I stood to salute and depart, and I walked back down the raised wood walk knowing full well that I was not being assigned to one of the few armor slots available, but was headed instead for a staff position. I immediately began to wonder how I was going to arrange to get to a job in a combat battalion. I certainly did not intend to spend a year in a combat zone doing the same work that I could do anywhere in peacetime.

We were back in Di An by six that evening, and, sure enough, three days later I was assigned as the adjutant of a brigade whose base camp was at Phuoc Vinh, some forty miles north of Saigon.

Somewhat resignedly I gathered my gear and headed for the helicopter. The roads, it turned out, were opened only once every two months between the division base at Di An and the brigade base at Phuoc Vinh for a resupply column; then it took a major effort that involved a brigade or more of troops. Flying, therefore, was the only way to travel. My major friend from Germany had been assigned as an adjutant in another brigade, and we said goodby at the helicopter pad. Three months later he was dead. He had taken advantage of a chance to fly as an aerial observer in a light, two-seater aircraft and had been hit by a rifle shot that had come up out of the quiet, lovely, green land below him. He bled to death before they could land.

Phuoc Vinh was an expanded version of the original village that had clustered on the edge of what had been Highway 1A, amid rolling French rubber plantations that the jungle was now rapidly reclaiming. There had been the original village and, a short distance up the highway, the French Foreign Legion post that had represented colonial authority in the area. Then, in the early days of South Vietnam's independence, an ambitious government had built a new model village between the original village and the Foreign Legion post—by then occupied by the Army of the Republic of Vietnam (ARVN)—and a new district capitol across the way from the post. It had all been very grand in concept. The model village had been built around a long grass mall, ending in a white-stone square containing a bust of a national hero, which was set in front of a low stage of the same white stone. The new district capitol buildings had been spaced around a two-story, steepled administration building, in front of which was a large, packed-dirt parade ground and a tall flagpole.

As the internal conflict in South Vietnam grew, the model village and the district capitol had posed a challenge to the opposition. The capitol had been overrun by the Viet Cong, the district administrators and their ARVN guards routed, the villagers dispersed, and the model village destroyed.

Shortly after American combat troops were introduced into Vietnam, one of our early-arriving brigades had been posted to Phuoc Vinh. It had taken possession, secured the area, and started building the standard low, wood buildings around the Foreign Legion post across the road from the district capitol, whose administrators, or their successors, reemerged and repossessed the remnants of their district cap-

itol buildings. The original village of Phuoc Vinh repopulated itself
with Vietnamese who were oriented toward "service" to the troops.
The village was never again attacked or used as an avenue to attack
the base camp. It was simply too valuable a tax source for the Viet
Cong: they levied a tariff on each owner of each "service" industry,
and they couldn't risk its destruction. To support that first brigade,
an airstrip big enough to accommodate four-engine cargo planes was
constructed, and storage areas were built for the supplies that were
flown in. Eventually, the brigade to which I was assigned inherited
the area.

By the time I arrived the base camp was a sprawling equilateral
triangle, one angle of which pointed south. The airstrip formed the
base of this triangle on the north. The remains of Highway 1A met
the triangle at its southern point and formed the eastern leg, though
the highway itself was no more than a dirt road and became completely impassable just north of Phuoc Vinh. The original village took
an irregular bite out of the western leg of the triangle just north of
where Highway 1A met its point and was separated from the base
camp by the high wire fence, set on concrete posts, that completely
enclosed the camp. This large triangular enclosure was divided up
internally by dirt roads, dusty or muddy, depending on the season,
with fences running alongside them that separated the various functional compounds: the district capitol, with its half-destroyed buildings, ARVN soldiers, and the American advisor team; the Foreign
Legion post with its original stone buildings and low decorative stone
walls and steps, now augmented by our unpainted wood additions; a
service complex, made up of some more low wood buildings housing
a PX and service club; and other subdivisions for our artillery battalion, engineer company, and medical company with its dispensary.
Between the internal dirt roads and the fences were overgrown grassy
strips that hid an assortment of land mines laid by the successive
occupants. Nobody knew exactly what kind of mines were where,
and the solution at this point was to post warning signs at intervals
and leave the strips strictly alone. The infantry battalions, who occupied enclaves of tents neatly lined up and set on wood frames and
raised wooden floors close to the outer fence on each of the three
sides of the triangle, took turns outposting the perimeter as they rotated in and out of the base camp. The bunker line that ran just inside

the wire fence was always manned to one degree or another. That was my new neighborhood.

My own home here was the brigade headquarters compound, which occupied the Foreign Legion post and a collection of tin-roofed, wood buildings, with louvered walls from waist height to just under the deeply overhanging eaves. An old French bunker in the middle of the compound served as the operations center. The brigade staff officers lived in four one-story stone buildings with deep verandas, built around a central grassy quadrangle, which was neatly quartered by white stone walks that met at a flagpole set in a small circle in the center. The aura of the Foreign Legion was so strong that even our newly dug steel culvert and sandbag shelters could not eliminate the distinctly "Beau Geste" quality of the place.

I had fallen into unexpected luxury. The stone walls were guaranteed to provide more peace of mind than canvas or wood with regard to random incoming mortar shells, but the big treat was the common French bathroom facilities in the center section of one of the buildings. Miraculously, they still worked—sort of. There were real toilets, serviced by overhead, chain-pull water tanks; real shower stalls; and real sinks. Granted, there was only cold water and we shared the toilet stalls with a large gecko lizard who lived above the water tanks and came to peer down disconcertingly when you used the toilet, but it was a far cry from the honey pots.

The bare, hard-used, stone rooms were all identical. Each had a screened window space that looked onto the veranda and the quadrangle beyond, and another screened window space that looked out the back. In the ceiling was a slowly turning French fan, the kind I had seen in countless movies set in the tropics. The final feature of my room was another large gecko lizard that kept close watch on me from an upside-down position outside and toward the top of one or the other of my screened window spaces. I am told that the name "gecko" is echoic of its cry, but the troops called it the "fuck you" lizard because that was echoic of its cry to them. That cry never failed to startle me. I would come into my room, see nothing on my screen, and settle down to some chore. After a few minutes, the sound of the softly repeated "fuck you" from the direction of my window would make me jump, and there would be my upside-down friend watching me intently.

After a very few days at Phuoc Vinh, my duties became familiar, and each day began to be very much like the one before. Unless there was a reason to be out on an operation earlier, we were breakfasted and in the headquarters building by a little before six in the morning, which gave us time to update the brigade commander, answer his questions, and get his instructions for the day before he flew off to start his rounds of the units operating in the field.

I was responsible for the administration and anything that remotely touched on personnel within the brigade. My section kept track of the strengths of our three infantry battalions and sent in the daily reports that triggered replacements for them from the division. We counted in those replacements, processed their decorations when their units or individual actions gained them recognition, and reported their deaths and woundings when it was necessary. I personally dealt with the division officer assignment people on the more delicate question of officer replacements, which increased in delicacy with the rank being replaced because of the specific demands of the job and the whims of the commanders involved. Most important, I supervised a myriad of administrative details that impacted directly on the soldiers of those infantry battalions: the supplies in the local PX, the operation of the mail system, the operation of the various makeshift clubs in which they could drink their beer when they were in the base camp, and the availability and scheduling of chaplains and doctors to support their spiritual and physical health needs.

Also, I ended up being responsible for any kind of research effort aimed at getting to the bottom of adverse press reports, which turned up from time to time, and whatever administrative support the brigade commander personally required. All of this was accomplished with an officer assistant, a sergeant, and several soldier clerks. Division headquarters was a series of voices at the end of one of my field telephones, which in reality were connected by wire to a radio van that talked to another van at division headquarters that was connected by wire to the various division offices with which I spoke. Another field telephone connected me by actual wire to the infantry battalions' headquarters in our base camp, where a captain or a lieutenant and his several enlisted assistants did the same kind of thing for their companies that I did for their respective battalions. The two phones, and the disembodied voices on them, constituted the administrative communication network for Phuoc Vinh and its inhabitants. The war was fought on the operational network, which ran through the radio sets in the operations center or the operations office, but we supported it on our telephones.

My job was a typical staff job, and the fact that I was doing it in Vietnam instead of somewhere else did not change its essential nature—and that rankled. It was one thing to come halfway around the world to Vietnam to practice my trade as a professional combat arms soldier, but it was quite another to end up performing only the routine chores of any Army garrison. Yet, with few interruptions, that would be my cut of the war for the next few months. I would be simply an observer, at one remove or another. There would be the frustrations that come from trying to force the cumbersome wheels of an administrative machine to turn efficiently, and there would be very few satisfactions, but there also would be very little danger and minimal discomfort.

The lot of the infantry soldiers in our three battalions was far different. They carried the burden of the war, as always. Aside from their week of R & R, with a couple of days for going out and coming back on either end, the infantry soldier's life was a succession of helicopter rides to a clearing; hot, tiring walks, interrupted sporadically by short, fierce fights with largely unseen enemies; and the night defensive positions that ended each day's walk in the early afternoon, where he dug the mandatory foxhole with overhead cover. The noncommissioned officer's lot was the same, with a few more privileges when he was back at Phuoc Vinh and a lot more responsibility when he was out with his platoon. The lieutenants and captains in the infantry companies led the same life also, but their uniforms were individually laundered sometimes, and sometimes their names and insignia were on them. And they, unlike their enlisted men, usually rotated to a staff job after about six months. The battalion staff captains and majors moved back and forth between the base camp and the night defensive positions, sometimes walking with the battalion commander, who stayed with his soldiers (or over them in a light observation helicopter) most of the time, sometimes flying back to the various meetings or supervisory responsibilities required by their particular job at our base camp. They all shared the same dangers as long as they were out in the field, but they didn't all have the right to command a helicopter ride. Creature comfort depended on mobility, and that depended on rank.

In the late afternoon, the helicopters would fly out to the night defensive positions, bringing mail, food, and ammunition for the soldiers; some form of shelter for the battalion headquarters staff; and the battalion mortars, which were too heavy to be carried during the day-long marches. The protective fires of the mortars and the direct-support artillery within range would be registered in around the position; then all would go quiet as the soldiers settled in for what rest they could get in their freshly dug holes while waiting for the mortar or sapper attack that came, more often than not, around midnight. In the meantime their only link to the rest of the world would be the softly humming radio. As dawn broke, if there had been no enemy contact during the night, there would be a numbing clash as the night defensive position's perimeter exploded with rifle fire and previously emplaced claymore mines, set to discourage would-be attackers lurking to ambush the troops as they uncoiled out of their positions and started on the day's march. After their weapons' "throats" had been cleared, the battalion headquarters shelter and the mortars would be lifted out by the helicopters that were bringing in supplies for the day. Then the battalion would be off on another walk to another night defensive position or a helicopter landing zone, from which they would be lifted to still another landing zone or, at intervals, back to Phuoc Vinh. These actions were all coordinated and fitted to similar actions of the other division units. In the aggregate they became operations with picturesque names that lasted for a set period of time and resulted in some planned objective being attempted, but the guys doing the walking and fighting never knew that until they read about it afterward in the Pacific edition of the *Stars and Stripes*.

This cycle of activity also drove the routine of the brigade staff. If any battalion was out, the brigade commander and his operations or intelligence officers would be off by half past six in the morning. They would spend the day in their command and control helicopter, with its battery of radios, hovering over each battalion, checking on its progress or joining the three-level tier of orbiting command and control helicopters that congregated over enemy contact on the ground: the first tier was the battalion commander in a light "bubble" helicopter; the middle tier, a thousand feet above, was the brigade commander; and the top tier, still another thousand feet up, was the division commander. They were all trying to help, and they all wanted to be involved in the war that was going on at that moment. If there was no contact, the command group would land the command and control helicopter at one or another command post to coordinate the next day's operation. For most of each day, therefore, the brigade headquarters at Phuoc Vinh was left to the adjutant and the brigade executive officer. We fielded all the questions from division, processed the eternal stream of paperwork in preparation for the commander's evening return, and dealt with any emergency that arose, without disturbing the people fighting the war, if possible.

We shared our dining hall with the Air Force forward air controllers—the "FACs" in the jargon of our trade—who directed the air strikes of the jet aircraft that supported our infantry soldiers from above. The FACs were usually Air Force captains or majors, and they flew light, single-engine planes that in those years looked like overpowered Piper Cubs. They had enlisted assistants who operated the radios and who acted as observers from the second seat, in back of the pilot. Between them, they spotted the targets and talked the fast-flying, jet fighter/bombers to those targets. A FAC had to be a very good pilot. He had to fly low and slowly to be really effective, and he had to be amazingly accurate with the marking rockets that hung under his wings in fixed brackets. To aim those rockets at the target to be marked, he aimed the plane at the target and held the course until the rocket was on its way. All that adds up to a very aggressive pilot with a lot of guts.

There were three FACs assigned to our brigade, and they were all very good at their work. They also tended to be a bit overzealous in their approach to their jobs, however, which caused them to go out "hunting" for targets on their own when there was no assigned brigade mission to support. This "hunting" was officially classified as a "visual reconnaissance mission." A FAC would fly out over what was a declared "war zone," a zone from which all civilians had been evacuated and in which no friendly Vietnamese were authorized to be moving, and look over the area. Everyone found in such a war zone was presumed to be hostile. In a society in which communication is as primitive as it was among the Vietnamese peasants, there were certain dangers inherent in that presumption, but those were the rules. If a FAC found an appropriate target, he called in an air strike on it, but if the target did not warrant the attentions of high performance aircraft, a truly aggressive FAC might take it under fire with his marking rockets or his own personal M16 rifle. Typically, that kind of target tended to be a group of people whose identities were impossible to verify. Granted, nobody should have been out there at all, and the odds were good that anyone moving in a war zone was at least a supply bearer for the Viet Cong. Still, there was some doubt. For that reason the procedure was officially discouraged, but it was hard to control what happened in a lone aircraft out over a war zone on a visual reconnaissance mission.

One day while I was eating lunch my attention was drawn to a noisy gaggle pushing through the rickety wood screen door. At the center of the obviously elated group was an intense FAC who took his job particularly seriously. As the group passed my table, I asked what all the excitement was about. The serious FAC, who had earned the nickname "The Hunter" because of the frequent opportunities he found for visual reconnaissance missions, told me that he had been flying over the war zone north of Phuoc Vinh when he had spotted six figures walking along a stream bank with large sacks on their backs. He and his observer had swooped down on them and taken them under fire, their M16 rifles held out the side windows of the plane while The Hunter flew with the stick between his legs. The results had been "great," he said with obvious pleasure. The figures had made no attempt to run and had been cut down as they walked. On the second pass he had flown close enough to see that all six were dead. The Hunter was still excited by his kill, and he passed on to his table, talking about how he had "really gotten Charlie this time." I thought there was a shadow of a doubt as to whether he had stopped food supplies from getting to the Viet Cong or alienated still another village by killing farmers taking personal belongings from their previous homes to some resettlement village. He had played by the rules as they were laid down, however, and there was nothing to be said.

Several days later The Hunter was flying another mission when he decided to return to the area where he had found the six supply bearers. This time he found a full platoon of figures moving along the same stream, but these figures were carrying weapons. They melted swiftly into the scrub along the stream bank at the sound of the plane. Down The Hunter dived, intent on churning up the scrub and flushing out some of his quarry. He fired off his marking rockets on the first pass, and, as the foliage started to smolder from the heat of the white phosphorus, banked around for a pass with M16 rifles. The figures had faded to the left of the stream, and his eyes were riveted on the line of scrub on that side as he made his pass. He didn't see the flash from the single gunner, hidden on the right side of the stream, who midway through his pass sent a single bullet up through the thin skin of the light plane. The bullet hit him in the lower back, and The Hunter instantly lost control of his legs. He had time to radio his position and the fact that he had been hit and to tell his sergeant in back of him to lock his harness for a crash; then he passed out. At this point the story should end, but it does not.

The sergeant had flown many, many hours as an observer. He calmly took the spare control stick from its bracket on the back of the pilot's seat and locked it into its floor socket. Then he unlocked his floor pedals to activate them and pulled back on the stick. The plane responded. The sergeant gained the altitude he needed and leveled off. Ahead and to the right was a column of black smoke that the sergeant knew had to mark the burning honey pots at Phuoc Vinh. After a little experimenting with the pedals, he managed to get the plane headed in that direction. By this time another FAC and one of our light observation helicopters had been attracted by The Hunter's last radio call. They had headed for the area of the incident immediately and were now flying near the sergeant, giving him encouragement and instructions over their radios. As they approached our airstrip, The Hunter regained consciousness. Fighting to stay conscious, he attempted to land the plane without using the pedals, but he overshot the airstrip. He pulled back hard on the stick to go around again and almost stalled the plane. Now a FAC on the ground took charge. He tersely instructed the sergeant on what to do with the pedals and talked him around until the plane was once more headed in on a ragged final approach course. The plane floated over the end of the runway, hesitated a moment, touched down, and rolled on. It was rolling too fast, however, and the sergeant ran out of runway before he could get the plane stopped. It rolled off the runway and hit a drainage ditch, where it came to rest with its tail in the air and the propeller dug into the far bank of the ditch.

All was quiet for a moment; then people and vehicles converged on the plane as if they were metal filings drawn to a magnet. There was no fire. The sergeant was shaken but unhurt. Quickly and gently The Hunter was pulled out. A medical evacuation helicopter was called in, and shortly The Hunter was on his way to the hospital, the paralyzed victim of his prey. The sergeant was awarded the Distinguished Flying Cross.

# II
# An Adjutant's View

As my second month in Vietnam began, my daily duties had settled into a pattern of coping with a variety of routine administrative problems, some aspects of which I soon found difficult to get excited about. It became apparent, for instance, that one of our infantry battalions had a disproportionate share of the brigade's malaria cases. Our tallies on sick soldiers showed that there were more than fifty cases in that battalion and that there were seventeen cases in one of its companies alone. Those figures were serious because they indicated that either the troops were not regularly taking their antimalaria pills or that we had encountered a new strain of malaria against which the pills were ineffective. In either case something needed to be done to stem the rising numbers of incapacitated soldiers.

We reported our information on the battalion to the proper division headquarters staff offices so that the problem could be properly examined, but the division commander had a more immediate solution. I found out about it toward the end of supper one evening when the brigade executive officer burst into the dining hall to announce that the division commander had personally directed us to ensure that all soldiers slept under their issue mosquito netting, took their antimalaria pills, and used insect repellent to ward off the mosquitoes when they were in the field. Having delivered himself of this news, he looked meaningfully at me and departed. It was my job to get the word out, I knew, but it seemed to me that I could probably finish my supper without incurring the wrath of the division commander or risking malaria for another soldier. I was wrong!

About fifteen minutes later, as I was on my way back to my office to pass on the general's words on malaria, I was approached by the executive officer and asked if I had gotten the word out on the commanding general's wishes. He was appalled to find that I had not yet accomplished that mission, though I was at a loss as to what effect fifteen minutes would have had on the long-term habits of our soldiers. The last troop formations of the day had been conducted already, and those soldiers who remained in the base camp had finished supper already. The supper meal would have been the last chance to check on antimalaria pill consumption until morning. Knowing that nothing I could do would have much effect until the next day, still I rushed off to take some action that would placate my boss. I relayed the instructions from the commanding general to the three infantry battalion headquarters over the field phone then called the division radio station to ask that the guidance be broadcast between the musical selections. Then I reported my actions to the executive officer, who was delighted that I had done something, even though no soldier would know about it for several hours and even though no meaningful changes in habits would take place probably for a lot longer than that—if ever. Wasted motion and unnecessary concern over the petty aspects of serious subjects seemed to be the norm in the routine duties of an adjutant.

One day I broke the routine by getting one of our light observation helicopters to fly me out to a tiny outpost just south of our base camp to check on the needs of the officer and three enlisted men from our brigade who were stationed there to train the local government militia, or Popular Forces, that manned the little fort. Our brigade sent out several of these mobile training teams to augment the regular advisory effort in our area of operations, but they tended not to get the same level of attention from the brigade staff as the combat operations of our infantry battalions, which were the major focus of my command group's interest. The officers posted to these mobile training jobs were assigned in response to a levy and frequently were those whom the battalions could most easily do without. The outpost that I visited was typical of the many that dotted Vietnam. Almost every village had one. Some had American advisors, but most did not. They were invariably set on a dirt road at the edge of the village, where they were supposed to be a symbol of government authority and provide protection for the villagers. Some did, but most did not.

This particular Popular Forces outpost consisted of an ammunition bunker dug into a hard mud central area; a dilapidated building near it that was divided into a kitchen, a common room, and a radio room; and three towers set at the points of the triangle formed by the raised dirt berms that enclosed it all. Firing positions were carved into the berms at intervals, and one point of the berm had an open latrine, which emptied into the dry moat that paralleled the berm on all sides. Its odor permeated everything. Outside the dry moat was a tangle of barbed wire and booby traps, all overgrown with tall grass. Entrance to the outpost was gained by walking along a very narrow path that was enclosed in its own barbed-wire walls. It made several right-angle turns through the booby-trapped area and ended at the dry moat, which could be crossed by using a single swaybacked board.

My helicopter landed on the dirt road next to the outpost, and I walked in through the mazelike entrance path. Inside the little compound it was hot, dirty, and smelly. Two of the corner towers were made of sheet metal and scrap wood. They were about five feet square, and the Popular Forces soldiers lived in the bottoms of them. Our officer and one of his enlisted assistants had set up a two-man wall tent in the center of the compound between the ammunition bunker and the dilapidated building. The other two American enlisted assistants lived in the radio room or the common room, which was used to store weapons and which also served as the classroom. Nothing was going on when I arrived. Only two of the American enlisted men and four Vietnamese were in the compound, and it did not appear that much training was taking place. The four Vietnamese soldiers lounged lazily against the perimeter berm, which was in disrepair, and the weapons that were in sight were rusty. All in all, it was a discouraging sight. My mission, however, was to see if our trainers were getting the support they needed from my brigade, and having determined that they were and that the other two Americans had driven back to the base camp on some personal mission, I left. That evening I made a short report of what I had seen, but my commander was not very interested in such small stuff when there were battalion-size combat operations to concentrate on.

September also brought my first taste of election activities, Vietnam style. Whenever there was a national or local election, the Viet Cong became especially active. Their purpose was to show the villagers that they had the ability to strike where and when they wanted, thus demonstrating the futility of elections for a national governmental authority that could not exercise sufficient control even to prevent their interference. The first election activity this time was an attack on the little outpost that I had just visited. It was hit the night after my visit, and two of the four Americans were wounded. Its proximity to our base camp and our ability to quickly send helicopter gunships to its relief prevented anything more serious from happening. However, an obvious point had been made to the villagers about the ability of the outpost to provide security.

Much of the paperwork that we processed through my office day in and day out, regardless of election-day activities or alerts, consisted of recommendations for awards. We reviewed all the submissions and put an endorsement on each, recommending approval or disapproval. These recommendations for awards poured in after any of the battalions were involved in contact with the enemy, and the narrative supporting statements ranged from the very good to the ludicrous. My little group did what it could to make the narratives understandable, to check out the ones that appeared doubtful, and to make reasonable judgments in forwarding the valid ones. We could not, however, be too picky because we were dealing with batches of one hundred or more per battalion at a time.

A related problem was the division practice of preparing a "packet" of awards for each departing battalion and brigade commander. The theory was that any successful commander of a battalion or a brigade who survived his command would have qualified for a range of valor and achievement awards in the normal course of performing his job, but that frequently there would not be a superior around to observe the deserving act and make the needed recommendations. To solve that perceived inequity, a system was set up whereby the division staff directed each departing commander's staff to submit justification for a list of appropriate awards that it had drawn up after due consideration. The range, unfortunately, tended to increase with the grade of the commander, and, as with most good ideas that become institutionalized, abuses resulted because the system took on a life of its own.

Shortly after the election-day activities, our brigade had a change of commanders in the normal course of events. My new colonel was a very different kind of commander from his predecessor. Where the former had been tall and slim, he was short and blocky; where the former had evidenced some interest in ensuring his own reputation, he was interested only in his soldiers; and where the former had achieved his position in nineteen years of service, he had taken twenty-four years. Older than most of the infantry brigade commanders in Vietnam, he had already commanded the division's support command for six months when he came to us. As a result, he was familiar with our supply and maintenance problems and with the operational methods that were in use in the division, so there was practically no learning period when he took command. He was a true professional who knew what the troops on the ground were experiencing and managed them accordingly. He was interested and knowledgeable about all aspects of the brigade's operations.

The first operation that the brigade conducted under his command was a road-opening operation. Highway 1A between Phuoc Vinh and Di An was not kept open because it was believed to be too expensive in men and equipment. Part of this decision to not maintain the road stemmed from an earlier philosophical decision to divest the division of much of its mechanized and armor capability prior to bringing it to Vietnam: the remaining single mechanized infantry battalion, with its armored personnel carriers, and the division's cavalry squadron, with its tanks and armored cavalry assault vehicles, could not be dedicated only to keeping the roads open. Though some unofficial Vietnamese traffic used this road routinely, and paid the Viet Cong tax collectors at their various roadblocks, we used it only after we had mounted a large operation to clear it of mines and gain temporary control of it. Such an operation was run every eight or ten weeks in order to relieve the burden on the aerial resupply system by replenishing the supplies at Phuoc Vinh and stockpiling the bulkier items that were not cost effective to bring in by air. Each road opening involved the division cavalry squadron, the mechanized infantry battalion, and several regular infantry battalions under the control of one of the brigade headquarters.

Typically, the road-opening operation would start at the southern, Di An end, and work its way north. First, the mine-sweeping teams would move out, overwatched and protected by the mechanized infantry and the cavalry, who would stay alert and move in force if any major opposition was encountered. When a section of the road was declared cleared, infantry troops would come up to outpost it, and the mine-sweeping operation would move forward again. It was a chain reaction of clear and take control, clear and take control, with everybody involved always alert for a major enemy effort to disrupt what we were doing. In about three days the entire stretch of road to the gate at Phuoc Vinh would be cleared and outposted. The mechanized infantry and cavalry elements would form the outer protection for a series of temporary fire-support bases from which the supporting artillery could fire and to which the outposting infantry soldiers would return each evening, only to set out on nightly patrolling, which attempted to forestall any planting of new mines. Each morning the infantry would uncoil from these fire-support bases and sweep their assigned sections of the road for new or missed mines and take up the outpost positions from which they guarded the entire length of road during the day. After the road had been opened and secured in this manner, the convoys of trucks would start to roll. A loaded convoy would move north on one day and return south empty on the next. After sufficient convoys had run to fulfill our supply needs and fill our depots, the troops would coil back to their temporary fire-support bases one last time to be lifted out by helicopter, and Highway 1A would be turned back to the Viet Cong for another couple of months.

Our road-clearing operation got under way two days after our new brigade commander came to us, and it provided my first opportunity to see how we did our operational business. Since my arrival, the headquarters at Phuoc Vinh had operated only as the rear administrative or back-up command post. The daily control of the operations had taken place at a temporary forward command post located nearer the action. Now, however, only the commander flew out to check on progress, and the actual tracking and coordinating of the operation took place in our base camp operations center and was monitored from the operations staff offices, which were equipped with additional radios and were right next to mine. I had a bird's-eye view of what went on.

The start was inauspicious. The mechanized infantry battalion, which was to lead off, was lined up at the Di An end to start the operation at seven o'clock in the morning, but it didn't move out until nine o'clock because of one problem or another. First, some radios did not work; then the mine-sweeper teams were not ready; next, the mine-sweeping equipment did not check out. By then the problems were snowballing as each delay led to another complication. The road-clearing elements were to have secured an initial artillery fire-support base a short distance from the starting point so that an artillery unit could occupy it and stand by to support the troops on the road in case they were attacked. As a result of the two-hour delay, the artillery unit moved to the starting point before the road was cleared, clogging the road and adding to the confusion. Then the commanding general became impatient from his observation post in the sky and ordered a cavalry troop to go around the mechanized infantry, which was still trying to get its mine-sweeping teams operational. The cavalry moved out without waiting for mine sweeping and promptly lost a tank to a mine before it had gone a mile. The commanding general in his ubiquitous command and control helicopter saw the smoldering tank waiting for a recovery vehicle to haul it off and decided that it should be pushed off the road, though it was not in the way and pushing it off would make the eventual recovery operation more difficult. Ten minutes of angry radio transmissions followed on that subject; then the clearing operation finally got under way.

It quickly became apparent to even a casual observer that our generals had too little to do and too much communications equipment with which to do it. In earlier wars commanding generals became involved in squad and platoon operations at the risk of losing control of their overall commands. Thanks to the helicopter and the radio, they now had the ability to micromanage the small actions, even down to how the soldiers were holding their mine-sweeper equipment, without losing touch with the rest of the division. Since actions of a scope that would really engage their talents were few and far between, they found the temptation to get involved in whatever little action was going on to be more than most of them could withstand. So they "helped" the ground commanders, though they frequently could not know all the problems that existed fifteen hundred feet below them. From their positions overhead, all they saw was the clean blueprint of the action; they missed the sweat, the dirt, the tall grass that obscured a trail perfectly apparent from the air, and the other complications that prevented actions from working out on the ground the way they were supposed to. The solutions appeared simple and straightforward from fifteen hundred feet up, and simple instructions were issued. When the response was not instantaneous, the commanding generals didn't understand, and more irate radio transmissions took place, with more confusion following. The road-clearing operation provided ample evidence of this phenomenon.

On the second day of the operation, I happened to be in the operations center when the lead mechanized infantry unit ran into an ambush. It had been overwatching the mine-sweeper teams when it had been taken under fire from the jungle undergrowth that started twenty or thirty yards from the road on both sides. All forward movement stopped as the troops, in and out of the armored vehicles, turned to face their antagonists. The radio transmissions reflected the momentary confusion that follows any sudden attack while antitank rockets and automatic weapons fire continued to crisscross the road above the prone soldiers. My brigade commander came in and took the hand microphone from the duty officer at the radio. He always looked uncomfortable with that microphone, and I always imagined that he would have been much more comfortable using hand and arm signals to direct his troops or shouting instructions directly to them. As was his habit, he pressed the transmission button, paused for a moment with the channel open and humming, took a deep breath, and asked the battalion commander on the scene for a situation report. Back came the terse detail. Yes, they were receiving antitank rocket and automatic weapons fire at a pretty good rate; yes, they had taken up defensive positions from behind what cover they could find and were returning fire; no, they were not advancing on the undergrowth because there was a good possibility that the open area between the road and the undergrowth had been plentifully booby-trapped in anticipation of just such a move; and no, there were no serious casualties. My brigade commander and the engaged battalion commander quickly agreed on a plan to bring in artillery fire from the artillery unit standing by. It had been positioned for just such an eventuality and was ready when the call for artillery fires went out.

The request for a fire mission was never completed, however. The division commander apparently had been listening to the brigade command channel, and he now broke in with his well-known, "This is 77," which was the radio call sign for the commanding general. There was a momentary silence; then, with a disregard for the rules of proper radio-telephone procedure that aim at preventing personal identification of a speaker or his position, he said:

"Butch," (which was my brigade commander's first name) "this is 77."

"Yes, sir?"

"Butch, I am over that enemy contact, and I have been monitoring what is going on down there. I agree that we need to give them some fire support, but I want you to use tactical air strikes instead of our own artillery."

"Sir, I think that artillery is the answer here," said my brigade commander after his usual pause and deep breath. "They are standing by and can respond quicker. It doesn't look like we really need to go for an air strike."

"Butch," came the response, "I think that it will be to our advantage to use tactical air, and I am having it called in."

"Yes, sir," said my brigade commander and placed the microphone on the table. A moment later he picked it up again to ask the battalion commander if he had monitored the conversation. When the expected "Roger" came back, he laid the microphone back down and stared at the radio.

After a thirty-minute wait, while the troops lay on the road and traded a desultory fire with their unseen antagonists, the planes arrived and swooped down. They dumped their armament on the offending sections of the jungle just off the road and pulled away. There was no more firing from the jungle, but we would never know if it was because of the Air Force or the passage of time and the desire of the Viet Cong to simply get away after having disrupted once again our road-clearing operations. What I did know was that the commanding general preferred to use tactical air instead of our own artillery to support our troops and that he believed he was a better judge of what was needed in a given situation than either his brigade or battalion commanders. A colonel's command in combat is a much-sought-after prize, but I wondered if the interchange I had just witnessed was what my brigade commander had envisioned during those twenty-four long years of working toward that prize.

I knew that there had been a drive on in our division recently to conserve our artillery ammunition and to use some of the other support means available to us. That made sense to me because there were times when Air Force ordnance was just as effective as artillery, and we did consume enormous quantities of artillery ammunition. Still, I was not so sure about forcing the choice of the type of supporting fire on the subordinate commanders who were engaged in combat. I worried about the inevitable lapse of time before aircraft orbiting on a standby station could be vectored to the mission location where they were needed. In this case no harm had been done except to hold up the road-clearing operation and to expose our soldiers to enemy fire for a slightly longer period of time. Unfortunately, no apparent harm had been done to our opponents either.

On the second night of the road-clearing operation, with about two-thirds of the road to Phuoc Vinh cleared and outposted, the division headquarters gave us a surprise. They flew in a team of inspectors just after dark and called a surprise practice alert in our base camp. Such a procedure is common in peacetime, when an alert is used to check the ability of a unit to prepare to move out for combat on short notice, but it is a bit uncommon when used on a brigade that is actively engaged in running a combat operation in a theater of war. Nevertheless, that is exactly what was happening.

The inspection team fanned out to check our various emergency defense procedures. In the meantime the bulk of the operations staff was engaged in trying to get artillery fire support and helicopter gunships for one of our battalions that had been attacked in its temporary fire-support base out on the road. It was engaged in a brisk firefight with a Viet Cong force intent on taking back control of a piece of the road. Eventually, the firefight and the inspection both ended without much bloodletting. At eleven o'clock in the evening, we all gathered in the briefing room to hear the critique of our practice alert by the inspection team. We were duly reminded about using the proper password out on the perimeter of the base camp and about speeding up our alert notification procedures, though several inspectors stated, with straight faces, that we might have been somewhat slower than usual because the radios and operators who should have been involved were distracted by the enemy activity out on Highway 1A. The critique finally ended after midnight, and the inspection team flew off while we tried to salvage what was left of the night for sleeping.

After three days, the clearing operation reached the gate at Phuoc Vinh and the road was declared open. Then our convoys of supply trucks started to run. Despite the clearing and outposting of the road, however, there were still mines that had not been detected and there was always the chance of an ambush from the jungle undergrowth on both sides of the road. Each morning before the convoys moved, a quick sweep of the road was made to make sure that the road was still clear. On the first day that a convoy was to make the trip north, the morning clearing sweeps cost us two tanks and a recovery vehicle; two soldiers were killed, and another ten were wounded. Then the convoy rolled, and the trip to Phuoc Vinh was made without further incident. The next morning the pre-opening sweep of the northern-most section of the road started at Phuoc Vinh. Just outside our front gate the first mine-sweeping team was hit by a command-detonated claymore mine, no doubt captured from us, which spewed fragments all across the road. One soldier was killed, and four others were wounded. The stunned security squad for the mine-sweeping team spotted two figures in black running away across the fields as the smoke cleared and fired *warning* shots over their heads!

Before the last empty convoy made its final return run five days later, our troops had discovered and destroyed 136 land mines in one twenty-mile stretch of road. That did not include the undetected mines that claimed two tanks, a recovery vehicle, and an engineer bulldozer. The Viet Cong had been laying mines in the soft dirt of that road for so many years that it was literally seeded with them. Some went off the first time pressure was placed on them, and some malfunctioned and did not go off until the third or fourth time pressure was placed on them. Many were constructed of plastic explosives and wood trig-gering mechanisms with only the tiniest metal contact points, which our mine-detecting equipment could not pick up. In addition, there were the command-detonated mines, which were buried in the road and which had no triggering devices. They were set off by a person hidden in the jungle who waited until he had a target on top of it before sending an electric spark along a buried wire to detonate it. The mines ranged from the small plastic and wood ones to the con-verted five-hundred-pound bombs, which could turn over a medium tank with the force of their explosions.

Everybody was delighted to see the end of the road-opening op-eration. The temporary defensive positions and the fire-support base guarded by the mechanized infantry and cavalry vehicles, which had provided irresistible targets for the Viet Cong each night, were va-cated, and the infantry outposts strung out along the road folded in on themselves as the last convoy heading south rolled past them. As they moved to designated helicopter pick-up points, the walking sol-diers stayed alert for the possibility of one last ambush or one last command-detonated mine. Then they were on their way to a base camp or another operation. The road was quiet again, turned back to its original owners for another couple of months, during which more mines would be planted and more ambush sites prepared.

With the end of the road-opening operation, our intelligence officer returned to planning and coordinating the "seal and search" missions that he ran in the immediate area of Phuoc Vinh. These operations did just what the name implies: a village was sealed off and isolated by a cordon of our infantry soldiers and then searched for material that could be used by the Viet Cong, which, if found, was confiscated, or for inhabitants who did not have proper identification papers, who, if found, were detained. It was a standard approach to gain control over our immediate area of operation, and it led to fierce engagements on those rare occasions when we selected a village that contained Viet Cong in force. These missions, like the mobile training teams, took second place to the combat operations in the war zones and were usually assigned to an infantry company of a battalion back for a few days' stand-down in the base camp. Frustrated by my own paper war, I asked to go along on a seal and search mission of a nearby village. The mission was postponed once when our helicopter support was pulled away for a more urgent mission; then all the arrangements were simply moved ahead a day.

On the morning of the operation, my alarm went off and I groped awake under my mosquito netting at four thirty, when the Vietnamese night is still dark and cool. It was a good temperature for sleeping, I thought, as I collected my shaving gear and stumbled down to the latrine to shave in the dim light. As I came fully awake from the cold water, I realized that I had few grounds for complaint. Not only was I doing this of my own volition, but out in the wet paddies the sealing force had been on the move for two hours already. Wading through knee-deep muck in the dark, they had quietly encircled the selected village, sealing it off from the rest of the country with a cordon of damp infantrymen. From the quiet of the night and the lack of excitement in our compound, I knew that the seal had been placed without any enemy contact. For the next hour and a half, the sealing force would lie behind their weapons behind the rice paddy dikes, waiting for dawn and the loudspeaker helicopter that would announce to the village that a search was about to begin.

I left the latrine, finished dressing, and headed for the dining hall, which was one building away from my bare cement room. I finished breakfast quickly and returned to my room for a moment to pick up my pistol, helmet, pistol belt, and small camera. I debated whether to wear my flak vest, which hung on a nail in easy reach by the door but decided that with the seal already set and no contact reported, it was an unnecessary burden. I closed my door and stepped ouside to fall in with my next-door neighbor, who was the intelligence officer.

Together, we walked to the brigade headquarters building and found the jeep that I had arranged for the night before. There was a moment's delay as my driver, new to his job, fumbled with the jeep's lights. I leaned over and released the lock lever that prevents the lights from being flashed on accidentally. We moved off toward the airstrip while I grumbled to the driver about becoming familiar with his vehicle before I got back. The intelligence sergeant and his radio had joined us, and the jeep was a little crowded, but the ride was short. As we came onto the airstrip, I sensed rather than saw another jeep parked in shadow. When we stopped and got out, I told my driver to return to the headquarters building. Beside the other jeep were two American enlisted men and the smallest Vietnamese I had yet encountered. The two Americans were trained interrogators: one had been at this kind of operation for ten months; the other had just started. The tiny Vietnamese was a "Hoi Chan," a Viet Cong who had deserted to the government forces and was earning his pardon by leading American units to Viet Cong base camps and by pointing out key Viet Cong personnel. This one was outfitted in a cutdown American fatigue uniform and carried an old World War II carbine. He stood a little apart from us and smoked his American cigarette with an air of total unconcern.

By now it was six o'clock and the horizon was starting to show light. Just as we started to worry about whether our helicopter would show up on time, we heard the distant noise of a "Chinook," the twin-rotor helicopter that could carry eight thousand pounds or thirty-three combat-loaded soldiers. As it started to let down, the intelligence sergeant pulled the pin on a yellow smoke grenade to mark our exact location for the pilot. In the dim light the column of billowing smoke was colorless. The helicopter landed and cut its engines. Still, we stood waiting. Then, silhouetted against the now rapidly lightening sky, a jeep and two trucks came into sight. The silhouette effect put the occupants into sharp relief against the sky, and the varied headgear and uniforms of the Vietnamese Regional Forces could be seen clearly. Some wore bush hats, and some wore helmets; some carried big revolvers, and some carried M1s, the universal military weapon in this era of massive American aid. When the trucks stopped, the troops jumped down and formed small chattering groups a short distance from the slowly turning blades of the big helicopter. Six figures, taller and bulkier than the rest, detached themselves from the mass and walked toward us. They were the American advisors for this district force, who would actually do the searching of the village. They carried the same weapons and radios as we, but they were dressed more like the troops they advised, with their bush hats and variously altered jungle field uniforms. We shook hands and joked for a moment about the differences in our jobs; then we started moving toward the rear ramp of the helicopter. As we did, another truck, with seven more Regional Forces troops pulled up. We speculated as to how many more might straggle in; then we were being carried into the helicopter by the current of jostling Vietnamese troops. I let them flow around me so that I remained near the rear of the helicopter.

A little behind the main crush came the district chief, a Vietnamese army captain who was in charge of the administration of the district in which we operated and who commanded the troops that were with us. He was accompanied by a sergeant and a body guard, a tough-looking guy who wore a tiger-patterned jungle field uniform with a matching vest. With the vest and a rakishly worn bush hat, he looked like an Oriental cowboy. I was introduced to the district chief, and we both saluted and shook hands. We separated, but the next thing I knew he was moving along the seats roughly ordering his men to make room for the Americans. Though I was perfectly happy standing by the open ramp, I accepted his gesture and settled into a nearby canvas-and-pipe troop seat as the helicopter started its engines.

We lifted off. The sun came fully up, and the ground, seen through the still-open rear ramp, came into view below a layer of light, early-morning cloud. The sky above was red and rosy and fresh looking. The flight was short. We landed on a dry spot in the wet brown paddies that surrounded the village to be searched. Watching the Vietnamese soldiers file off the helicopter, I realized that we had fifty-nine instead of the authorized thirty-three, but the small stature of the troops made it a safe load nevertheless. The Regional Forces troops moved quickly away from the helicopter toward the village, which was only one paddy width away. We were inside the sealing cordon, and our own soldiers were only barely visible from their positions. The village children were already lined up at the edge of the village, attracted by the helicopter landing. They watched our approach with curious dark eyes set in impassive faces. They were dressed raggedly in short-sleeve pullovers and dirty shorts. Both boys and girls had the same black bangs. The dirt was all the more apparent because their clothing was made of light-colored material. Ahead of us the Regional Forces troops were spreading out and disappearing into the village. We followed. Our intelligence sergeant took a slightly different route and suddenly was floundering waist deep in muck, weighed down by his radio. The intelligence officer went back and pulled him out.

Once inside the village, we were hedged in by small, insubstantial thatched huts, miniature groves of coconut trees, and foul-smelling pens containing water buffalo. The buffalo did not like this intrusion by strangers, and they strained at their ropes and the encircling wood rails. Overhead two helicopter gunships circled in case they were needed; the loudspeaker helicopter flew slowly around the village while the broadcasting voice explained the purpose of the search and directed all males to report to a designated central location. We passed men who were headed toward the specified collection point. Some looked annoyed, but most were expressionless. They had been through this before. In and around the huts the women continued sweeping their floors and tidying up the hard-packed little squares in front of their doorways. Some children were playing, and some were still eating their breakfast bowls of rice. The living areas and the cooking facilities were very primitive, and the huts were open to the weather, though the closeness of neighboring huts and the thick overhanging groves of trees gave some protection. Deeper into the village we found that the women and children had stopped their routine to watch us. I wondered what they thought of the intrusion and how they felt about their Regional Forces countrymen who were moving in and out of their huts, poking here and pulling there. The soldiers were neither careless nor rough. They were merely thorough, with all the invasion of personal privacy that is implied by that. No area of the huts escaped their prying, but there was no protest from the watching villagers. Their thoughts and allegiances remained impenetrable to me.

Toward the center of the village, we found our two American interrogators and their interpreter. They had two fifteen-year-olds in tow. Apparently, our surprise had been complete this time because we had found young men. On the last search of this village, there had been no young men present, which was a sure sign that the village had been alerted. These particular young men were dressed in sport shirts and slacks and seemed a cut above the rest in appearance. One claimed to be an ex–Viet Cong, which was probably as close to an admission as we would get. The two were herded off to the collection point. By now it was eight o'clock in the morning, and it was getting very warm.

The searching continued, with the soldiers methodically going through all the likely hiding places. At first nothing of interest turned up. Then word was passed that sixteen full sacks of rice, which was about two thousand pounds, had been found in a house at the other end of the village. We picked up our pace and went off to see. On the way the American advisors and the district chief joined our group. When we reached the rice, an interpreter explained that he had gotten two different stories from the occupants of the house. One claimed that the rice had been moved in temporarily to protect it after a neighboring house had burned, and the other said that the rice had just arrived from out of town and had not yet been distributed. The markings on the rice sacks looked suspicious to the district chief, and he questioned the householders more closely. Finally, he decided to have it brought to the tiny triangular Popular Forces post on the outskirts of the town. If a bill of sale could be produced, he told the two, the rice would be returned. Meanwhile, one of the American advisors had found a motorbike in a nearby shed. It was of a kind that the Viet Cong were known to have acquired the previous December for their supply couriers. Still, the evidence was not conclusive. We walked back toward the collection point.

The doctor from our sealing unit had arrived and was conducting a sick call in the Popular Forces compound for the villagers. The compound was left over from the French days when the town had been a district capital. It was a triangular dirt-bermed fort with two artillery-battered buildings sticking up in the center. Ironically, American artillery, through some misunderstanding, had done the battering on a previous occasion. The outpost was completely surrounded by barbed-wire mazes, booby traps, and mines. A number of 81mm mortar shells were hanging from poles by the gate. They could be detonated by wires from inside the guard bunker. We guessed that it would take a battalion to actually overrun this post. The entrance to the interior was gained through a single narrow cut in the berm. Inside there was ample evidence of the very professional, French-trained Vietnamese sergeant who commanded it. It was clean and neat and ready for instant action. In the center, sunk into the soft ground, was a very substantial concrete command bunker. There was a marked contrast between this outpost and the one I had visited with our mobile training team earlier in the month. The effectiveness of this military efficiency was attested to by the fact that this post had never been overrun, despite its location at the edge of a village that was acknowledged to be sympathetic to the Viet Cong. Or maybe the sergeant had made an accommodation with his neighbors!

In one of the two battered buildings inside the fort, our battalion doctor was doing his business. He was surrounded by silent, wide-eyed children and worried-looking, patient mothers, and he worked as though he were in his own office instead of in a bare, roofless building. I walked back out of the little fort and headed toward the crowd that had gathered at the collection point for the male villagers. Along the way my eye was caught by the incongruity of the American war materials that had been incorporated into the village architecture. C-ration cartons and sandbags formed walls, and soda cans left by previous searching troops were used as containers of every sort. All the houses had bunkers, usually built right under the hard, wooden sleeping platform that formed the center of each hut. The more affluent even had mat floors in their bunkers. The external impact of the war on this tiny, close-built village was plain enough; the internal impact was beyond my understanding.

At the collection point there were eighty-five men who had been rounded up. The district chief and his assistants were walking among the squatting, patient group, checking identification papers. It was eight thirty by now, and the sun was hot. Nothing remained to be done but to complete the check and move out. The group of men was being divided and redivided as papers were checked and accepted or rejected. Directly in front of me was a father with his young son cradled in his lap. The son was clutching his father's neck. I wondered if the father would be taken. After a while, the little boy got up and joined his mother, who was watching from a short distance away with a group of village women. Finally, the group to be taken was narrowed down to fourteen men who could not be identified by their papers or by the Popular Forces sergeant who commanded the local outpost. Then the Chinook was called in, and a yellow smoke grenade, brilliant this time in the glaring sunlight, was thrown to mark the desired landing spot. We loaded up on the helicopter with the fourteen detainees squatting in the aisle. The silent, staring children lined the edge of the paddy, watching as the helicopter lifted off.

By nine thirty in the morning, I was back at my office sifting through my papers. I was hot, gritty from the dust that the helicopter had thrown at me, and a little sleepy. Out by the village the sealing infantry soldiers were forming into a march column to move to a landing zone and be lifted out. The results were two thousand pounds of confiscated rice and, as of noon that day, three confirmed Viet Cong from the fourteen detainees. It was not a very impressive tally for the hours and equipment that had been invested, but it was typical of "population control" techniques. The techniques were as old as war; only the helicopters were new. This particular seal and search had been smooth and easy. They were not all as inexpensive in lives, and they got less interesting and more frustrating the more one participated in them.

# III
# Infantry Operations

October brought increasing heat, decreasing rain, and word that we would be moving our brigade headquarters north to Quan Loi. Our main operations now took place primarily to the north of Phuoc Vinh in War Zones C or D, and it made sense to locate our permanent brigade headquarters closer to the center of these areas of operation. More and more frequently, a small command post had been going out and staying out for the duration of an operation at one temporary fire support base or another to direct the day-to-day combat operations of our brigade. Phuoc Vinh was too far away for good radio commu nications, and it was rapidly becoming an administrative haven south of the combat zone, useful mainly as a place for an infantry battalion to stand down for a few days respite from the much more primitive life of the night defensive position. Quan Loi had been selected be cause of its geographic proximity to our projected combat operations and because it already had a good airstrip. Though the French-run Terre Rouge rubber plantation was still operating there on a marginal basis, a series of infantry battalion task forces had been using it on a rotational basis for the past several months as a temporary base of operations.

Quan Loi sat on a ridge overlooking rolling jungle and rubber trees about thirty miles north and west of Phuoc Vinh, as the helicopter flew, but no road provided such a direct link between the two loca tions. It was situated five miles east of Highway 13, which was the main road running almost due north into Cambodia from Saigon. That highway ran through Lai Khe, where the division headquarters was located some seventeen miles north of Saigon, and on to An Loc, another thirty-four miles to the north. There a road split off to the east to Quan Loi. Beyond An Loc, fifteen miles farther to the north on a much-narrowed Highway 13, was Loc Ninh and the Cambodian border. An Loc and Loc Ninh would have their moments of publicity as the war visited them again and again in the months and years ahead, and even now they were not newcomers to combat. There had been a major French defeat in an ambush just north of Loc Ninh, when the Viet Minh controlled the area, and the rusting hulks of the French vehicles could still be seen from the road. My job took on welcomed variety as I became involved in the details of moving our brigade headquarters to Quan Loi, a move that was projected to take place in November.

In the meantime the infantry battalion combat operations continued to the north of Phuoc Vinh. Their mission was to locate and destroy the main force Viet Cong regiments that made their homes in bunkered encampments in War Zones C and D, from which they forayed whenever a likely target or politically opportune moment presented itself. To accomplish that mission, our battalions were airlifted by helicopter into a series of landing zones. Sometimes these landing zones were quiet and calm, and sometimes they held unpleasant surprises for the lead sticks of infantry squads and platoons that came to them. The landing zones, however, were always a major attraction for the division's senior commanders, and we could always count on there being at least one general to supervise. To assist the generals in their supervisory work, a system of colored smoke grenades was used to mark the outer limits of advance of the succeeding echelons of infantrymen as they spread out from the center of a landing zone to secure it for the rest of their battalion. The system came to be called a "Christmas Tree" because that is what it looked like from the air, with the multicolored smoke grenades identifying the squads in a precisely prescribed pattern as they fanned out from the helicopters that were hovering inches off the ground, forward movement barely stopped, while the soldiers leaped and hit the ground running. On several occasions a considerable amount of energy was expended on the command radio nets regarding the failure of a ground unit to adhere strictly to the prescribed smoke-grenade pattern. It sometimes seemed that proper marking was the most important part of an air assault into a landing zone, and it is true that the commanders in the air could not "help" if they could not identify the players.

Once a battalion was landed, it would set up a night defensive position with a quickly dug perimeter of foxholes, all with overhead cover, enclosing a command post and, if possible, a helicopter landing pad. The perimeter would be quickly reinforced by rolls of barbed concertina wire and claymore mines that were flown in. Then the position, totally dependent on the helicopter for supplies and evacuation, would be in business to act as a base of operations for the daily searches of the adjoining jungle or rubber trees. A skeleton force secured the night defensive position during the day while the majority of the battalion struck out on a planned search route in one direction or another to try to locate one of the main force Viet Cong regiments that our intelligence people always "knew" were operating somewhere close by.

The heat and the thickness of the foliage made these sweeps tough, and the shadowy presence of the main force regiments made them dangerous. Though we had the ability to inflict heavy casualties on any main force regiment that we could pin down, such regiments were well armed and well disciplined. They were far more formidable than the groups of local Viet Cong that harassed the villages, outposts, and roads in the more populated areas closer to Saigon, and their knowledge of the terrain gave them the capability to inflict considerable damage on the unwary. The current doctrine of our division called for the searching infantry to find this enemy and for the artillery, within whose range these operations always took place, and the Air Force to destroy them. From this doctrine evolved a set of tactics that can be described as follows. The infantry moved out each day along a line of march looking for evidence of the Viet Cong, with the lead elements probing to the front and sides in a cloverleaf pattern that aimed at discovering an ambush before it could be sprung. Once contact was made, either through sighting the lurking enemy or by triggering an ambush, the infantry would direct an overwhelming volume of rifle and machine-gun fire at the enemy and withdraw about fifty yards under cover of that fire to set up lines parallel to the enemy. Then the artillery and air strikes were directed into the target area to kill the enemy force. The idea was to inflict maximum damage on the Viet Cong at minimum cost to ourselves.

It did not always work as planned in the heat and closeness of the jungle and the untended rubber trees that were our battle ground. One morning early in the month one of our battalions started out from its night defensive position on a sweep and was attacked only one hundred yards from its own perimeter. The night defensive position had been set up very close to some previously prepared Viet Cong bunkers, which had remained undetected through the night, and that closeness caught the infantrymen still thinking they were secure and still straightening out their march order as they started their clover-leafing movements. In moments the lead company had seven dead and twenty-six wounded. Then, as they withdrew in accordance with the division doctrine to establish a line parallel to the enemy and to call in the killing supporting fires, the remainder of the lead company got into a firefight with its own uneasy sister company further back in the march column. By the time it was all sorted out and the artillery had ranged in on the bunkers, the occupants had drifted away into the jungle. The blocking force of additional infantrymen, who had been waiting on alert at a division airstrip and were quickly flown in behind the enemy, arrived too late to do anything but investigate the empty bunkers. Though some particularly unfortunate mistakes had been made in the surprise and confusion of finding a fortified position right outside their own base, the outline of the action was not especially unusual. The thick vegetation and the triple canopy of overhead tree cover prevented spotting the enemy from the air, and it was just very difficult to see the antagonist. Most encounters, therefore, occurred very suddenly at point-blank ranges, and the theory of killing the enemy with indirect fire turned out, more often than not, to be nothing more than a tearing up of empty jungle after a brief contact in which a few soldiers on both sides had been killed or wounded. Certainly, it was difficult to visualize a decisive battle under conditions such as these.

Our commanders were exposed to an added danger in these brief, fierce encounters in the jungle. The presence of the backpack radios, with their telltale whip antennas, was a certain marker of the location of the company or battalion commander in any group of moving soldiers. Without the radio nearby the commander could not keep the tracking artillery and Air Force observers informed of where his troops were and could not call for the needed fire support when contact was made; with the radio near at hand the commander was a marked man. Since the Viet Cong frequently placed snipers in trees, the commander and his radioman were frequently the first to be hit by enemy fire.

During the second week in October, the brigade headquarters established a forward command post next to Highway 13 near a minor crossroads village named Chon Thanh, which was about half way between Lai Khe and An Loc. From that central location the brigade directed a series of search operations in War Zone C, which ran west from Highway 13 toward what once had been a thriving Michelin rubber plantation. The brigade forward command post shared its location with a battery of eight-inch guns and was protected by a perimeter formed by a platoon of armored cavalry with its assault vehicles and tanks. It was a dusty, marginally secure location.

The temporary brigade operations center consisted of several large connecting circles dug waist deep into the dusty red earth and covered by tentage. Sandbags were built up around the tents to give protection up to about the height of a man. Also, they effectively kept out whatever breeze there might be and ensured that the interior, with its constantly humming radios, was stifling. The sleeping arrangements consisted of some two-man tents near the operations center with canvas cots inside. This tight complex was literally under the guns, and every time the battery fired, the concussion hit us in a wave. Sleeping under these conditions at night was a real trick because we had to wear earplugs to have even a prayer of dozing off, and the guns lifted us off our cots every time they fired. To add to that discomfort, the helicopter pad for the large Chinook helicopters that delivered artillery ammunition and other supplies was located between the guns and our headquarters. Each time one hovered in or lifted off, it threatened to blow down all the tentage and drove a storm of stinging dust into all exposed surfaces.

Almost daily I traveled back and forth between this fire-support base and our headquarters at Phuoc Vinh. My time was split between doing administrative chores at Phuoc Vinh, continuing to arrange for our move to Quan Loi, and ferrying the inevitable papers out to the fire-support base for the brigade commander to ponder when he returned from a day of directing our combat operations. More often than not I was at the forward location for the daily briefing that we still conducted in the late afternoon each day, and I frequently stayed the night to take part in staff meetings on the forthcoming move and to

have access to my commander for various items that required discussion. In those cases I flew back to Phuoc Vinh in the first helicopter out in the morning. The routine, and the poor sleeping conditions under the guns, soon took its toll, and the permanent residents
of the fire-support base, particularly, began to look tired and worn.
Even our husky operations officer showed the effects of the hectic
daily pace on just five hours of sleep a night with the guns firing
directly over his cot.

One day it dawned bright and very hot, which, in combination
with the flu shots that had been mandatorily given to all members of
the brigade, slowed us down as we went about our business in the
headquarters building at Phuoc Vinh. Even being in the combat zone
did not alter the inevitable Army cycle of the fall flu shots. It had the
makings of a slow day, with only the late afternoon trip to our forward
base to spice up my life and break the routine.

Then, toward midmorning, the brigade command channel on the
radios in the next room started to carry reports of a heavy enemy
contact in War Zone C, with the possibility of heavy casualties. Next
there were reports that the battalion command group of the battalion
in contact had been wiped out and that our brigade commander was
on the ground trying to put it all back together. Soon after came a
report that our own brigade operations officer had been killed. Everything stopped in the headquarters building, and we all clustered around
the operations center radios, trying to make sense out of these fragmentary reports and to understand what was going on in the jungle
to the north. In another twenty minutes there was a radio call for me
and the deputy base commander, another major, to get up to the brigade forward command post to take over the normal duties of our
brother staff officers who had been flown forward to the night defensive position of the battalion under attack. Very quickly we stuffed
some basic essentials into waterproof rubber bags, got our weapons
and helmets, and were on our way to the helicopter landing pad. The
brigade commander's command and control helicopter was coming
in for us as we arrived at the pad, and we jumped aboard.

As we gained altitude and headed northwest, the battery of radios,
which formed a center island in the passenger compartment of these
command and control helicopters, came alive with the voices of the
battalion and brigade staff members who were trying to sort out the
situation. During a momentary pause in the transmissons, an unfa-

miliar voice came on the command channel of the battalion that was in contact.

"Dauntless, Dauntless, any Dauntless station, this is Pfc. Costello."

"Dauntless" was the call word that represented the engaged infantry battalion on the radio. Used the way it had just been used it was a request for any Dauntless radio to answer. Again it came, sounding like a voice in the wilderness.

"Dauntless, Dauntless, any Dauntless station, this is Pfc. Costello."

"Pfc. Costello, this is 79'r," came the response from our assistant division commander, who must have been monitoring the engaged battalion's command radio channel. There followed one of the most poignant radio conversations I have ever heard. Pfc. Costello was one of the radio operators for the battalion commander. He was, he told the assistant division commander, wounded in three places and lying in the middle of the battalion command group, all of whom were dead. He was also the only link between the battalion and the outside world at the moment, and he was the first contact that had been established with the fighting elements after the confusion of a plainly heard fierce fire fight, which had eliminated the normal communications that had existed between the part of the battalion on its sweep and its command post in its night defensive position. Everybody in the night defensive position knew that there was a fight going on—the beginnings of the fight had been clear—then, however, there had been a sudden increased volume of fire and loss of radio contact. The assistant division commander assured Costello that help was on the way and pressed him to provide what details he could about the situation on the ground. Based on Costello's information, artillery fire was brought in on the attackers firing from the jungle undergrowth, which provided momentary relief for the hard-pressed troops.

Shortly after Costello's radio message, we were landing between the battery of guns and the brigade forward command post and running for the operations center. All was carefully controlled and calm in the hot, airless tents that covered the dugouts in which the radios and field desks sat. Reports were starting to come in, and supporting fires were being coordinated. The quiet tension expressed itself in exaggerated politeness. There was much shoulder squeezing as people passed each other on their way from one radio to another or to a desk, and arriving officers sent to take up temporary staff duties were greeted with solemn handshakes. The conversation was subdued, and there was a constant background chatter from the radios that served the artillery. A high volume of artillery fire was being directed against the edges of the area where the fighting was going on in an attempt to shield the remainder of the battalion, which was still caught in the grips of the trap. Our brigade commander was making his way out to the besieged companies from the night defensive position to take command on the ground. In the meantime the assistant division commander had taken over the brigade and was coordinating our efforts in the operations center. As we listened to the radios, we began to realize that the artillery was being directed by an artillery forward observer lieutenant who was with the battalion. He had been badly wounded but had recovered from his initial shock and was steadily adjusting the artillery fire. He finished his latest set of adjustment instructions over the artillery radio channel and paused to observe the effects of his work. Then his voice came on the radio again.

"I know I'm going to die," said the voice of the lieutenant, whose name was unknown to us at the time, "but I just want to tell you that the artillery fire is good—don't bring it in any closer."

He continued to make minor adjustments to the artillery fire until he could no longer talk. They found him later, slumped over his radio, dead.

At about the same time the earlier rumor that our brigade operations officer had been killed was confirmed. By now it was afternoon, and we all knew that we had a disaster in the making. Our focus was on helping to regroup the survivors and to get them back to their night defensive position while trying to evacuate the wounded at the same time—and to do it before dark. There was beginning to be some order in the confusion on the ground as the brigade commander pulled the survivors together. They started to become a coherent unit again, but the evacuation of the wounded who could not be carried back to the battalion's night defensive position was still a major problem. There was a hole in the jungle canopy over a crater near the center of the fighting, and one helicopter at a time could go down into it, pick up the wounded, and come back up. The firing that was occurring all around the crater made it a touchy business at best, but the helicopters kept going down into the hole in the jungle and coming back up with loads of wounded. The lieutenant colonel who commanded the division aviation battalion was flying one of the helicopters himself when he was hit by a rifle round that came up through the floor of his ship, entered his foot, and ran up his ankle. Somehow he kept control of the helicopter until his copilot took over. He survived but never walked normally again after that trip into the crater.

By nightfall all the wounded who had been located were evacuated and the survivors of the morning's sweep were back inside the protection of their night defensive position, where the battalion executive officer had been keeping things going all day. With full dark came an uneasy quiet, broken by the artillery shooting their random harassment and interdiction fires into the battle area to keep any enemy in the vicinity off balance.

In the morning the survivors were airlifted back to their base camp at Lai Khe, and fresh troops were lifted in. They reentered the battle area, recovered the remainder of our dead, and tried to assess the damage that had been done to the attackers. The weapons and radios were still by our dead, which showed that the enemy had not loitered to pick up loot, and the enemy weapons recovered indicated that our soldiers had inflicted some casualties in return. Our brigade commander took back control of the brigade. A major from the division staff, who had been brought in the previous day, took over as our operations officer for the time being, and the normal pace of operations resumed.

It soon became apparent that there was nothing more that I could contribute to the ongoing operation, so I was directed to go back to the battalion's base camp and help sort out the names of the killed and wounded and get an accurate accounting of who was still alive. The death of so many of the leaders and the quick work of the tropical heat on the bodies of the dead, combined with the evacuation of wounded to several different field hospitals, had made it very difficult to sort out who was dead and who was missing. I spent the afternoon back at the battalion's base camp going over rosters and cross-checking with the survivors about whom they had seen around them for certain. In the course of those conversations, I obtained a very clear picture of what had happened.

The battalion had been lifted in by helicopter several days before to search for a Viet Cong main force regiment that was thought to be operating in the area of jungle that lay between Highway 13 and the

Michelin rubber plantation. Several caches of rice had been found close by, as well as several other intelligence indicators that pointed to that area as a likely hiding place for a regiment. Our infantry battalion had been landed in a clearing and had set up its night defensive position. The next few days were spent searching the surrounding jungle without finding anything. Exhausting and unprofitable searches into three of the four major compass-point directions from the night defensive position had been made on successive days; the search into the fourth direction, the south, was to be made on the battalion's last day in the area. The commanders of the two companies that were scheduled to be the searching force were concerned about the plan and had asked the battalion commander not to go back out. They reasoned that they had remained too long in one place and had allowed the Viet Cong to get too good a fix on their position and pattern of activities. They were also concerned that they would be taking the only direction that they had not tried previously and that seemed a bit too obvious to them. They were overruled. Some ingrained sense of orderliness seemed to require this last sweep in order to complete the search of the targeted area, which had thus far yielded nothing, despite the potential of the intelligence indicators.

So two rifle companies and the battalion command group moved out to the south on that final morning. The lead elements of the first company followed a draw to the beginning of the heavy jungle about four hundred yards away from the night defensive position, with the rest of the company, the battalion command group, and the second company following in a loose column. As they entered the jungle proper, the lead elements began the cloverleaf movements that were meant to prevent the bulk of the column from falling unexpectedly into an ambush or a Viet Cong defensive position. About one hundred yards inside the jungle, the point man of the lead squad froze when he saw two shadowy figures in black in the undergrowth ahead of him just off the track. He passed back the word. When nothing happened, it was decided that the point man had not been detected. The battalion commander then directed an ambush to be set at the edge of the track to try to catch whoever was out there. The lead company set up a hasty ambush, while the following company simply moved off to the side of the track and waited alertly in the undergrowth that began at the trail's edge. Unfortunately, this hasty ambush was set up inside the so-called killing zone of a prepared ambush that the Viet

Cong had in place. Their ambush was in the typical L pattern, with its short leg across the trail that the infantrymen had been following, and its long leg parallel to the trail itself. The Viet Cong spotted by the point man apparently had been part of the short leg.

It took about five minutes for the lead company to set up its hasty ambush. Then the quiet that followed their settling in was broken by a withering fire of automatic weapons and antipersonnel mines from the waiting Viet Cong concealed farther back in the undergrowth. A number of our soldiers were wounded in this first hail of fire, including both the battalion commander and the battalion intelligence officer. The battalion commander, however, could still fight his battalion, and he directed the lead company to fall back while he called for supporting fire. Doctrine called for this withdrawal to take place along an imaginary diagonal line drawn from the interior junction of the two legs of the L, but the jungle undergrowth made that difficult. The lead company thus fell back more or less along the trail, which was parallel to the long leg of the ambush, while the following company moved forward just off the trail in an attempt to broaden the line. Since that company was also moving inside the long leg of the L, there was sporadic firing from the flanks, but nothing to indicate a problem that the two companies could not deal with. While this adjusting of positions on the ground was taking place, the battalion commander called for air strikes in accordance with the division policy of using outside supporting fire before using our own artillery, and the wounded were gathered to where the command group was huddled at the edge of the trail in the approximate center of the two rifle companies. Then they waited for the air strikes to come in.

The planes arrived in about twenty-five minutes and hit the point where the first contact between the lead company and the waiting Viet Cong had been made. Air strikes, however, can hit only one point at a time, and they prevent the artillery from firing on other nearby points for fear of hitting our own planes. Therefore, the battalion commander requested that the air strikes be called off and that artillery fire, which could hit simultaneously all along the perimeter from which fire was being received, be brought in instead. The Viet Cong, meanwhile, had taken advantage of the twenty-five-minute lull before the arrival of the first planes to extend the original L into a U, with the opening at the end of the trail leading back toward the night defensive position. The infantymen were beginning to receive fire from both sides of the track. When the battalion commander asked for artillery, he was asked to set off some smoke grenades so that the observers in the air could plot his location and range in the initial artillery rounds. By this time the two companies were receiving very heavy automatic weapons fire from both sides of the trail, and the situation was becoming dangerous. When the smoke grenades were set off to mark the center of the unit's position, the Viet Cong used them as a guide and moved through from one side of the trail to the other, killing or wounding everyone near the smoke grenades. The battalion commander was killed; the intelligence officer, who had already been wounded and was on a stretcher, was killed by a shot through the head as he lay there; and the command sergeant major was killed. The radio operator was wounded, as was the artillery forward observer, and for a time there was no radio contact with the various listening headquarters as individual infantrymen tried to fend for themselves against the intense automatic weapons fire and the whirring fragments of claymore mines from both flanks. Effective command and control of the two companies was gone.

Now everything had to be judged from the sounds. Back at the night defensive position the volume of firing indicated serious fighting going on, and the sudden breaking of radio communication indicated the possibility that key leadership people were out of action. At this point our brigade commander decided to land and take control on the ground. He was accompanied that day by our intelligence officer. They both jumped off the command and control helicopter and ran to the battalion operations center when they landed. Without radio communications, however, the situation was not much clearer from there than it had been from the helicopter overhead, so they set off to try to reach the battlefield to determine what could be done. They were eventually successful in rallying the survivors and extricating the remainder of the battalion by the end of the day.

At about the time the brigade commander and intelligence officer set out, somebody requested additional smoke grenades for the battalion over the brigade radio net, and our brigade operations officer took the opportunity to fly them in himself to be nearer the action in case he was needed. He delivered the grenades, stopped in on the battalion operations center, and stood around looking for some way to help. The wounded who could be moved the distance along the sniper-ridden trail between the battlefield and the night defensive position were starting to be brought back in by then, and after fifteen or twenty minutes, he saw his opportunity to get into the action. He borrowed an M16 rifle, told a nearby sergeant to get a machete, ignored the battalion executive officer's advice to stay put, gathered up a medic and another soldier, and led his three new-found teammates out at a dead run to see what they could do to help cut a path and speed the evacuation of the wounded. He got his one hundred yards, but not even the power and drive that had made him the most valuable player of an Army-Navy game could protect him from the sniper in the tree ahead where the trail forked. Two rounds from an automatic rifle did what no tacklers had ever done permanently. The medic got to him and found him still breathing, but the sniper was not finished. He opened up again and hit the sergeant in the arm. The medic ducked. By the time the sniper was eliminated and people could move again, our brigade operations officer was dead.

The cost of the day's action was fifty-nine dead, seventy-seven wounded, and three missing and presumed dead. Most of the leaders had been killed or wounded, and my review of rosters indicated that no more than thirty managed to survive unscathed. The well oiled enemy weapons that the relieving troops found on the following day indicated that we had run into an estimated two reinforced companies of a very professional force; their fire discipline and cool tactics indicated that there were probably a fair number of regular North Vietnamese Army soldiers among the attacking force. I was not amused to read the statement of a senior Army officer in the newspaper a few days later, which said that the engagement did not have "the flavor of an ambush" because the "Communists did not fire mortars or recoilless rifles." I was sure that the survivors did not agree with his assessment.

Once more the division's awards program showed its weaknesses. My brigade commander had made his way out to the disorganized remnants of that battalion under fire, had reorganized them, had directed the evacuation of the wounded and the tricky extraction of the survivors, and had spent the better part of the day and night voluntarily acting as the battalion commander on the ground. I had eye witness reports that supported an award for gallantry, and I submitted a recommendation for the Distinguished Service Cross for him. The division headquarters studied that recommendation for the nation's second-highest award for gallantry for several weeks then returned it without action because they did not think that an ambush was the kind of event that they wanted associated with two such awards. The commanding general had decided that the dead battalion commander, the son of a previous division commander, should be awarded the Distinguished Service Cross. It seemed clear that awards were based occasionally on the whim of the senior officer present instead of on actual observed facts.

A few mornings later at about nine o'clock, as I was working with my clerks to finish up the casualty reports and awards recommendations from the ambush, the phone from our base camp operations center jangled. I was told that an unarmed troop-carrying helicopter had been shot down as it lifted off from our airstrip. The pilots had managed to land it fifteen hundred yards outside our perimeter, and the crew was unhurt. As the senior officer present in the camp at the moment, I was in charge. I ran to the small operations center and quickly arranged to call in two helicopter gunships to protect the downed ship from above while we figured out how to secure and extract it. Then I alerted the rifle company that was guarding our bunker line to move its quick-reaction platoon to the airstrip and to be prepared to go out to secure the helicopter on the ground. While the operations center staff made the detailed arrangements for helicopters to lift the troops from our airstrip to the downed helicopter, I checked on the radio frequencies in use, marked the approximate location of the forced landing on my map, and had my weapon and helmet brought to me. Then I got our aviation officer to let me use one of our light observation helicopters to take me up so that I could see the situation for myself and provide what assistance I could until the troops could be lifted in. By the time the helicopter was ready, I knew that the quick-reaction platoon was on its way to the airstrip in trucks, that the helicopters were on the way to lift them out, and that the assistant division commander was flying in to direct the operation. It was 9:10.

We circled up directly over the base camp to one thousand feet, mindful that if the other helicopter had been brought down by ground fire, a lower altitude in our much lighter and more vulnerable ship could be a particularly unhealthy position. From our one-thousand-foot altitude, everything looked peaceful on the ground. The downed helicopter was easy to see, and we could tell that the crew had skill-

fully settled it on one of the dirt tracks that crisscrossed the area between scrub woods. It appeared to be undamaged. Below us the two
gunships were already circling protectively in a tight orbit over their
downed sister, and there was no threatening activity to be seen among
the rice paddies and villages. We circled and listened to the radio. I
told the operations center that I was in position to help, and I gave
the exact map location of the downed helicopter. In return the radio
told me that the platoon of troops was at the airstrip, that the assistant
division commander had arrived and was briefing them, and that the
requested troop-carrying helicopters were arriving. A few minutes later
it appeared from the radio traffic that the executive officer of the infantry battalion to which the platoon belonged had also arrived and
was making a last check of the troops and their equipment.

The radio channels were becoming very crowded, and the proper
people were taking charge, so I told the pilot to take me back before
the air space became as crowded as the radio channels. The two gunships were still flying orbit, and our FAC's light aircraft passed us
on the way in, which meant that we had an observer on station to
direct artillery or air strikes should they be needed. The activity below, around the artillery guns, in the base camp indicated that they
were ready to respond to any request for fire. Only thirty-five minutes
had elapsed since the first notification, but those minutes must have
seemed like hours to the crew standing nervously around their downed
ship.

I walked back to my office and into the operations center to listen
to the radio transmissions that would tell us the progress of the recovery operation that we had set in motion. There had been no further
indications of enemy activity on the ground, and no attempt had been
made to attack the downed ship or its crew, but an area around the
helicopter had to be cleared and secured so that a big Chinook could
be brought in without unnecessary risk. The Chinook would also bring
a crew that was expert in rigging disabled ships for liftout. Securing
the area had to be our first objective, even though all this was taking
place only fifteen hundred yards outside our base camp. The shot that
brought down the helicopter to begin with was supposed to have come
from closer in than that, and nobody could be sure that it was not
part of a plan to lure in more soldiers and helicopters. So we played
it as though there were more than just one marksman out there.

The platoon of infantry landed at ten o'clock in a clearing some

150 yards away from the dirt track and the wounded helicopter and anxious crew. Overhead the gunships were still circling and the assistant division commander was monitoring the operation. It looked like an easy walk to the dirt track for the platoon. It was not. In thirty minutes they had covered only half the distance and had three wounded. One soldier had lost a foot, one had a badly mangled leg, and a third had shrapnel wounds in the mouth. The platoon had encountered booby traps and mines in the scrub woods, and everybody was now alert for some sign that the Viet Cong were lurking farther back, waiting to ambush the entire group. We could not tell if the casualties resulted from good planning on the part of the enemy or from bad luck on our part, but the recovery operation was becoming costly. It took another thirty minutes for the platoon to sweep through the dirt track and beyond it. They found no trace of enemy, and there were no more casualties. A medical evacuation helicopter was brought in to take the three wounded soldiers back for treatment.

It was now eleven o'clock in the morning, and the waiting Chinook was told that it was safe to come in. After it landed on the dirt track near the downed helicopter, its crew began rigging. An anxious hour passed, with the platoon forming a watchful perimeter around the busy helicopter crew members. When the rigging was complete, the Chinook took off, hovering over the downed helicopter while its hook was attached to the prepared rigging. Out came the downed helicopter. Ten minutes later the platoon had closed back in on the dirt track and was being lifted out. By 12:20 everybody was back inside the base camp perimeter, and by 12:30 we knew that the helicopter had gone down because of engine failure rather than because of hostile fire. Damage to the ship had been light. The three casualties, it turned out, resulted from mines that an American unit had emplaced more than two years earlier and had failed to record. A simple engine failure and our own carelessness had cost us three wounded, and the day was only half over. Not to have put the platoon on the ground, however would have invited other, far graver risks. As always in Vietnam, there was no simple solution.

# IV

# In the War Zone—
# Quan Loi

The first day of November brought very hot weather, no rain, and the advance party from an Army division that was still in the United States and that was to take over our base camp at Phuoc Vinh as part of the American military buildup that was then under way. Fourteen officers, including the division commanding general, descended on us that day to look over the base camp and to plan where to put the various parts of their division. They carefully checked the state of repair of the facilities that they would take over and noted what we would leave behind inside the buildings. Since our brigade was moving to a tent city to live under somewhat spartan field conditions, there was not much in the way of fans, lights, and other such amenities that we needed to take with us, but our visitors had the traditional Army suspicion that when we left we would strip off everything that could be carried—and in the end they were right to have been suspicious. There is something in the make-up of the American soldier that prevents him from leaving anything for his successor that he has "scrounged" for himself.

The commanding general of the incoming division was a notorious figure in Army circles, with an earthy manner and an irrational temper that could explode quite unexpectedly. As a result, we all walked very gingerly around him and provided information only when asked. Our jeep drivers were even more edgy than we were as they drove him around the camp. The combination of these circumstances operated to keep the general from learning that we had service club women quartered in our compound, and we had not had occasion to let our service club women know about the personality of the general. The director of our service club and her two assistants lived in a small, homemade bungalow close to the brigade headquarters building. It was set off a little from our other buildings and was situated so that the military police gate guard at the entrance to our headquarters compound could see it clearly. It was also in plain sight of our headquarters building. The scrub grass around the bungalow was surrounded by barbed-wire entanglements and trip flares to discourage amorous soldiers from gaining entrance through any of the windows—or even getting close enough to invade the women's privacy. The only safe entrance was by the walkway to the front door, unless you wanted to chance the barbed wire and the flares, and that walkway was in plain sight of everybody. Because the women kept the service club open until eleven o'clock each night and had closing-up chores to do after that, they were in the habit of sleeping in during the morning hours and lounging in the comfort provided by a window air conditioner. They were protected from the world of men with which they had to deal daily by the combination of their highly visible location and the field fortifications that surrounded them.

The visiting general noticed the bungalow and apparently had ideas for its use, though he had not indicated his interest to any of us. During the course of his walk through the brigade headquarters area that morning, he decided that he wanted to inspect the bungalow along with the rest of his soon-to-be-inherited domain. He marched up to the door, trailed by his chief of staff, and knocked peremptorily on the door. No answer came. He knocked again. Still no answer came. He pushed open the door. Three pair of eyes looked at him over lowered newspapers, behind which the women, still in their bathrobes, had been enjoying coffee.

"Who the hell are you, and what are you doing here?" demanded the general.

"We live here," replied one of the women, "and who the hell are you?"

The general was taken aback, but he stood his ground and informed them that he was the incoming commander of Phuoc Vinh. The women replied that they were the service club women. An uncomfortable silence followed this terse exchange of information. It dragged on. Finally, the general wavered under the stares of the three women and backed out, which was the closest thing to a defeat in an encounter of personalities that any of his staff had ever witnessed.

Early in November an engineer major who had been on the faculty with me at West Point was out with his mine-sweeping teams on a routine clearing mission. He was checking on progress when one of the teams stopped suddenly. An operator had spied a heavy piece of paper lying on the edge of the road and was staring alertly at it. The major, who was the battalion executive officer, came up to the team, asked what the hold-up was, and started walking toward the paper. He reached down to pick it up and disappeared into a cloud of dirt, rocks, and the acrid smell of cordite. When the cloud settled, he was dead. Nobody ever figured out exactly what had happened: some kind of triggering device had been set off, but whether it was attached to the innocent-appearing paper or a trip wire on the road or a pressure-sensitive plate buried in the road, we never found out. We lost a couple of men like that every few days; I just happened to know this one.

November was also our month for media sensationalism. One of our battalions seemed to have an uncanny ability to attract one or another of the television crews that wandered about Vietnam. Each contact invariably resulted in another piece of uncomplimentary, but dramatic, publicity. Maybe it was their black scarves that attracted the media, or maybe it was just luck, but if the black-scarved battalion was involved in anything that could be construed as not quite proper, the television crews were there to record it. For instance, there was the matter of the reliability of our M16 rifles. These rifles were still new at the time, and there was an admitted problem with jamming. The round would fire, and as the bolt came back to pull the spent shell case out, it would frequently rip off the end of the expended cartridge, leaving the remainder of the casing inside the breech. That could be a bit annoying, to say the least, in a firefight because until the casing was removed, no more rounds could be fired. The only way to get the casing out was to ram it out with a cleaning rod from the muzzle end. The Army was very sensitive to this problem, which was eventually solved by a combination of better weapon-cleaning habits, better lubricants, some modifications to the weapon, and a change of propellant powder in the ammunition. In the meantime every

M16 was issued with a cleaning rod attached, which obviously showed recognition of the problem. The Army, however, remained more than a little defensive about the whole subject—primarily because the problems should have been identified in development before wholesale procurement and issue to the troops began. Nevertheless, the M16 was the right weapon in concept for the theater.

One day a television camera crew happened onto the scout platoon of its favorite battalion, and those black-scarved soldiers volunteered the information for coast-to-coast broadcast that they did not trust the M16 and that some of them were in fact, by preference, using captured Communist weapons. The interview that followed on the relative merits of the two weapons was an instant thirty-second news hit. I, of course, ended up investigating the circumstances of the interview and who was using what weapons in the scout platoon. In fact, we had found the AK-47, which was the Communist weapon in question, to be no more reliable than the M16, but for different reasons. Its weakness was in its magazine, which had a spring that was not strong enough for the job. The result was that its ammunition frequently did not feed properly, the same problem experienced with the old World War II carbine and which finally contributed to its being eliminated from our arsenal. None of that was known to the black-scarved scouts, of course—nor should it have been. They were simply users who had identified a problem that was known already to the Army establishment, but their short-term solution was bizarre enough to be ideal for television drama. So once more the Army establishment was made to look foolish, and the American public was led to believe that our privates had uncovered another example of the incompetency of the American military. The full story, unfortunately, was never presented, and the incident remained an example of our supposed ineptness, broadcast live for the general public's pleasure, without any counterbalance or any mention of the fact that the Army in Vietnam was not responsible for weapons development—just for fighting a war with what was provided.

Later there was the "ears" story. Throughout the conflict in Vietnam, there were recurring tales of atrocities committed by our soldiers, and some of our soldiers certainly did do the kinds of things alleged. Of those who stepped beyond the line of proper conduct, most were caught and quietly punished, though after My Lai the

American public never believed that completely. One of the more common tales had to do with the particularly repugnant practice of disfiguring the dead bodies of the enemy by cutting off parts of their bodies. During November I had to investigate an incident involving an ear, and it was recorded for posterity by the ever-present television cameras that happened to be standing by. This incident really got our attention. The rifle controversy had been merely embarrassing. This matter was more than that. None of us was into mutilation. It really struck at our professionalism. We were astounded at what had been recorded on television, and I was promptly given the task of finding out what had happened. The answer was not hard to find, and it was no prettier than what had been reported on television; it was, however, certainly different.

In this case the television crew had been out looking at a battlefield right after the black-scarved battalion had been engaged in a very sharp fight with the Viet Cong. The crew was looking for something dramatic to reflect the intensity of the skirmish but found only the standard dead bodies and wounded soldiers that usually accompany such actions. An Army public information specialist, an enlisted man from the public relations staff whose job it was to escort the television crews, had an idea. He called aside one of our black-scarved fellows and offered him a hunting knife and the proposition that he show how tough his outfit was by cutting off the ear of the nearest dead Viet Cong. The response to this challenge was predictable, and the television audience was treated to the sight of an American soldier mutilating a dead Viet Cong as though it were a routine occurrence in the "brutalizing" war in Vietnam. It did reflect "brutalization," but not the kind that was projected to the folks back home. They thought they were seeing a real-life, tacitly condoned practice of the frontline infantry soldier. What they were really seeing was a noncombatant's misplaced attempt to "help" his television crew. Obviously, several people other than the pictured infantryman bore some responsibility for this particular "media event"; that, however, never came out. Certainly, actual incidents such as this one may have occurred from time to time, but it was equally certain that they were not nearly as widespread as the media were trying to depict.

Generals like to make gestures to show that they care about their troops, and the troops like to take advantage of that inclination: that dynamic has been around as long as there have been armies. The advent of the helicopter and the radio, however, has increased the power of the soldier to make his dreams come true and decreased the likelihood that a general will investigate the situation thoroughly before trying to remedy it. Instant communication means instant gratification, and a general could listen to the complaints of a private without losing contact with the tactical situation of his division, while using those same communications to resolve any perceived deficiency. All of this was illustrated beautifully one day in mid-November. An infantry battalion had occupied a night defensive position on the previous afternoon and was busily at work reinforcing its temporary home before starting out on the routine searches of the surrounding area. Our division commander had landed his command and control helicopter to look around inside the perimeter and was checking on the battalion as it went about its preparations.

At about ten fifteen, the morning calm at Phuoc Vinh was broken by the imperious voice of the commanding general on the radio in the next room.

"This is 77," said the general, "I'm landing at your location in five minutes, and I want ground transportation to meet me."

After I sent my jeep to the helicopter landing pad, I checked with the operations center to see what was going on. From monitoring the various radio nets, they had pieced together the information that I was sending the jeep to meet a private, not the commanding general. It seemed that our general had been walking the battalion's position when he came across a private carrying ammunition to his squad's machine-gun position.

"How are you doing, soldier?" asked the general.

"Just fine, sir," came the answer from the saluting private.

"Sure you don't have any troubles, soldier?" (As if there ever was a soldier that did not have a problem he could come up with for a senior officer.)

"Well, sir, I'm supposed to go to Hawaii in a week to meet my wife, and I haven't gotten a letter from her saying that she will be there," blurted out the soldier.

"Don't worry, son. Get on my helicopter and we'll take care of that," responded the general.

Leaving his ammunition by the trail, the private got on the helicopter with his commanding general and was flown to Phuoc Vinh.

Forewarned by the radio, I had the jeep there to meet him and to take him directly to the semiofficial radio-telephone station that could be used to call the United States via reflected radio beams and the good offices of "ham" radio operators. The private arrived at 10:23, and by 10:37 he had assured himself that his wife was going to meet him in Hawaii and was back on his way to the field aboard a passing helicopter. Not a bad gesture, and the soldier and his wife would have a story to tell.

The general, meanwhile, had returned to his walking tour of the battalion position after dropping off the private at Phuoc Vinh. He headed off in a different direction and found another dusty soldier.

"How are you doing, soldier?" queried the general.

Again, the soldier replied, "Fine, sir," and again the general probed. "No problems at all, soldier?"

"Well, sir, we don't have any water to fill our canteens out here."

No water! The radio again crackled alive in the headquarters. Our general was furious that his soldiers did not have water available, and he directed us to get water out to the position immediately. We stopped all other work while we made arrangements for two water trailers to be filled and brought to the airstrip. Then I made a series of phone calls and radio calls to divert two helicopters that were working other missions in our area. They flew to our airstrip, were rigged to carry the water trailers as external loads, and flew off with them to the battalion position. There they set down the water trailers at the battalion water point, next to the fifteen full five-gallon water cans that had been stacked five-hundred yards from the dry private since early that morning.

Still ignorant of the outcome of his last gesture, our general had continued his patrol of the defensive position. He found another sweaty private working on improving his fighting hole.

"How are you doing, soldier?"

"Fine, sir," came the answer as the soldier paused in his digging.

"Sure there is nothing I can do for you, soldier," pressed the general.

"Well, sir, we haven't had any soda in a long time." That was the final straw for the general. Obviously he had uncovered a unit that did not take care of its men. This time he called my brigade commander and told him to get his battalion taken care of. My brigade commander, who was flying over the search operation of another battalion, called me and told me to get soda out to the battalion even if our headquarters had to donate it. Not feeling quite that charitable, because I knew the soldiers had been in the field less than twenty-four hours, I phoned the battalion's rear detachment. Sure enough, they had ample soda available. While they were trucking a pallet of soda to the airstrip, I went to work to find one more helicopter to divert. I found the helicopter and had it come to our airstrip, where it picked up the soda and ferried it out to the battalion. Once it had lifted off, I radioed my brigade commander that the soda was on the way. End of another mission, I thought. Only later in the day did I find out that the battalion had used two cargo helicopters to lift sixteen thousand pounds of something out to its position that morning.

The pressure on our brigade to move to Quan Loi increased as the month passed. The driving force now was the arrival date of the incoming division, not the readiness of our new accommodations. It soon became apparent that we would have to move in the third week in November, before Quan Loi was ready for us, in order to make room for the arriving soldiers. We set about preparing to move to Quan Loi as if we were simply moving to the field for good. The tent pads would not be ready in time for our move, nor would our command bunker. We would live and work in the area that the rotating infantry battalion task forces had been using as their command post. We would leave behind all the convenience items that had made Phuoc Vinh resemble a stateside Army post.

Just before Thanksgiving we made our move. Cargo helicopters carried our personal and professional gear to Quan Loi in relays one day, and by evening the antennas were up and the tents pitched, and the brigade headquarters was operating from the abandoned plantation workers' bungalows that had served so many different infantry battalions as temporary headquarters.

The rooms were damp and musty. Mine was particularly stuffy because the single window looked out onto a veranda that had been converted into our operations center by using sandbags to create walls and by extending the eaves with old tentage. There was no air circulation inside, and it was far more pleasant to work outside. My sleeping tent was pitched next to the side of the building, and I soon took to working in front of it on a field desk. Close to this building were the other elements of the brigade headquarters. The commander had his sleeping tent pitched a little ways off, toward the mess tent, and he worked out of it from a field desk when he was in. The operations staff set up in a large general-purpose tent that easily accepted its map boards and drafting tables. Interspersed around the area were the two-man sleeping tents for the principal staff officers and the large general-purpose tents in which our enlisted personnel slept in barracks style. Field phones connected this maze to the operations center's switchboard, though we could probably call to anybody we wanted because the walls to all the tents were rolled up most of the time to expose the canvas cots and work areas to whatever breeze was available.

To protect the headquarters personnel from the mortar and rocket attacks that we knew would eventually find us, we brought in a mechanical ditch digger to cut trenches out of the hard red earth adjacent to the cluster of tents and the main bungalow. These trenches were then covered by sections of galvanized metal culvert laid next to each other so that only the ends of the trenches remained open. With a covering of three layers of sandbags, we had sturdy shelters into which to dive if we were shelled. From this setting the routine of the brigade headquarters went on much as it had in Phuoc Vinh. The transition caused barely a ripple in the flow of papers moving in and out of my office, in the coordination of helicopter movements by the aviation officer, in the direction of combat operations by the operations staff, and in the conduct of the evening briefings.

Much of my time was taken up facilitating the construction of the area that would become the permanent home for the brigade. We had arranged with the French plantation manager to take over for this purpose a section of young rubber trees, which were not yet producing, across the airstrip from our current location. There were more and more contacts with the French plantation manager and his staff as our paths crossed more frequently in daily routines. Inevitably, there were conflicts that resulted from roads being blocked unexpectedly by our trucks, units moving into areas that the French had not cleared for our use, and the casual abuse of property that always seems to occur when troops occupy an area in a combat zone. I did a lot of the negotiating that was required to resolve each conflict, and we tried to make amends as best we could for the invasion. Toward the end of November, several of us who dealt most frequently with the French were invited to the home of the plantation manager for supper one evening.

Since the wives of the French plantation staff spent their weeks in Saigon, it was an all-male setting. As we relaxed, the conversation turned to how the manager felt about the current situation and why he stayed, given the increasing danger of his position. He told us very frankly that he stayed on because it was a great deal better than being a bank clerk in Paris, which is about all he could aspire to, he said, in metropolitan France. Looking around at the furniture, servants, and the comforts that went with his position, it was easy to understand his attitude, even in the face of the steadily encroaching war. He also told us that the plantation had been only marginally productive for a number of years and that it stayed in operation because it was subsidized by the Vietnamese government in various ways. That government apparently believed that it was absolutely essential to have some exportable products for the international market, despite the ravages of war, and rubber was the best available product. The low productivity, however, was not only a function of the war and the disrupted transportation system and economy, the manager told us. The decline had started when he could no longer hire North Vietnamese workers, but had been forced to make do with South Vietnamese peasants when the countries were partitioned. It appeared that soldiering was not the only thing that the North Vietnamese were better at than their southern neighbors, at least if this long-time plantation manager was to be believed.

It was a lovely and memorable evening for me, and it turned out to be my last social contact with the French at Quan Loi. Thereafter our relations became progressively more strained as our presence made itself increasingly felt. Our artillery batteries set up between the neat white plantation villas and chopped off the tops of the screening trees in order to obtain clearance for firing in a 360-degree arc. Those same batteries then fired intermittently over the houses throughout each night. Then our soldiers, fresh from the primitive living conditions of their search missions in the jungle, abused the French hospitality. They had granted us the use of their club swimming pool, and our troops used the changing rooms as a latrine. Though we could attempt to explain and apologize for these situations, it was hard to erase the image of the elegant white-stone changing rooms smeared with shit. I was just thankful that the French women were no longer living at

Quan Loi because I could guess at the problems that sooner or later would have attended their presence.

As the last days of November passed, more and more vehicles arrived to support our growing operations, and more and more large planes landed each day. The red dirt, from which the Terre Rouge plantation took its name, was churned into a perpetual red dust cloud that hung in the air as a result of constantly turning wheels and propeller blades. Eventually, all of this activity attracted the mortar, rocket, and ground attacks that we knew from the beginning were inevitable, and all semblance of an operating colonial plantation ceased to be. By that time I was gone from Quan Loi, and I never found out what became of the urbane French plantation manager and his Terre Rouge plantation as the war finally engulfed it.

# V
# Ambush, 31 December 1967

December found me worrying about three different base camps at the same time. I was responsible for the smooth functioning of the temporary headquarters area into which we had moved upon our arrival at Quan Loi; I was responsible for pushing the completion of our new cantonment area across the airstrip from that temporary headquarters and for planning a service-complex addition to it, which would consist of a post-exchange facility and a service club for the brigade soldiers; and I was trying in vain to disentangle the brigade from Phuoc Vinh.

Since the end of November, however, pressed on by fears of serving a year in Vietnam doing the same type of work I could have been doing in any peacetime assignment, I had been hoping for a new position in a combat battalion. Using the personnel channels that I dealt in day to day and from friends in other assignments, I heard of an opening in a cavalry squadron in another division. I was able to arrange to be assigned there in return for having an incoming major diverted to our division as my replacement. At last I had orders in my hands to report to my new assignment as a cavalry squadron executive officer on 21 December. In the late afternoon of 20 December, I said goodbye to my fellow brigade staff members and loaded my footlocker, duffel bag, and a waterproof bag onto a helicopter that was flying south. We lifted off from Quan Loi and followed Highway 13, passing over Chon Thanh, where our temporary command post had been set up during the ambush in October. As we flew over, I found myself staring to the west, to where the sun was setting over the ambush site. It was peaceful out there this evening, but my thoughts turned to the dead and wounded and the confusion of that day as I watched the sun tint the tops of the dark jungle canopy a deep red. Then we were past Chon Thanh and over Lai Khe, which was now the main division headquarters complex. In a few more minutes we were letting down at Di An, where only the division support troops still made their home. I spent the night with a friend who had taught English with me at West Point then borrowed a jeep, trailer, and driver from him the next day for the drive south past Saigon to my new division. I left behind some good friends and some bad memories after four and a half months, but I was also leaving behind directed awards packets, paralyzing overcentralized control, and an unwarranted elitist attitude that prevented this historically famous Army division from realizing its full potential.

The twenty-mile trip south the next morning took me over the same road that had originally brought me to Di An then on to the main highway into Saigon, with its heavy traffic. From there I drove south on Highway 15 past the big American headquarters complex at Long Binh. South of Long Binh, even though the countryside became less populated, the traffic continued unabated. Before long we were turning into the road to Bear Cat, which was the name given to the base camp that housed my new division headquarters and many of its major elements.

The division had moved into this area more than a year ago, when the first elements had arrived in Vietnam from the United States to start developing the camp. The maps showed that there had been a military installation of some kind at this place for a long time—or the regular outlines of a military encampment would not have appeared on the map—but I never had the time to learn the history. When I arrived, it was a flat, sprawling, dusty area inside a low perimeter marked by an embankment, some concertina wire, and machine-gun emplacements. It was totally devoid of trees, and the buildings and tents were a uniform dusty color. Driving into the base camp toward division headquarters, I realized that it must be very wet here on the northern edge of the Mekong Delta during the monsoon season because the dusty roads were bordered by very deep, five-foot-wide drainage ditches whose bottoms had cracked into an intricate web of geometrical shapes. Obviously, they had been designed to carry large volumes of water, but today any vehicle movement threw up a cloud of dust that obscured everything until it settled.

The division headquarters was located in a group of silver-colored Quonset huts clustered around a semicircular driveway and a set of flagpoles erected on a patch of scraggly brown grass. It was neat and unimposing, but functional. I had the driver stop in front of a building marked by a sign that indicated the personnel office, and I unloaded my gear onto the ground by a corner of that building before sending my borrowed jeep and trailer back to my host of the previous evening. I walked in and introduced myself to the division personnel officer. He took a copy of my orders, confirmed my assignment, took my records, and put in a phone call to my new unit to come get me. That was the extent of the processing. I was instructed to join the division commander at his table for supper that evening in the division head-quarters dining hall; then I was back out to my gear, waiting for transportation. There had been no delays, no interviews, and no foolishness. In twenty minutes I was on my way to the area where my new unit lived; in another five minutes I was entering the cantonment area of my cavalry squadron. My first look almost made me question what I had done. Clearly visible against the noon glare were the outlines of nine fifty-ton tanks, 90-millimeter guns pointed haphazardly into the air, engines out. Those tanks—standing idle in the hot dust in varying degrees of disrepair—were one-third of the squadron's tank force.

The squadron area was nearly deserted because the cavalry troops were out on a mission, and the completely mobile headquarters had set up near them, as was usual in a fire-support base with the supporting artillery. They were scheduled to march in on the following day because of a change in mission, so there was little point to trying to go out to join them. Besides, a squadron executive officer's business was as much in the base camp with the maintenance problems—namely, why those nine tanks were standing idle, gaping at the sky—as it was anywhere. I introduced myself to the adjutant, who normally remained in camp, and was shown where to bunk and to put my gear. Then I went out to get familiar with the squadron area and to see what was going on.

The squadron, which consisted of three ground line troops, an air cavalry troop, and a headquarters troop, was set up in a series of small adjoining tent camps clustered around the squadron maintenance area and the vehicle park. The central location of the vehicle park was appropriate because the vehicles and the mobility that they provide are the heart of a cavalry squadron. Each ground line troop had nine medium tanks and twenty-three armored personnel carriers, most of which were fitted with the extra side-mounted light machine guns and gun shields that converted them into armored cavalry assault vehicles—called ACAVs in the vernacular. Each troop also had three mortars mounted in specially adapted armored personnel carriers, which had sliding roofs to allow the installed mortar to fire; a powerful tank retriever on tracks to recover disabled vehicles; and several trucks and jeeps. At full strength, 180 officers and men worked and lived in these line troop vehicles.

The headquarters troop owned no tanks, but it had six specially built-up armored personnel carriers under whose raised roofs the command radios and map board lived. With the radios in these command vehicles, the squadron staff could control all the troops operating at once and still talk to supporting and higher headquarters over great distances. There were seven additional armored personnel carriers in the headquarters troop that were dedicated to the commander and various staff sections, to include the squadron maintenance platoon—or that portion of the platoon that did not ride in the two headquarters troop tank retrievers. Because of the availability of the air cavalry troop scout helicopters to carry the commander and staff to wherever the troops were operating, five of these armored personnel carriers had been converted into ACAVs and were used as a security platoon for the commander and the headquarters command vehicles. Taken all together, this squadron represented more than one hundred tracked vehicles thundering along on the road, and that did not take into account its supply trucks, fuel tankers, and other administrative-use wheeled vehicles.

Each of the troop areas consisted of a low wood building, in which supply and administrative business was conducted; a wood building that served as a dining hall; and a series of tents pitched on the typical wood frames and raised wood floors that served as home to the officers and men alike when they were in the base camp. In deference to the flat terrain and the monsoon deluges, the wood floors were raised more than what I had been accustomed to, and the tents stood some three feet above the ground. The entire cantonment area was parched, with dusty weeds growing up in the meager shade of the raised tent floors. The wood on which the tentage hung had been thoroughly soaked during the monsoon season that had just passed and was badly warped. The resulting sagging and leaning tents gave a run-down aura to the whole cantonment. It was apparent that this squadron had not spent much time living in its base camp.

Only the air cavalry troop presented a well-kempt appearance. There, because its entire complement worked in the base camp when not actually flying missions, the tents had been replaced by neat wood buildings, and the pilots had actually constructed a two-story complex divided into two-man rooms. Air cavalry troops had a talent for that kind of work—and the transportation to scrounge whatever necessary building materials were not easily available. This one had made the most of both capabilities. Our air cavalry troop owned nine light scout helicopters, eleven troop- or cargo-carrying "Hueys," and another six "Huey" gunships. (The name "Huey" derived from the official designation for that helicopter—UH1.) The permanent flight operations center and the maintenance facilities for these aircraft adjoined the squadron area at the edge of the large airstrip that occupied most of the center of Bear Cat; the living area was built back from there. The pilots, forty-four officers and warrant officers, and their maintenance crews lived close to the airstrip and worked long hours; however, because they could not all be flying at once, there were always men available to take care of their area. The air cavalry troop area, therefore, gave an appearance that was closer to a peacetime Army camp than any other area of the base camp—except for where the other aviation units lived.

After a slow walk through the squadron area, I returned to the headquarters to talk with the people in the rear detachment in order to get an idea of the personnel and supply problems that I would be faced with as I tried to coordinate the logistical, maintenance, and administrative support for this diverse nine-hundred-man organization. The maintenance problems would have to wait for the next day because the maintenance platoon and the maintenance officer were in the field with the squadron. By the time I had finished looking around, the afternoon was gone and it was time to think about going to division headquarters to meet my new commanding general.

I changed to a clean jungle uniform, washed the dust off my face and arms, and found a jeep to take me over to division headquarters. On entering the dining hall, I saw that a table was set aside for the commanding general and his party. Several other newly assigned officers joined me, and before long the commanding general and one of the assistant division commanders arrived from their evening briefing.

The conversation centered on the day's operations, and each of us was carefully drawn into it in turn. The general obviously had been given some basic information about each of us. He commented on our new assignments and questioned us about our previous experiences. It was a pleasant dinner hour, and by the time it was over, I had met my division commander face to face and had been welcomed into the division. Now the commander would be able to place a name with a face for each of his new field grade officers. It had been accomplished with style, and I could not help contrasting this hour with the ritual that I had been put through when I joined my previous division upon arrival in Vietnam several months earlier.

The next day toward noon the squadron came in. A cavalry squadron on the move is an awesome sight, and despite my years with armored vehicles, I got a thrill watching my new outfit come home. Roughly one hundred tracked vehicles rolled in column through the main gate of the base camp. I saw the dust cloud on the road long before I actually saw the vehicles, and I watched from a corner of the squadron area as the noise of the diesel and gas engines grew and the long, swaying antennas and squarish shapes of steel materialized out of the cloud. Mixed in the dust were the trucks and jeeps that carried supplies, kitchen equipment, and those of the headquarters staff who were not riding in tracked vehicles. As I watched, most of the tracked vehicles peeled off and headed for the vehicle park; the trucks and jeeps headed for the administrative buildings to unload, and the headquarters command vehicles eased into their home stalls next to the building in which the adjutant had been reigning supreme. Almost without slowing, the vehicles slid into their positions in line, and fuel trucks started moving in. The headquarters command tracks had moved into their standard configuration, with three of them backed together to form a command post, with connecting tents especially designed for that purpose. Then the engines were cut and the dust started to settle.

I went to report to my new squadron commander, who was standing with his operations officer and several others watching the command post set up. He was a slim, casual officer I had not known. I dropped into the background and listened to the conversation between the commander and his key staff officers, trying to size up the dynamics of this group that I was joining. After a little while, he detached himself from the group and asked me to accompany him to the vehicle park to look over the newly parked cavalry troop vehicles. As we walked along, I took the opportunity to question him about what in particular he wanted from his executive officer. He told me that he believed in mission-type orders and that I was to do what needed to be done. Though I had to admit that his guidance lacked a certain amount of specificity, it was apparent that it was all I was going to get. After walking the vehicle park with my new boss, I went off to start doing what needed to be done.

For a cavalry squadron executive officer, what needs to be done invariably centers on the vehicle park and the squadron maintenance platoon, and that is where I spent the rest of the afternoon. In the following two days I introduced myself to the troop commanders; took notes on the supply, maintenance, and personnel problems that they told me about; tried to master the details of why we had nine abandoned tanks; and visited the various division support maintenance and supply elements who held the key to getting them back into operation. When I learned what our problems were, I started coaxing the support needed to resolve them from the various division sources. I also made some headway toward turning in for salvage those tanks that were beyond repair so that we could draw replacements. What was left of each day I used to begin to instill some order in our supply system, which had suffered from the squadron's long periods in the field and a preoccupation with combat operations.

The orders that had brought the squadron back into its base camp required it to prepare to move to Camp Blackhorse, the base camp of an independent armored cavalry regiment located some eighteen miles across the jungle and rice paddies to the east of Bear Cat. We were to relieve the last squadron of that regiment remaining at Blackhorse and assume responsibility for the area of operations surrounding the camp by 26 December. The squadron we were replacing was moving north to rejoin its parent regiment, which was operating in War Zone C.

Once we assumed responsibility for the Blackhorse area of operations, we would have to secure the base camp and its tenant supply and medical units, keep the road network open between it and the Saigon area, and perform several other routine patrol missions that went with the territory. Also, we would take on the job of escorting the ground elements of an assault aviation battalion from its current base camp at Vung Tau to its new permanent home at Blackhorse. The move was scheduled to be made in three separate convoys, moving on different days along Highway 2, which ran north direct from Vung Tau to Blackhorse, or along Highway 15, which ran northwest from Vung Tau by a more circuitous route past Bear Cat to a junction of other highways that ran east and south to Blackhorse. Two of the three convoys were scheduled to move after 26 December and would therefore be our responsibility. We had to be prepared to escort them on 27 and 31 December on either of the routes.

I had to get to Blackhorse to coordinate the transfer of responsibility and to make arrangements for using the vehicle parks, living quarters, and eating facilities of the absent regiment. I arrived at the large, central airstrip after a fifteen-minute treetop flight in one of our scout helicopters. From the air it was a bleak picture: another patch of scored red earth enclosed in a bunkered perimeter. Clumps of ramshackle buildings marked the living areas, and discarded ACAV parts marked the empty vehicle parks. With only one squadron still in residence, there was little activity. It was flat and treeless, and the regiment's tracked vehicles had ground the surface of the roads and vehicle parks into fine red dust that lay inches deep everywhere. The slightest movement of a vehicle or the slightest breeze gathered the dust into a red haze, which hung in the air for minutes before settling and coating everything it touched. In the heat and glare of the dry-season morning, everything had a red tint to it. As a result of my stay at Blackhorse, some of my personal equipment retained a red cast for years afterward.

I borrowed a jeep from the regimental rear detachment and went to the headquarters complex to meet with the regimental executive officer. I then drove around the camp. Back at regimental headquarters I negotiated some adjustments in the facilities that had been offered to us and went over the details of how and when we would take over the security and communications for the camp.

The remaining squadron was anxious to rejoin its parent regiment, but our orders were to move on the twenty-sixth, and we still had to obtain road clearance for the three-hour march the squadron would

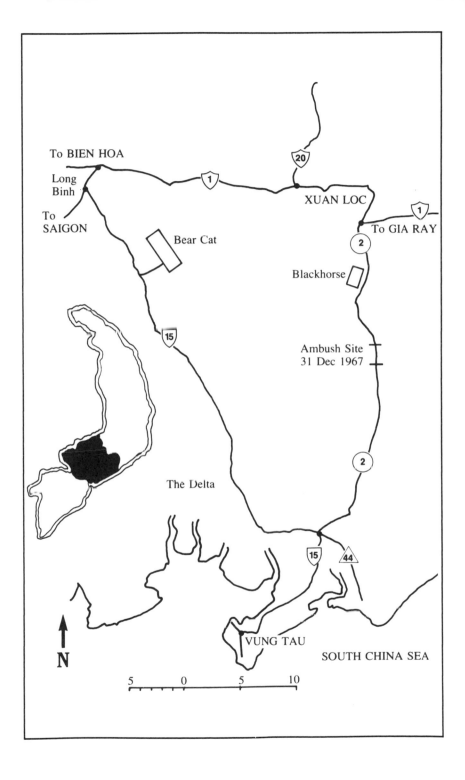

To BIEN HOA

Long
Binh

To
SAIGON

Bear Cat

XUAN LOC

To GIA RAY

Blackhorse

Ambush Site
31 Dec 1967

The Delta

VUNG TAU

SOUTH CHINA SEA

N

have to make from Bear Cat. Unfortunately, we could not march the direct eighteen-mile route across the jungle and paddy that I had just flown; instead we would have to march forty-seven miles around three sides of a distorted rectangle on some very congested supply routes to get to Blackhorse. With the details of the march still to be worked out and coordinated with the supply convoys using the same roads, all I could do was to make general arrangements for the final change-over of responsibility and agree on some code words that we could use to pin down dates and times later on the phone or radio. That done, I climbed back aboard our scout helicopter and flew to Bear Cat, where I briefed my commander and our staff on what I had learned. It was Christmas Eve.

Christmas Day was a holiday for all but those on guard, and it was ushered in by a spectacular and totally unauthorized display of fireworks at midnight as soldiers all over the division base camp fired off whatever flares and star shells they could get their hands on. On the perimeter there were bursts of tracers fired at random into the warm black sky. Though it was wasteful of expensive ammunition and strictly against all rules, cutting it off was done fairly slowly and with good humor. It was very early in the morning by the time quiet returned, however, and it was a good thing that Christmas Day was a holiday from normal routine because nobody had had much sleep. The soldiers passed the day writing letters, enjoying a traditional Christmas meal of turkey and ham with all the trimmings at noon, and just relaxing. They crowded the little makeshift clubs or gathered in small groups to consume huge quantities of beer. When darkness came, there were a great many very happy soldiers who had drunk far too much beer, and there were a number of attempts to replicate the fireworks displays of the previous night. This time, however, there was more prompt enforcement of the rules and less good humor, so the amount of pyrotechnics and tracer ammunition expended did not reach the level of the Christmas Eve display. Still, there were enough attempts at it to keep most of the majors and lieutenant colonels on the base up and making rounds until well after midnight.

The squadron had received a Christmas present of its own: its departure for Blackhorse was postponed until 28 December. This delay gave us more time to shape up our maintenance and supply situation and to get a few more tanks back in working order before we moved out on our new mission, which was to last for an indefinite period of time. It also relieved us of responsibility for convoy escort missions for the time being.

Early on the twenty-eighth the squadron moved out in a long column. I watched it disappear into its own dust cloud and then flew to Blackhorse in order to guide the troops to their new areas. I had already sent an advance party with representatives from each troop.

The squadron commander had told me to take charge of the advance party and the reception of the squadron, get them bedded down and topped off with fuel, then fly back to Bear Cat to continue the job of getting our tanks back in running order. I had hoped to be back by midafternoon. The projected three-hour road march took much longer than planned, however, because the slow supply convoys used the same heavily trafficked road net and because of our own lack of good march discipline. The timing of our starts and stops was off, and gaps developed within the march units that caused elements of the same troop to become separated. The lack of march discipline was understandable, in part, because we had spent so much time slogging along jungle trails in recent weeks, but the great gaps in the arriving column led to confusion and certainly were not the hallmark of a truly professional unit. The squadron commander did eventually shepherd in all the elements of our column from his helicopter, however, and we finally did get everybody settled down so that I was able to fly back to Bear Cat in the waning light of the day.

I spent the next day again making the rounds of our supporting maintenance and supply units. Finally, I managed to arrange to turn in those tanks that could not be repaired. They had to be thoroughly cleaned out, which meant stripping off the equipment that was not to be turned in. Then I arranged for flatbed trucks to haul them to the turn-in point. For those tanks that could be repaired, my problem was still trying to get delivery of the engines, track, or suspension system parts that were needed to make them run again. Partial crews had been left with each tank to do the work, and a large part of the squadron maintenance platoon had remained at Bear Cat to lend its support. We all became good friends quickly in the course of those two hot days of scrambling to set things right. We even began to clean out the junkyard that had grown up next to the squadron maintenance tents, with its bits and pieces of captured equipment that nobody could bear to part with. Also, there were stacks of heavy Navy cables, still boxed up, that had been ordered for vehicle recovery use in the Mekong Delta area to the south and a Kansas windmill that had somehow made its way to Bear Cat when the division first came from Fort Riley, Kansas—it was lying on its side, rusting. By 30 December we had accomplished all that we were going to: the cleaned, stripped tank hulks had been lifted onto the flatbeds by the ingenious combining of several tank retriever vehicles and their giant booms; those engines that could be obtained had been installed; and all but two of the repairable tanks were ready to move. In midafternoon on 30 December, the squadron maintenance platoon marched off to Blackhorse with its maintenance vehicles and the repaired tanks, and I flew over to join the squadron. On the short flight over it occurred to me that New Year's Eve was the next evening. It did not seem that there would be much to celebrate at dusty Blackhorse.

I arrived at Blackhorse at about four o'clock in the afternoon. At five o'clock I joined the squadron commander and staff for the first operations briefing that I had been available to attend. It was run by the assistant operations officer, who was standing in for his boss, who was on midtour rest and recuperation leave. Apparently, nothing much was going on. The intelligence report was routine, and it appeared that things were quieting down in preparation for an alleged truce that was to start on New Year's Eve. When the meeting ended, I made sure that the squadron maintenance column was properly settled in after its road march from Bear Cat. After supper, I wandered around the squadron area in the dusk, talking to various members of my new outfit. My commander had gone off to the borrowed bungalow he was using, which was at some distance from the operations center, and several officers had been invited to join him there to play cards. Not being a card player, I had chosen to stay around the operations center and turn in early.

At 4:10 in the morning, I was shaken awake by a frantic radio operator from the operations center who was shouting at me that we had enemy contact. I did not understand! He repeated that we had enemy contact and ran out. I grabbed my trousers, stepped into my jungle boots, and ran after him to the operations center without stopping to lace my boots, scooping up my helmet, shirt, and pistol on the way out. The only possible enemy contact we could have, I thought, was on the perimeter of the base camp, and that would be very close indeed. Inside the operations center it became clear that the perimeter was not the problem. We had enemy contact on the road somewhere south of us where a column of our C Troop vehicles had been ambushed, but nobody was quite sure where they were. At that, they were ahead of me because I did not even know that unit was out. I mentally reviewed the afternoon briefing that I had attended, but I could recall nothing about any troop going out. Since I was the senior officer present, I did not dwell on that riddle very long. Probably the operation had been in progress and I had not been briefed because everybody else already knew about it. I turned to making sense out of what was coming in over the radios. The radio traffic made it clear that there were a number of vehicles in a fight; however, it sounded as though the intensity of the fighting was slacking off. Finally, we got a lieutenant on the radio who was with the column. He verified that firing was slacking off and that they had been hard hit, but he could not tell us exactly where he was.

That was unheard of in a cavalry unit! All I could find out was that they had been moving south on Highway 2 from Blackhorse and had been stopped on the road by an ambush. I did not know why they were there, but I did understand that they had been badly hurt. The enemy appeared not to be pressing the attack, though, and our cavalrymen had rallied around some relatively undamaged vehicles and in the drainage ditches beside the road. Since our headquarters security platoon with its five ACAVs was standing by, I launched them out onto the road to try to relieve the column while I alerted the cavalry troops in the base camp to prepare to move and to tell me when they were ready. About then the squadron commander arrived from his bungalow. His first words were, "Who's out? I didn't know anybody was out!"

I was stunned. I thought that I had simply missed something because of having been at Bear Cat until the previous afternoon, but to find that the squadron commander also knew nothing about the unit out there was almost beyond belief. It was not, however, a time to ponder all this. The squadron commander sent our two remaining cavalry troops out to join their unfortunate brethren, called for a helicopter, and told me to organize a recovery operation to bring back the damaged vehicles as soon as the area had been cleared and secured. Then he left for the airstrip, and I went to put together a recovery column that would consist of all our available tank retrievers pooled under control of the squadron maintenance officer. I also left instructions to obtain some flatbed trucks and to send them out to us later in the day. Then I headed for my jeep.

On my way out into the quickly brightening day, I passed our division commanding general on the stairs. He had been alerted by our first radio reports of the ambush and had quickly flown over from Bear Cat. He stopped me to ask for the latest reports then sent me on my way. As I climbed into my jeep to join my recovery column, I compared this commanding general's quiet presence, which allowed us all to do our jobs, with the overwhelming pressures that would have been generated by the division commander of the division I had just left. Here no commanding general had broken in on our radio nets to demand special reports or to tell us in detail what actions to take; instead, he had quietly come to our location to find out what was going on and to determine what needed to be done, while leaving the immediate business to the people whose responsibility it was.

I drove to where the tank retrievers and maintenance armored personnel carriers had gathered at my instruction, quickly formed them into a column, and got moving. Once out the gate, we all watched the road edges warily. The heavy machine guns on the tank retrievers and maintenance armored personnel carriers were continuously manned by their very alert mechanics. By now it was fully light, and our two cavalry troops had already swept down the road ahead of us, but we were all keenly aware of the possibilities. It turned out to be merely an uneventful, dusty march, however, and I was soon searching the road ahead for the first signs of the ambush site.

Then my jeep topped a slight rise, and I saw spread out before me in an almost straight two-thousand-yard stretch of road the remains of our unit. Eleven vehicles, facing in different directions, were scattered along the road in various stages of ruin. The road in between the vehicles was littered with pieces of equipment and empty machine-gun ammunition boxes. One of our cavalry troops was still sweeping the jungle edge on the left side of the road, and those troopers from C Troop who had survived the ambush without serious injury were walking among their vehicles in a dazed way, collecting the serial numbered machine guns and undamaged gear that could be salvaged from the burned-out vehicles.

The first vehicle I came to was what was left of a mortar carrier—

an armored personnel carrier fitted out with a floor mount and a sliding top that enabled the mortar to fire from inside the vehicle. The frame of the floor and the steel ring on which the mortar traversed were all that remained. It looked for all the world like a large, blackened sledge waiting to be pulled along the road. The engine was a charred, but still identifiable, lump in the middle of the road ten yards in front of it. This vehicle had been last in line, and it had literally been blown to bits.

The next vehicle in line was an ACAV facing straight ahead in the center of the road. It was completely burned out inside, and the heat of the burning gasoline fuel tanks had actually melted its front slope down onto the dirt road as if it were lead from a melting pot. Next was an ACAV that had run off the road to the left and had come to a stop, facing the distant woodline, some ten yards away. It, too, was completely melted down inside. Then there were two vehicles that bore the typical marks of antitank rocket hits—the distinctive round sunbursts with the small, deadly hole in the center that always indicates where the rocket impacted and penetrated into the interior. They were whole except for the telltale marks, and their back ramps gaped amid a litter of empty ammunition boxes. Slightly ahead and off the road to the left was one of the two tanks that had been in the column. It had run off the road and stopped, and it now stood smoldering in the sunlight, with its tracks and road wheels literally melted into the ground. It was still far too hot to approach. And so it went up the column to the first vehicle in line, which was a tank. It stood in the middle of the road facing forward, still leading the column, with several rocket holes in its suspension system and the distinctive spall marks under its main gun shield right above the driver's hatch. Having hastily surveyed the wreckage, I went back to my maintenance people, and we made our plans for repairing what we could and preparing the rest to be put on the flatbed trucks that we had requested to haul off the debris of the ambush.

We decided to work our way forward from the tail end of the column, concentrating on those vehicles that looked as if they might be quickly put back in running order. Then we would move to the vehicles that were left, breaking loose those that had melted into the road and positioning them for lifting onto the flatbeds. We already knew by looking that the smoldering tank would not be cool enough to move until the next day, so we left it in its blackened circle of

ground some twenty yards off the road. Our plans made, the maintenance crews started their work and I turned to take stock of the
situation. The last of our wounded were being evacuated by helicopter
now, and the surviving crews were just about finished stripping the
machine guns, or the blackened remnants of machine guns, off the
burned-out ACAVs.

On both sides of the road near the barely identifiable remains of
the last vehicle in column, troopers were picking through the weeds
looking for parts of bodies. We had found no bodies by that completely demolished vehicle, and we were looking for the grisly evidence that would verify how many had died in its explosion. It was
a very unpleasant search, but eventually they found sufficient parts
to place in plastic bags to account for the three men that we believed
had been riding in the mortarless mortar carrier when it hit the mine.

About that time I became aware that our B Troop was lined up
on the road stretching back and away from the ruined last vehicle.
The troops were spaced out evenly on one shoulder of the road, machine guns and tank guns pointing toward the woodline that began
some two hundred yards from the road. I wondered what was going
on, and I walked back to the lead vehicle, keeping a wary eye on the
woodline at which all that firepower was pointing. Crewmen of the
first vehicle told me they were covering the area on orders from the
troop commander, but that they did not know why. I walked back to
the next vehicle and was told the same thing. Finally, I found a platoon leader and was told that the troop was covering the troop commander, who was scouting the woodline on foot. I shook my head in
disbelief. The troop commander had left the bulk of a cavalry troop
lined up on the road to cover him while he went on a foot patrol by
himself. When he was pointed out to me, I could see him, pistol in
hand, moving in and out of the edge of the woods. I signaled for him
to come in, and in a little while the captain was back on the road. I
asked what he thought he was doing, and he told me that he had
decided that he should personally make sure that the woodline was
clear. I suggested a little testily that there were better ways to accomplish the mission than by making a solitary patrol while a whole
cavalry troop stood motionless on the road without its leader, and I
mentally marked this young man as somebody who would bear watching. A month or so later, under a new squadron commander, he was

relieved for a similar lack of judgment, but I do not think that he ever really understood what he had done wrong.

By midmorning the searching and gathering by the C Troop survivors were complete. We had all the equipment and all the body parts that we were going to collect. Our mechanics, by patching and improvising, had managed to get three ACAVs running and had hooked up a fourth for towing. They were lined up in column now and were being checked over. I called in on the radio to have C Troop's guidon flown out on one of our scout helicopters, which had been circling over us looking for signs of enemy activity. When it arrived, we mounted it on the lead ACAV, loaded up the nine unscathed survivors on the four vehicles, and marched them back to Blackhorse under their own power and under the control of their own platoon leader.

I was left with my maintenance crew and a cavalry platoon that was providing continuing security by sweeping the area on both sides of the road. They would remain with us for the rest of the day. We turned our attention now to the totally disabled vehicles. By noon we had positioned several of the burned-out ACAVs for loading, and we gratefully took a break to eat the hot meal that had been brought out on a kitchen truck at my request. In the midst of the ambush site, we stopped and gathered around the truck to eat our meal from trays. None of us had eaten breakfast before we moved out, and the unusual setting did not disturb our appetites at all. As we finished eating, the flatbed trucks came into view down the road, and we went back to work in the heat and the dust to load our burned-out ACAVs onto the trucks. I kept in contact with the cavalry platoon, still working the wood edges, through my jeep radio, but all was quiet out there.

Later in the afternoon, I walked out to the lead tank, which had been stopped in its tracks, literally. There it stood as though it were ready to move out. It was a pretty good distance from the next vehicle because it had been out in front to begin with and because the third and fourth ACAVs in line behind it had been ones that were still operational and had been moved. As I approached the tank on foot, I heard voices from inside. Though there was a platoon in the woods within sight and though my maintenance crews were working less than five hundred yards away, I suddenly felt very alone. Drawing my pistol, I cautiously climbed up on the tank. To my surprise the voices came from the radios, which were still working. Looking around a little sheepishly to see if I had been observed, I replaced my pistol in its holster and walked quickly back to get a mechanic. Together, we examined the tank more closely. Though there were three rocket hits on it, it was obvious that nothing had burned and that there were no fuel leaks. We checked the various fluid levels. Then the mechanic climbed into the driver's seat. After a moment, the engine cranked, and we had one more running tank. The mechanic turned it around in place and headed it back down the column while I gleefully went to my radio to report to squadron headquarters that there had been one less vehicle loss than we had at first believed.

The remainder of the afternoon was spent loading the burned-out hulks onto the flatbeds, two per truck, and getting them lashed down for the trip back to Blackhorse. By four thirty that afternoon, we had done all we could. The only vehicle left was the tank that had burned. Although it was still too hot to move, it had cooled down sufficiently so that I could climb up on it and look around to ensure that nothing of value remained that could be collected by an alert enemy. I looked down into the turret and was confronted with nothing but gray ash and molten metal. Only the breech of the main gun was identifiable: the rest was a misshapen mass of slowly cooling melted steel. The heat and the explosions from the burning ammunition had been so intense that the turret had been lifted off its ring and now sat loosely on the lower body of the tank. It was clear that nothing of value had escaped the intense fire and explosions.

For the march in, I split the cavalry platoon that was still with us so that we had combat vehicles in front and in back in case of trouble. The tracked tank retrievers, one towing a disabled ACAV that could be pulled, and the loaded flatbed trucks were alternated in the column, and the tank that we had revived from the head of the ambushed column was placed up front to lead the way. I positioned myself toward the rear of the column where I could see any problems that might occur; then I gave the signal to move out. The vehicle directly in front of me was a flatbed truck with two burned-out hulks on it. It moved only about twenty yards before it blew up in a spectacular geyser of dust and smoke. A mine had been detonated under the flatbed. Fortunately, the mine had gone off after the tractor was past it, so the explosion was somewhat dissipated by the open space behind the tractor, where the flatbed arched over to its coupling. Though the driver had escaped injury, the rear axle of the tractor was gone.

A squad from our securing cavalry platoon immediately launched itself out toward the woodline on the side of the road nearest the mine, but nothing was found. We all started looking rather suspiciously at the road under us. We had swept this stretch of road for mines when the area was first cleared by the arriving relief column, and we had been working up and down the road all day, yet we had obviously missed a mine. My whim of placing sandbags under the seats and on the floorboards of my jeep that morning to provide a little protection for us against mines made even more sense at the moment, and I determined to make it a standard in the squadron. It had been a standard operating procedure in the division that I had just come from, and it seemed like it was an idea worth retaining.

The flatbed was obviously not going anywhere, so I arranged for a cavalry platoon to come out to secure it. I then started the column for Blackhorse one more time. The platoon that came out to secure the area found the wires that indicated that the exploding mine had been command detonated. Somebody had been watching us all day, it would seem, despite our sweeps of the area, and had pushed the plunger down on the blasting mechanism when the truck moved over the mine. The platoon also found, and disarmed, another set of hidden wires that led to a second command detonated mine within the perimeter that they established for the night.

In the meantime our column moved into Blackhorse without any further problems. It was almost dusk, and there was the sound of small-arms fire in the near distance, but the perimeter was quiet when we finally passed through the gate and closed in. By the time the maintenance vehicles were in our vehicle park and cleaned up so that they would be ready to go again if needed, it was almost seven o'clock in the evening. I went back to my quarters for a shower and a fresh uniform before going to an officers' meeting that the squadron commander had called for eight to review what had happened. It was important that we try to learn from the ambush itself. By then we knew that we had twenty-five wounded and eleven dead from the forty-five troopers who had been out. Three of the dead were beyond recognition and had to be listed as missing because their remains could not be positively identified until the parts were matched against their medical and dental records. Miraculously, many of the wounded had suffered only burns and would be coming back to duty in a day or so. Of the two tanks and nine ACAVs that had been in the column, one tank and four ACAVs were good only for salvage. The others needed repairs of some sort, but we would eventually get them running again. It could have been worse; even so, it was a stark lesson about what could happen if you stopped being quick enough and good enough even for a moment. Although the riddle as to how and why the troops were out without the squadron command group's knowledge remained to be unraveled, we put it off until the next morning. It had already been a very long day.

Emerging from the review meeting at about ten thirty that night, I realized that I had truly become part of a combat cavalry squadron. Until today, even though I had been with my squadron for over a week, there had been no shared experiences to make me feel that I was really a part of the group. Now I had gone through a crisis with my unit and had played a part: I had been on the radios in a combat emergency and had started the relief going; I had worked with the wounded and the dazed at the ambush site, and I had helped to solve the problems of recovery during the long, hot, fourteen hours on the road—and I had just missed being blown up by a mine. After ten years of preparation, I had finally come to war and become an officer in the true sense of the word; my stint as an adjutant did not count. As I walked into the dark, I felt older. And I also felt a great exhilaration at having been equal to the task that I had been trained for—and at just being whole in body and alive after what I had been close to.

Simultaneously with that thought came the realization that I was very hungry and that it was New Year's Eve. I went off to an officers' club that served the base camp tenant units and belatedly had a steak. Suddenly, the idea of actually celebrating the new year sounded very good. I joined several other majors with whom I had served in various parts of the world, and we welcomed in the new year. I felt more joy than I had thought I was capable of a mere twenty-four hours earlier. Despite the dust and the bleakness of a base camp in Vietnam and the eighteen hours of toil just past, it was very nice to be alive. In a very real sense, that celebration of the new year was a celebration of life.

# VI
# TET

On the first day of the new year, I began to piece together the events that had allowed C Troop to fall into a deadly ambush. The reconstruction of the chain of events that ended in a terrible ten minutes on Highway 2 on the morning of 31 December 1967 was very revealing. No one event had been the fatal flaw, instead, a series of minor oversights had combined to cost us dearly. We had, of course, been aware of the escort mission for the ground elements of that aviation battalion located at Vung Tau from the time that we were first alerted to take over the Blackhorse area of operation. The last-minute delay in our move from Bear Cat to Blackhorse on Christmas Day had relieved us of the convoy escort mission because we would not be at Blackhorse in time to perform it. The regular occupants of Blackhorse took on the second escort mission, and the third convoy became a remote possibility to the squadron from its location at Bear Cat. It slipped way down in our priorities for planning. We did not even keep ourselves informed about the conduct of the first two moves. We did not know, for instance, that both of the alternative highway routes between Vung Tau and Blackhorse had been used, which meant that any interested observer of those roads would have noted the unusual convoy activity. Very little more information would have been needed to enable an alert enemy to figure out the identity of the unit being convoyed and to determine that there were still more to come. Then the perceptive enemy could be prepared to ambush either of the available routes, and our potential danger would be much greater.

Shortly after we had made our delayed move to Blackhorse, our operations officer was reminded by division headquarters that we once more had responsibility for the third and last escort mission, which was scheduled for 31 December. That simple reminder was received in clear text over the regular telephone, and our operations officer, who was about to leave for his midtour rest and recuperation leave in Hawaii on the thirtieth, passed the problem to his assistant for action in his absence. That assistant, aware only that the reminder had come over the regular telephone, saw no reason to be secretive about the remaining arrangements and made a number of additional phone calls to discuss the details of the convoy mission with the various affected parties.

Anybody could have monitored those conversations about the convoy route and its composition. The details developed during the phone conversations were provided to the C Troop commander, who had originally been selected to perform the convoy escort duty and who now was reassigned to the mission. Having given the mission back to C Troop, our assistant operations officer backed out of the problem, assuming that some previously approved plan would be implemented. He also assumed that the renewed convoy agreement must have been passed along to all the staff; he, therefore, did not include it in the first operations briefing that he ran on 30 December, after the operations officer had departed. Both assumptions were wrong. As a result, he was the only staff member who knew that C Troop was going out, and he did not know what its plan was. The squadron commander and I were not even aware that the responsibility for escorting a convoy had been given back to us.

The C Troop commander knew the Blackhorse area of operation from previous missions and believed that the sector had been quiet, which led him to look at his escort mission as a routine precaution: more an exercise in road marching than anything else. In reality the lack of recent enemy contact did not represent a quiet sector; it represented the absence of aggressive patrolling by the one squadron of the regiment that had remained back until we relieved them. It had been too busy responding to the other Blackhorse operational requirements to mount the normal probing operations in the direction of Vung Tau, but that information had not been passed to us—nor had we asked about it.

The C Troop commander, believing all was quiet, planned a routine night road march that would enable his escort elements to arrive at Vung Tau, some eighty miles to the south, at the agreed-upon rendezvous time of nine o'clock in the morning on 31 December. He elected to employ two platoon-size elements on the mission, while he remained behind at Blackhorse with a third platoon to render assistance in the "unlikely" event that it was needed. He planned for both platoon-size elements to leave Blackhorse at three thirty in the morning on 31 December and to march south in the predawn darkness on Highway 2, which had been designated as the route for this third convoy. About one-third of the way south to Vung Tau, the Blackhorse area of operation met the Australian area of operation, and at that boundary, the trail platoon of the two would drop off. It would spend the remaining hours of darkness running the road between the boundary and Blackhorse to ensure that the road remained secure after the escort column had passed south. The lead platoon would continue on through the Australian area to Vung Tau to pick up the sixty vehicles that made up the final convoy of the aviation battalion and escort them back north. On the return trip the other platoon would rejoin the column at the boundary and complete the security measures for the run up to Blackhorse. Since nobody but our assistant operations officer had been reminded of the escort mission, nobody checked the troop commander's plan: nobody asked why he was staying back while the bulk of his troop was on the road, nobody asked why he had not designated checkpoints at which to report the progress of the march to the squadron operations center, nobody asked why he had not arranged for on-call artillery fires along the route in case of need, and nobody asked why he was making an avoidable night movement, which is always the most risky kind. The better part of a cavalry troop was about to be put on the road at night without normal marching fires or normal control measures, and many of the details of the march had been discussed over the telephone!

As the column moved out from Blackhorse and passed onto Highway 2, which ran next to the base camp, flashing lights were observed momentarily in the dark wooded area across the road. Nobody in the departing column thought enough of that somewhat unusual event to break radio silence to report it, and squadron headquarters remained unaware that some of our vehicles were moving. Apparently nobody in the column was sufficiently bothered by the flashing lights to be extra alert during the march that followed, and the composition of the column militated against truly coordinated action.

The lead platoon in the column consisted of one tank from C Troop's third platoon, two ACAVs from its second platoon, the troop maintenance section's armored personnel carrier, and the troop commander's command ACAV. It was commanded by the second platoon leader, who was riding in the lead tank. The trail platoon in the column consisted of one tank from C Troop's second platoon, two ACAVs from its third platoon, two ACAVs from its first platoon, and the first platoon's mortar carrier, which did not have its mortar tube mounted in it. It was commanded by the third platoon leader, who was riding in his command ACAV. Each platoon-size element was led by its tank in the order of march, and the driving lights and tank searchlights were used at intervals to illuminate the road and search the sides of the road as the march column got under way. There was no rationale for the mixture of vehicles and the breaking up of the normal platoon integrity other than simple expediency and the availability of vehicles.

The first part of the march in the warm predawn dark was uneventful, and the sleepy troopers undoubtedly relaxed their guard as they rumbled down the empty dirt road that was Highway 2. About six miles south of Blackhorse, the road crested a slight rise and dipped down to run straight for about two thousand yards until it climbed up another slight incline. The lead tank of the march column crested the northern rise and flashed its searchlight down the straight stretch of road in front of it. Nothing suspicious there. The column moved over the crest and down the gentle slope without a hesitation. By the time the lead tank was starting up the southern rise, the last vehicle in the column, the mortarless mortar carrier, was leveling off at the bottom of the northern rise, which meant that the march interval had spread to about two hundred yards between vehicles. At that moment the first rocket came out of the dark and hit the lead tank on its main gun shield right above the uncovered driver, who was killed instantly. The unguided tank simply shuddered to a halt, blocking the road. That action signaled the beginning of the ambush, and the entire lead platoon came under intense antitank rocket fire and automatic weapons fire from the left side of the road. The rocket fire either started fires in the ACAVs or wiped their top decks clean of the troopers who had been sprawled out by their machine-gun mounts.

No effective, coherent fire was returned by the platoon. Whenever a trooper attempted to get a machine gun into action, the whole line of the enemy ambush was at liberty to concentrate on that one vehicle until the gunner was driven from the gun, instead of having to disperse its fire along the whole column, as would have been the case if there had been an instantaneous return of fire from all the guns on all the vehicles. In many cases troopers had been knocked off the top decks several times by the concussion of the antitank rockets hitting the sides of the vehicles. Since the floors of these ACAVs were layered several tiers deep with machine-gun ammunition boxes, there was little room inside for people. The lack of space, combined with the added protection from mines that came from riding on the top deck, caused the whole crew except the driver to ride on top of the ACAVs most of the time. Fortunately, therefore, nobody was caught inside any of the vehicles. The lead platoon leader, in the lead tank, had not even had his map in his hand when the column was hit; and since no checkpoints had been established, he had not been keeping track of his location. He did not know where he was, and he could not, therefore, tell his troop commander where to send help. All he could do was to duck down into the protection of his tank.

The trail platoon leader saw the ambush developing in front of him and directed his platoon vehicles to herringbone in place—to angle left and right alternately so that each vehicle presented the smallest target to the sides of the road and could bring the maximum number of machine guns to bear. Unfortunately, a gap of several hundred yards had developed between the two platoons, and stopping in place had the effect of further diluting the potential firepower of the column by keeping it well spread out. As the trail platoon herringboned, its lead tank was hit in its fuel cell by a rocket. The tank exploded when hit and ran crazily off the road until it lurched to a halt and burned, the ammunition inside adding to the heat of the fire. At about the same moment the last vehicle in the column was blown up by a command-detonated mine. Since this vehicle was loaded with mortar ammunition, the detonation of the mine under it literally disintegrated the vehicle and all that was in it.

In ten minutes it was all over. The ambushing force had hidden in the clumps of fallen trees that remained, ironically, from the effort to clear the road edges of growth for one hundred yards on both sides to prevent the enemy from lurking in the undergrowth. The enemy had been in this deadfall, no farther than ten yards from the road edge, we learned the next morning. At that range, they could not miss.

When fire slackened, the lead platoon leader had been able to call in, but that was all. Since no artillery fires had been planned, there was nothing we could do to help except to send out a relief column. It took us fifteen minutes to figure out where the ambush was on Highway 2.

In the harsh light of the first day of the new year, the mistakes were obvious, but knowing them could not bring back the dead or make whole the vehicles. The division commander also realized that there had been a few too many mistakes; the planned change of squadron command was quietly moved up, and I had a new squadron commander within three days.

The new squadron commander and I went over the ambush and the squadron's operating procedures in great detail, and together we started reintroducing the basic policies and procedures that we hoped would prevent any repetition of the events of 31 December. These practices were the same ones that we had followed in Germany in my earlier years; there, however, failure to follow them had resulted in failing a training test; it had not resulted in death. Stressing these basics, I now realized, was what my own experience could contribute to the "combat veterans" of my squadron.

My new commander was a thorough professional with a good eye for detail, and he soon was out checking and prying into what made our cavalry troops work—or not work. March discipline was tightened up, more attention was paid to alertly manning the ACAV machine guns and ensuring that the sound practice of having half the column's guns covering each side of the route of march all the time was enforced. To check the responsiveness of the squadron, he started calling surprise stand-tos in the early morning hours. We timed the interval between the alert notification and the movement of the first troop from the vehicle park. In the process of checking, we discovered that some of our troop commanders were prone to call in their ready-to-move times a little prematurely as a result of not being checked—and the practice had probably extended into other checkpoint reports, an effort to look more disciplined in their movements than they actually were. In short, all the practices that make a well-trained, professional unit had to be reintroduced into the squadron. Making them a habit would be a matter of constant checking, prodding, and rechecking over the next months, but the concepts were quickly established.

The reorientation of the squadron had barely been accomplished when the demands of the Blackhorse area of operation started to disperse our troops. One cavalry platoon was given the mission of guarding a rock quarry some sixteen miles away. There it protected the engineers who were making crushed rock for surfacing roads, and it escorted the truck convoys that carried the crushed rock to engineer depots close to Saigon. The remainder of that troop stayed at Blackhorse and ran local missions each day to keep the area surrounding the base camp under our close watch. Another troop was posted some eighteen miles north and west of Blackhorse at an artillery fire-support base on Highway 1 between Xuan Loc and Saigon. There it protected the artillery and ran the road to keep it open between the fire-support base and the logistical base at Long Binh. The remaining line troop was responsible for opening the road between Blackhorse and that fire-support base on Highway 1.

These road-opening missions consisted of running the road at night at irregular intervals with a platoon to prevent the enemy from planting new mines then sweeping the road at first light to make sure that it was safe before the endless supply columns started to roll. The platoon running the road would make two or three runs on a time schedule that varied each night. To confuse the enemy and to keep him unsettled, the platoon would frequently split into sections and run the tanks alone, for instance, then follow five minutes later with the remainder of the platoon. These runs were made at top speed in order to surprise anybody working in the road and to protect the vehicles by making it likely that they would drive through any ambush before it could do much damage. The effect was that the opposition could never be sure when a platoon of armored vehicles would show up, or whether there was time to plant a mine before the next group came by. Of course, the rest of that troop stayed on alert and ready to move out at a moment's notice to reinforce the platoon making the run if it made contact with the enemy. In addition, checkpoints and on-call artillery fires were meticulously plotted to ensure instant identification of location and the capability of quickly putting supporting fire on an ambush before it could get a good head up. The method worked. It kept the enemy off the road at night and held down the number of new mines that could be planted in the road. Tension was always high, however, and there never was quite enough sleep for the troopers when their troop had the road-running responsibility.

As hot, dusty January dragged on, though, the big problem became the mines on the morning road openings and the daily probes along the local roads and trails. Despite our nightly forays and our care with mine sweeping to clear the roads, we never found all the mines before they exploded. Day in and day out we lost vehicles and people to mines despite our best efforts. For a while we lost a vehicle a day. If the roads were cleared without incident in the morning, then some stream ford that a probing column used in the afternoon would contain a mine that had escaped detectors. The tank crews were relatively safe. Unless the mine was unusually large, the track and part of the suspension system would be damaged when a mine detonated under a tank, but the crew would normally escape with only a good headache from the concussion. Only once did we encounter a mine large enough to turn over a tank, and that apparently was an unexploded five-hundred-pound bomb that had been recovered by the enemy, converted to a mine, and buried by a stream ford.

The ACAVs, however, were far more vulnerable. They were not as heavily armored, and the crews' only protection was to ride on top of the vehicle, where they would be blown clear. The driver, of course, was unable to make such arrangements. Though his head was outside the hatch under normal conditions, his feet reached down to the floor to manipulate the controls. He knew that a mine would either trap him in the overturned vehicle or open the floor under him like a giant can opener, and the tension created by that knowledge built each time he drove out the gate. To add to the tension, there was no pattern indicating which vehicle in a column was likely to detonate a mine. Most of the mines had been in place for a long time. Their wooden pressure plates contained old nails, which completed an electric circuit when they touched. The wood might bend with the weight of the first vehicle, but not quite enough to touch the nails together. Each succeeding vehicle would press the nails embedded in the bamboo strips a little closer together as their weight hit them until finally a good contact was made. Then the mine might detonate, or it might not. If battery power was required, the battery might be weak and it might take some time to build up enough spark to blow the mine. There simply was no pattern. The first vehicle, the third vehicle, or the last vehicle, all were equally vulnerable; and leading with the tanks, which was our normal practice, did not give sure protection to the ACAVs against the mines. It was nerve-racking, and there was nobody to fight back against.

I often wondered what kept our troopers going out. I pondered what I would say and do if one morning an ACAV driver said that what we were doing was dumb and that he was not going to drive. It never happened, but the nagging worry was never far from my mind. That it did not happen is a tribute to the dirty, dusty cavalrymen who manned those vehicles. Nobody observing the war from the newspapers and the television even knew about that kind of heroism, but to this day I marvel at the courage that enabled men to move out in armored vehicles day after day to open a road for supply convoys knowing that one vehicle or another probably would be blown up despite their best efforts. You really have to try it to understand what it takes!

As if we needed a counterpoint to this deadly tension, the administrative gods turned up two new ways to devil us. First, we were arbitrarily informed that we could not put more than 250 miles of travel on our tanks during any one thirty-day period. It seemed that some logistical genius had calculated the mileage-to-repair-parts ratio and determined that the supply of repair parts available would support only that amount of usage. Unfortunately, nobody changed our various road and patrol missions, which typically caused us to travel far more than 250 miles a month, and we were not about to add to the danger of our missions by leaving our tanks at home. We ignored the edict (nobody ever questioned us) continued to piece together our fifteen-year-old tanks as best we could from the repair parts that we managed to "expedite," and wondered at a policy that sent new tanks to Europe and old tanks with only inadequate repair parts available to the combat zone. Somehow we managed to keep enough tanks operational to do the job safely, but it was only through the use of a lot of ingenuity and out-of-channels procurement.

Second, a new equipment readiness reporting system was implemented, with its attendant forms and criteria designed for a peacetime army. The system was supposed to measure readiness to deploy to a combat zone, and the fact that we were already there did not change the requirement. The various ratings involved measuring the potential for extended vehicle operation in the event of a deployment, and they were partially related to the cumulative mileage amassed by each vehicle. That led to a fuss with the division's chief supply officer, who naturally wanted all "his" vehicles to have the highest possible rating. No amount of talk could persuade this infantry officer that we had no control over the total mileage of our vehicles and that a less-than-top rating reflected the vehicle age and usage, not the caliber of vehicle maintenance. Eventually, I turned in our reports, reflecting the real mileage of our vehicles, and he wrote his own version to obtain his ratings. And that was my introduction to a readiness evaluation system that has been the center of one controversy or another ever since.

In mid-January, the troop that had the base camp security mission for the week was probing with its two platoons along one of the hilly jungle trails to the south of Blackhorse when there was a sudden puff of smoke from the thick jungle wall that ran beside the trace. Seconds later, as its crew scrambled to safety, the lead ACAV burst into flames. Before the puff of smoke had dissipated into the heavy, hot air, the rest of the troop was returning machine-gun fire and deploying to counter the ambush.

The new discipline and professionalism had taken hold, but this time there was no ambush. Probably, it had been a two-man rocket team looking for a quick hit, and probably the two were already making their escape through the jungle underbrush as the aluminum hull of the AVAC started to crack under the intense heat of the burning gasoline from the fuel tanks and the internal bombardment of the thousands of rounds of machine-gun ammunition that had been stored in metal boxes layered across the floor.

As suddenly as the action had started, it was over. There was silence except for the crackling flames and the exploding ammunition. The one lightly wounded crewman, grazed by the passing white-hot plug of molten metal from the rocket on its way to ignite a fuel tank, was attended to; and the column clanked on its way, leaving the still-burning ACAV and a problem peculiar to Vietnam: even the wreck of a vehicle was too valuable to be left to our enemies because it provided an endless source of metal and wire for making booby traps and for rigging mines. We would have to recover the hull from this trace, which was surrounded by an expanse of thick jungle through which the Viet Cong roamed at will.

Other operational commitments prevented us from immediately freeing up the resources necessary to go back the ten miles into the jungle to recover the wreck, so several days passed. Then one morning one of our aerial scout teams, which had been given a secondary mission of routinely monitoring the wreck, spotted two figures sifting the now-cool wreckage. We knew that we would have to move quickly to prevent the Viet Cong from taking all that they needed. We also had to consider the possibility that by this time they had set mines and booby traps to inflict damage on any recovery attempt. In addition, contact with a roaming band of Viet Cong was not out of the question. Finally, there was the stream that cut the jungle track just before the spot where the wreck sat. It was a fast-running stream with fairly steep banks, and though it had not been an obstacle to the tracked vehicles in the original column, it would be an obstacle to the flatbed tractor-trailer that we would use to haul the burned-out ACAV back to Blackhorse. We could not just drive a flatbed out to recover the ACAV, so I set to work on the details of still another recovery operation.

I decided that to recover the ACAV, I would need a flatbed truck, two tank retrievers, a portable bridge that rode on a tank chassis, and a cavalry platoon for security. To fend off the possibility of mines and booby traps at the only possible stream-crossing site and around the wrecked vehicle, I would fly in the aero-rifle platoon from our air cavalry troop. It would be lifted in on Hueys and land on the trace about one thousand yards back from the stream. From there the troopers would work their way down the trace to the stream, supported by our gunships overhead, to make sure that the approaches to the stream crossing and the crossing itself had not been mined. Then they would clear the space between the stream and the wreck and spread out into the jungle edges to secure the area for us. In the meantime my column would be marching along the trace to join them, timed to link up, I hoped, with the aero-rifled platoon as it finished its clearing business. To protect against ambush on the march, an aerial scout team would fly ahead of the column and marching artillery fire would be planned along the route where it was closed in on both sides by uninhabited jungle. I would control it all from a light observation helicopter.

At ten thirty the next morning the column got under way in the dust and heat of the dry season. The first part of the march was accomplished at a good pace because the ground was open on all sides of the road and the road itself was used routinely by Vietnamese going to and from market and was frequently reconned by our troopers. The possibility of encountering mines was minimal, and a plume of dust, visible from the air, clearly showed the rapid pace of the moving column. Then, as the road became a trace and entered the jungle, it narrowed and the column slowed. It now became necessary to stop to check likely locations for mines, which meant dismounting troopers and their mine-sweeping equipment. Despite the delay that was caused by our mine sweeping, the jerky forward progress of the column continued at a good rate. As soon as the column moved through the abandoned rubber plantation area, which bordered the trail closer to our base camp, and into true jungle, we called for our marching fires. The explosions on both sides of the trail ahead of us and the faint smell of cordite gave a reassuring feeling to the moving column. It was doubtful that an ambush that had escaped detection by our aerial scouts would stay to surprise us when artillery fire was hitting around them for no apparent reason.

Meanwhile, out near the ruined ACAV our gunships started their runs. They fired into the jungle on both sides of the selected landing zones on the trail then pulled off to make room for the troop-carrying Hueys. These ships came in, quickly disgorged their infantry soldiers, and pulled off. The aero-rifle platoon formed up and in moments was moving toward the stream as the dust of the departing helicopters started to settle. No sooner had forward movement begun than the point troopers saw two figures in black running into the thick jungle that lined the sides of the trace. They immediately fired at them, but the figures faded into the thick undergrowth and intertwined vines before anybody's aim could become accurate. Doubly alert now, the platoon continued on its move toward the stream and the ACAV hull, while our gunships, brought back by the aero-rifle platoon leader's radio call, returned to make strafing runs over the jungle on both sides of the trail. Soon the stream was reached. One squad quickly checked the approaches for mines while the remainder of the platoon moved through the stream to search the hull and surrounding area for booby traps. The search completed, the platoon fanned out to secure the edges of the jungle around the trace while the platoon leader called me on his radio to tell me that the stream-crossing site and trace adjacent to the hull were clear.

Just as the aero-rifle platoon was moving into the undergrowth to take up its position, the lead tank of the column poked its gun tube into sight around a bend in the trail. Our timing had worked. The tank moved through the stream and took up a position on the trail facing a relatively clear break in the jungle that led away to the right. The two ACAVs right behind the tank in the column also clanked through the stream then swept up and past the area that the aero-rifle platoon had just cleared. They went on around the burned-out hull and took up blocking positions some one hundred yards farther down the trail, just below the crest of a slight incline. The rest of the platoon spread itself around the perimeter of the area, leaving two ACAVs covering the route we had just traveled. I landed in the center of this secure island in the middle of a potentially hostile jungle and walked back to meet my maintenance chief, who was sizing up the stream banks before launching the portable bridge across the stream. It was just past noon.

After a quick check with the cavalry platoon leader to assure myself that our security was well tied in and that over the vehicle radios we had good communications on the ground with the squadron operations center, I returned to the bridging site. By then the bridge operator and the maintenance chief had tested the banks and were ready to lay the bridge. In short order the bridge had been hydraulically unfolded from its chassis and was in place across the stream. We sent one of our tracked tank retrievers across first to seat the bridge with its weight and to level the ground on the opposite side with its tracks so that the flatbed truck would meet no obstacles. Then the tractor-trailer was guided across the bridge and up the narrow, rutted trace, which tended to be quite soft near the stream. The tractor-trailer was driven past the hull, turned around so that it faced back the way we would go when we were through, and parked close to the hull. In the meantime our tank retrievers had pulled up at right angles to the hull on the jungle side and had dug in their stabilizing spades while their crews rigged the huge A-frame booms for lifting. When all was set, the hull was attached to the boom hooks with heavy chains and slowly lifted to the maximum height that the A-frames allowed. The retrievers then inched backward, after retracting their spades, until there was room for the flatbed to be driven under the dangling hull. The retrievers then inched forward toward the trace until the hull was centered over the flatbed, where it was gently lowered to the bed. The lifting chains were released, and the wreck was securely tied down. We were ready to recross the stream.

The soft ground near the streambed had made us all wary, though, and we sent one of the retrievers down the trail toward the bridge first so that we would have a way of towing if the tractor-trailer had difficulty negotiating the soft ground with its load. Sure enough, about fifty feet from the bridge, the heavily burdened tractor lost headway in the sandy ground and sank to a halt with its drive wheels still churning. We hooked up the waiting tank retriever and held our breath as the slack went out of the cable and the retriever strained forward. Slowly the flatbed started to move again. We sighed with relief as the rear wheels of the tractor hit the bridge and the tow cable went slack. The flatbed was moving under its own power. The retriever unhooked its cable from the tractor and moved across the bridge, closely followed by the flatbed, which kept moving until it had reached the solid ground on the trace that led back the way we would go. As it hit the firm footing of the trail, I fired a green star cluster from my flare gun, which was the signal for the aero-rifle platoon leader to call in his waiting lift ships and gather his men for extraction.

While the lift ships were coming in, we recovered the bridge, settled it back down on its tank chassis, and sent it up the trace to join the flatbed. The lift ships settled in by the spot where the burned-out ACAV had been, and the aero-rifle platoon soldiers quickly climbed aboard. As the dust of the departing helicopters started to settle, the two ACAVs that had secured the far end of the recovery site clanked back through the area and the stream to fall in on the end of the forming column for the return trip. I climbed into my light observation helicopter and lifted off as the column made its final checks and adjustments. Then it was moving out on the return trip. It was just two o'clock in the afternoon.

The march back was accomplished in good order, with the column adjusting its rate of march to the slow speed of the heavily burdened flatbed. The trace we were marching over had been under the observation of our aerial scout team since we had passed over it on the way out, and I now moved ahead of the column at treetop level, looking for signs of freshly dug dirt that might indicate newly planted mines. There was nothing to be seen. As the jungle thinned out and the dangers lessened, I put the escort platoon through various battle drills to break the monotony and sharpen the reactions of this platoon, which had been involved in the ambush on 31 December and had since received wholesale replacements for its losses in equipment and men.

At one point, as I hovered over the column, I asked the platoon leader over the radio to tell me his exact location—he was the one who had not had his hand on his map the night that he had been ambushed. Instead of a crisp reply, there was silence on the radio. Looking down at the top of his vehicle, I saw him fumbling for a map. I was appalled, and I spent the next few minutes in a one-sided radio conversation about why a cavalry platoon leader must always know where he is on the ground in relation to the map, as if the idea should have required emphasis in view of his recent personal experience. It proved once again how quickly you can block from your mind an unpleasant experience and all that goes with it.

By four in the afternoon the column was closed in at Blackhorse, performing the eternal after-operation maintenance on its vehicles. Aside from the slight contact encountered by the aero-rifle platoon initially, it had been a quiet operation. A lot of time, effort, and equipment had gone into recovering a burned-out hulk, good only for scrap, but at least we knew that the enemy in the jungle would not have access to that particular source of materials, which they could later use against us. Whether the enemy had ever planned to make trouble for our recovery effort or whether our preparations had discouraged any enemy action, we would never know. All that we did know was that we had completed a routine mission in a routine manner without any loss of equipment or personnel. In one sense the operation was a microcosm of our overall efforts in Vietnam, where every small success was the result of detailed planning and a generous expenditure of time, effort, and equipment. Our losses were always in inverse proportion to that expenditure.

The second half of January passed in a series of hot, dusty days filled with road openings and local mounted patrols, during which we rarely saw our enemy but regularly encountered his handiwork, as the ground erupted under a vehicle; minor skirmishes, which seemed to cause no great injury to either side; and a steady recovery from the effects of our ambush of 31 December. There was a growing sense of discipline and professionalism that resulted from our new commander's approach to running the squadron. One of the most rewarding aspects of this improved professionalism was the improved teamwork between our air cavalry troop and our ground troops. Whenever division did not use up our helicopter assets on its own larger missions, we made sure that our air and ground elements worked together. A gunship team would be included routinely in every ground troop movement, which gave us an added edge in case of an ambush. It got so that our air and ground elements could sense each other and what had to be done. No sooner would a platoon leader request support to counter fire that he was receiving from the side of a trail than the laconic "rolling hot" response would come back from one of our gunship pilots, indicating that he was already starting a gun run on the suspected enemy location. The immediate response was gratifying to the platoon under fire, and it reciprocated by being willing to go anywhere and do anything to get to our pilots if one of our ships went down.

Such was not always the case when our air cavalry was tasked out to support other elements of the division. One hot day we heard that one of our light observation helicopters had gone down while scouting for an infantry unit on the other side of the division area of operations. We listened intently on the division command radio channel to find out if it could be rescued. It could not be done, at least, not with the equipment available to the infantry. When they finally did get to the downed ship, they found the bodies of our two pilots on the ground near the ship lying foot to foot. They had defended themselves and their aircraft until they had been overwhelmed. Though we really knew better, we could not help believing that our ACAVs would have gotten to them in time if we had been the ones working with them.                                                                          .

Whether or not that was true was really irrelevant to the deep feeling of mutual support that it represented. What was truly significant was that for a short period of time we had accomplished the kind of air-ground integration that was meant to be in a cavalry squadron and was so often thwarted by having the organic aircraft siphoned off to other division missions. Aviation assets always seemed to be too scarce, and the division couldn't resist the temptation of taking ours away. In the years to come, that temptation was to become institutionalized to the point where the organic air cavalry troop finally was eliminated from the cavalry squadron. By then there were few people around who had seen it work as it was meant to, so there was no concerted effort to save the organic squadron aviation element.

On 29 January 1968 the enemy offensive that was to become known to the world as Tet erupted to the north of us. Over the years since then much has been made of the complete surprise of the Tet attacks, but at the tactical unit level—the battalion level—in the area adjacent to Saigon, we knew that it was coming before we were actually caught up in it. I cannot speak to the strategic surprise or to what the higher echelons had projected in their long-range estimates of enemy capability, but I know that we had two days' warning after the first attacks to the north. What we did not know was the where and the when, and we certainly did not foresee the magnitude of the effort that the Viet Cong and the North Vietnamese would mount against us. In part that underestimation was attributable to the cunning of the enemy and the nature of guerrilla warfare, but in part it was also the result of our own cynicism about the routine intelligence reports that were forever coming to us from "unspecified" sources. These reports always announced that one hundred or two hundred Viet Cong or North Vietnamese were concentrating at some grid square in the jungle, and we were always sending out troops to find them. After having participated in a number of such futile marches into the jungle only to find no trace of any human passage, we tended to take all such reports with little more than a grain of salt. And when it came to Tet, it turned out to be our mistake.

For two days we listened to reports of heavy fighting in the northern sections of the country. It was apparent that the series of attacks were moving south—either because of a lack of coordination or according to some plan—and that it was simply a matter of time until our turn came. By the night of 30 January, we were all alert and tense. Our A Troop was located to the north of us on Highway 1, securing an artillery fire support base named Apple, which was midway between Xuan Loc and Bien Hoa. Both our B and C troops were in the base camp at Blackhorse, performing the road and local security missions that made up our routine responsibilities. Then at six o'clock in the morning on 31 January, Tet reached us. Suddenly the division radio channels came alive with reports of large attacking forces moving against Tan Son Nhut Air Base, Bien Hoa Air Base, Long Binh, and the city of Saigon itself. We listened particularly closely to the reports being sent in by one of our division's mechanized infantry battalions that had been sent to Long Binh during the night, and we eventually switched to its internal radio channel to get a better idea of the fierce fighting it was involved in—and that we were sure we would be caught up in shortly. All was still quiet around Blackhorse. We had been alerted by our division headquarters to have A Troop ready to move to Bien Hoa to protect that air base, and now we waited. At seven in the morning, the command came for it to move out.

We directed the A Troop commander to leave one platoon at Apple to protect the artillery unit operating there and to march the rest of his troop toward Bien Hoa. Our squadron commander, who himself had only a fragmentary order on the mission, told the troop commander to start marching, that he would brief him later over the radio while the troop was moving. The troop had barely started its march along Highway 1 toward Bien Hoa when it ran into its first fight of the morning at Trang Bom, a village close to the fire support base. The troop's orders were to move to Bien Hoa, though, and the men drove through the ambush without slackening speed, concentrating the fire of their ACAV machine guns on the road edges as they continued to move. The shock of this fire suppressed the enemy fire sufficiently for the troop to get through without suffering any serious damage, and it continued to move toward the air base. Next, it encountered a gauntlet of strip villages—villages that were built one house deep on both sides of the road and which stretched out for almost a mile. Each house seemed to contain a gunner of one kind or another this morning, but the troop managed to keep moving. Farther along the highway, the lead tank came up to a concrete bridge that crossed a stream. It rolled on across the bridge without stopping; then a tremendous explosion dropped the entire short span into the stream behind it before any of the other armored vehicles could follow. Our ACAVs quickly turned off the road, skirted the bridge, and found a place to ford the stream, but the heavier tanks could not get across and had to be left there. A Troop moved on toward Bien Hoa, now with only one of its tanks. It was now beginning to move out of radio range of the squadron operations center at Blackhorse, but it still had not been able to make radio contact with the air base.

When the troops entered the city of Bien Hoa, which lay between it and the air base, the lead platoon found the city's central city square filled with people. Because of the pressure on them to reach the air base quickly, they just kept moving, dispersing the crowd by the force of their passage. It was only after they were in the midst of the crowd that it dawned on them that they had hurtled into several companies of Viet Cong and North Vietnamese soldiers. The enemy soldiers quickly recovered from their surprise at seeing an American column burst into their midst and opened fire on the passing vehicles, disabling two ACAVs. The second platoon in column, alerted by the firing, drove into the square with all its machine guns blazing and was able to push the two disabled ACAVs off to the side, pick up their crews, and continue on. The troop now consisted of one tank and eight ACAVs.

At this point the squadron commander joined the troop overhead in his light observation helicopter and reestablished the communications link between it and the squadron operations center. He stayed over the column and directed it through the narrow maze of city streets and out again toward the air base by the most direct route. As the column approached the nearest entrance to the base, the squadron commander spotted several hundred Viet Cong and North Vietnamese soldiers in the ditches ahead on both sides of the road, where they were apparently waiting to stop just such a relief column as ours on its way to reinforce the besieged base. Forewarned, the remnants of A Troop swung off the road and drove parallel to it, but behind the waiting enemy. As they passed, the ACAVs raked the waiting ambushers from their rear, inflicting heavy casualties on the enemy, who had suddenly become vulnerable because of our quick maneuver. Then the troop was through the gate and into Bien Hoa, where it joined up with an infantry battalion. They moved with hardly a halt to one end of a runway that was about to be overrun by sheer force of numbers, arriving just in time to stop the penetration.

At about this time the squadron commander, who was still circling above the troop, was almost blown out of the air by the force of an explosion that we actually heard a moment later at Blackhorse, some twenty-three miles away. The ammunition bunkers at the Long Binh ammunition depot had gone up in a blast of orange flames and black smoke that had almost engulfed his helicopter flying some thousand feet above it. Our report of the incident, relayed by radio a moment later, was the first information that division headquarters had of what the explosion meant, though they were located much closer to Long Binh than we were.

The remnants of A Troop fought on for the rest of the day, combining with the infantry battalion to fend off one attempt after another to penetrate the outer defenses of Bien Hoa Air Base. Late in the afternoon they launched an attack together to try to clear one corner of the sprawling base that had been occupied during the initial attack by the enemy forces. The concentrated firepower of our automatic weapons finally told on the Viet Cong and North Vietnamese, and they attempted to withdraw, but the quick-moving ACAVs cut them off and killed them as they ran. Thereafter, the troop, now down to six ACAVs and a badly beat-up tank, acted as the fire brigade for the air base, going where it was needed to supply the extra firepower to ward off attackers as pressure built up at first one point then another. By the time darkness fell and the situation at Bien Hoa had begun to stabilize, the tank had been hit nineteen times and the crew had been replaced twice. It was, however, still operational as night closed in, and it had done what it was supposed to do.

With full dark came relief as more reinforcing units began to move into the Saigon area, and the pressure on Bien Hoa began to lessen. A Troop had lost two killed and twenty-one wounded in its sixteen hours of fighting. Late that night we flew the weary troop commander back to Blackhorse for a debriefing. With him came our dead. I vividly remember meeting the helicopter as it landed and helping to unload the already-stiffening bodies of our troopers. The troop commander stayed with us long enough to have a hot meal and to give us the details of the day's fighting and the status of his remaining vehicles. Then he flew back to his troop, tired but exhilarated at having been able to fight back after weeks of running the roads and taking hits from unseen rocketeers. His feeling was shared by the troopers who marched back down Highway 1 without incident the next morning to rejoin the platoon that had stayed at Apple.

What enabled A Troop to move back to Apple unmolested on 1 February, and caused friendly operations in the Saigon area to become a mopping-up exercise instead of a continued defense, deserves mention here. Unfortunately, it was completely overshadowed by the media's concentration on the temporary, and militarily insignificant, occupation of the American embassy, and on the other well-publicized, overdramatized pockets of enemy resistance within Saigon as the Viet Cong and North Vietnamese continued to harass us from their encircled positions in the metropolitan area, located conveniently close to the television cameras. While A Troop had been fighting for its life and the life of Bien Hoa Air Base on 31 January, unknown to us, other armor units were being set in motion. From War Zone C to the north and from other division areas of operation to the northeast, cavalry squadrons were moving. They pulled out of their jungle operations on receiving radio instructions—in some cases breaking off actual enemy contact to do it—and moved to the roads leading south. Marching as many as seventy miles after pulling out of those jungle trails where they had been operating, they converged on the Saigon area, guided only by the standard fragmentary radio orders under which cavalry routinely operates. Some had to fight their way into the Saigon area, and the last stages of their marches were made in darkness. Amid the dust and confusion they moved into their designated positions that night almost without a halt. Friends who took part in those marches still talk about driving through the night at top speed with all lights on, scarves over faces to keep out the suffocating dust.

It was an exercise in mobility that is the heart of cavalry operations, but it was never reported on television. I can still remember the feeling of pride we had in our own operations center the next morning when we heard the squadron commander's initial report as he flew over A Troop's position and saw from the air that Saigon, Bien Hoa, and Long Binh were literally ringed in steel in the first light of the first day of February. Five cavalry squadrons had moved through the previous day and night, converging on the Saigon area. When dawn broke, they formed an almost-continuous chain of more than five hundred fighting vehicles around the outskirts of the metropolitan area. We actually cheered as we heard the squadron commander's astonished report. We had been braced for another day of just hanging on, but the odds had suddenly changed. There was still some heavy fighting ahead of us to clear out embattled pockets of tenacious enemy, and there were some tense moments still to come, but from that morning on the outcome was never in doubt. We knew that our enemy could never match our mobility, flexibility, and firepower.

To our complete bewilderment in the weeks that followed, nobody ever publicized this feat. Instead, we read that we had been defeated! None of us who were there has ever quite understood that. I am not referring to political appearances or some abstract idea of total victory in Vietnam, whatever that might have meant; I am referring to the reality that American soldiers in armored vehicles and on foot were better and quicker than their opposition and were quite simply beating the hell out of them after they had launched what was touted as their coordinated attack to end the war. Maybe you had to see the low walls of dead enemy bodies, stacked like the proverbial cordwood outside that ring of armor near one of our major headquarters installations, to understand our bewilderment. It had been close, but close does not count in war, and the casualties that we inflicted on the enemy in the process were of such a magnitude that he could not repeat the effort again any time soon. I think that those who were not actually part of Tet have never understood what our soldiers did and how quickly we regained the initiative. Their feat of arms may not have affected the final outcome in Vietnam, but its recognition by the media and the American people would have gone a long way toward giving the participants the credit they are owed. The media remain responsible for that situation, and most of us have not forgotten that yet.

While Tet was over for A Troop by late afternoon on 1 February, it was not yet over for the squadron. C Troop, which had remained at Blackhorse during the first hours of the action on 31 January, had moved to the town of Xuan Loc, nine miles north on Highway 2, to reinforce the American installations located there. Its three platoons had been split up among the various key installations in the city, and they were separated by some distance. They got no action on 31 January, but throughout 1 February the signs were ominous and sporadic firing was reported from different points in the town. As darkness fell on the first, our attention in our operations center focused on Xuan Loc and the situation reports from C Troop. During the early evening hours, one platoon or another was kept busy moving from one threatened point to another. They traded fire with the enemy soldiers who were slowly moving in, took some casualties, but were never stopped. At about three thirty in the morning of 2 February, while I was manning the operations center so that our weary squadron commander and operations officer could get some well-earned sleep, the combat activity suddenly picked up.

The enemy had concentrated around the special forces compound, and that post was now under heavy enemy pressure. One platoon of C Troop started moving through the narrow streets of the town toward the compound, but the going was slow because it kept encountering small moving groups of Viet Cong. The voice on the radio from the special forces compound was becoming more urgent in its request for additional reinforcement, but there remained only two cavalry platoons at Blackhorse. I was reluctant to commit them to a night road march, with its potential for an ambush, unless I was sure that it was absolutely required. As I hesitated over stripping Blackhorse of its last remaining fighting troops, the requests for reinforcements from the compound grew still more insistent. I was torn between my responsibility to protect an as yet unthreatened Blackhorse and the need to prevent the special forces camp from being overwhelmed. The platoon from C Troop was still moving, however, and though it reported fairly heavy concentrations of enemy soldiers, its movement had not been stopped. I decided to wait a little longer before taking any action. Then everything quieted down. No more requests for assistance came from the special forces, which a moment ago had been reporting heavy pressure on their compound, and C Troop reported dwindling enemy contact from its platoon moving through the town. By four thirty in the morning, it was over, and the enemy that had been pressing so hard twenty minutes earlier had faded into the predawn dark as if to be gone before daylight. Tet was over for us. After that one last moment of tension, the radios went quiet. Only the routine periodic situation reports came in to reassure us that there was nothing happening.

Three hours later our battered cavalry troops moved out on their respective normal road-opening missions. Aside from the remnants of some crude roadblocks, which were unmanned and easily cleared, and some blown bridges, the roads were open again. Convoys could move to resupply the outposts that had been under such heavy attack only a few hours before. Up north, Hue was still in enemy hands, and a lot of hard fighting still lay ahead in order to reduce the various pockets of Viet Cong and North Vietnamese soldiers who were trying to hold what they had captured. Now, however, they were the besieged and the defenders. The initiative had passed over to us between 31 January and 1 February, and it could not be regained by the enemy. The best proof of that was that twenty-four hours after the Tet offensive began in the Saigon area, and despite the enemy's best efforts, the roads belonged to us once again.

Tet cost my squadron about 10 percent of its strength in killed and wounded, but we had inflicted enormous casualties in return. And the frustrations of taking casualties from mines and hidden two-man rocket teams as we went about our patrolling and securing of the roads had been dissipated by finally having an enemy to fight against. The squadron fought well, and A Troop more than deserved the awards for heroism that were showered on it by the division commander (not from our own, who had been in charge of the defense of Bien Hoa— the same irascible general who had taken over Phuoc Vinh from the brigade in which I had been the adjutant). So it was a professionally proud and confident squadron that set about refitting after Tet. Unlike the folks back home, we did not know that we had lost.

# VII

# North to Danang and Hue

As soon as our involvement in Tet ended, my attention turned to a very unwarlike subject: my midtour rest and recuperation leave. R & R, as it was called, was a seven-day, paid vacation. Each soldier was authorized to go on R & R once during his tour in Vietnam. It was taken normally toward the middle of the tour, and its purpose was to get you away from the war and the hardships of living under field conditions in a combat zone so that you would have the same energy and alertness to deal with the second half of your tour that you had ostensibly brought with you to start your assignment in Vietnam. You could spend the week in any of a number of selected R & R sites, but you could not go to the United States, proper. During my tour in Vietnam, the available locations were Hawaii, Hong Kong, Australia, Japan, Kuala Lumpur, and a couple of other lesser-known locations in the Far East. You could fly free of charge to any of these locations to rejoin civilization and forget combat for a while.

My wife and I had been discussing possible plans for meeting in letters and tape recordings almost since my arrival in Vietnam. Selecting the location was the first step, and the economics of the travel pretty quickly made us settle on Hawaii: the government paid only for my flight; my wife's flight, if I wanted to meet her for my R & R, was our responsibility.

R & R began for me with a short flight from Blackhorse to Bear Cat. In preparation for the trip to Hawaii, I had exhumed my two tan uniforms from my footlocker several weeks earlier and had sent them to be washed and pressed after their five-month sojourn in that damp container. Though my tan uniforms were ready and I was packed for the civilized world, this first part of the trip to Tan Son Nhut airport was just like any other jeep ride in Vietnam. I wore my steel helmet and flak vest and carried my usual weapons as we made our way up the highway to Saigon and around the scattered pockets of Tet resistance that were still holding out in the face of our mopping-up operations. Saigon appeared to have returned to normal in the areas through which we drove, and the pedicab and bicycle traffic was at its normal overwhelming level as we picked our way through the city. We weaved through the crowded streets and reached the airport processing center without incident.

Then, and only then, did I turn over my helmet, flak vest, and weapons to the driver for safe keeping until my return. That ritual completed, I put on my soft cap and walked into the impersonal world of the R & R processing center. I was immediately caught up in a series of lines in which even majors lose their identities to the rules, the harried clerks, and the checklists. It was an efficient operation, however, and in short order I found myself assigned to a bunk in an open, screened building crammed with triple-decker bunks. I also had been assigned to a flight and given a reporting time for early the next morning. The intervening time was mine. I would have preferred to have been occupied at that juncture, but there was nothing to do but to lie on my bunk and read or chat with the others while trying to submerge unseemly excitement. All the officers who were going out the next day were in this one building, though, so there were plenty of people in the same boat I was in with whom I could trade war stories.

I slept fitfully that night, partially because of my excitement and partially because of the sounds of artillery in the near distance, the meaning of which was not at all clear to me. The last time I had been in a replacement center, I had been too new to wonder at the firing. Now, however, after months of being in a position to know what every weapon noise meant, it was difficult to be part of a herd of humanity without contact with the command structure and with no radio to tell me whether the firing meant an attack or just the normal level of nighttime activity. My temporary situation brought home very clearly to me how an enlisted soldier must feel all the time. He rarely would have access to the radios that eliminated uncertainty by giving information on the situation from moment to moment. In the back of my mind, too, was the thought of what a mess a mortar attack would make of this jammed processing center, with its three-tiered bunks and close-built screened barracks buildings. How ironic it would be to be injured or killed in your bunk as you prepared to go on R & R! It was not a comforting theme to dwell on, but I could not shake it. Somehow the night passed, though, and then it was time to change into my tan uniform and store my jungle uniform for my return. Then I was on the plane, lifting off from the airport to start the transition back to normal civilization, the first indicator of which was the stewardess on this commercial charter airliner that was winging me toward Hawaii and my wife.

It was a wonderful week of complete forgetfulness, of closeness with my wife, and of talking. Everything conspired to make it a truly idyllic time: the beach actually looked like it did on the posters, the people were friendly, and the weather was magnificent. Before we were ready, it was time to start the trip back to reality.

I found that I had gained a brand-new appreciation for the normalcy of life in the United States. It may be that you have to spend some time with a gun on your person twenty-four hours a day, with your eyes and ears alert for a noise that can kill you, to really understand how wonderful it is to walk unarmed on a street without fear or the need for constant alertness. Though I knew that our streets might not have been as secure as they seemed, even back then, it was still a far cry from the kind of streets that hide men carrying automatic weapons, men waiting to catch you off guard just once. Such thoughts, combined with having to say goodby to my wife once more, made the morning of departure particularly difficult for me. I am convinced that the walk from my wife's arms to the charter airliner waiting to take me back to war was the hardest walk I have ever made.

My flight back was unexpectedly lengthened by a stop at Guam. Tan Son Nhut airport was still liable to mortar attack at night and was therefore closed to commercial air traffic after dark. As a result, we had to lay over at Guam in order to make a daylight approach to Saigon in our commercial charter. We had pleasant accommodations in an old stone bachelor officers' quarters, and we took full advantage of a very nice officers' club during the evening. The next morning we were back on our way. Some four hours later we were heading down into Vietnam. On the ground, I quickly reclaimed my jungle uniform and called the squadron rear detachment for some transportation. In an hour I was strapping on my pistol, putting on my helmet, and shrugging back into my flak vest as I climbed into the jeep that would transport me the final miles back into the reality of Vietnam. The ride back to Bear Cat through Saigon was uneventful, and the dusty highway seemed to have the same supply trucks moving along it as when I had driven in the other direction. It was hard to believe that I had been away from the humming radios and the clinging dust for a week, and it was even harder to believe that my wife and I had been lolling on a white beach in another land only three days before. The ability of the human being to adapt to changing environments is truly amazing.

One event did occur on the ride back to Bear Cat that did not seem significant at the time, but which would grow in meaning in the next few years. The rear detachment driver who routinely piloted the jeep that I used when I was at Bear Cat was a black soldier. I had noticed that he frequently gave an upraised, closed-fist salutation to other black soldiers as he passed them. On this ride I asked him about the significance of the salute. He replied that it was simply a sign of recognition between brothers, and I let the subject drop. I had not noticed these interchanges in the squadron up north, but I now began to realize that it was very common in the rear areas. It carried no threat at the time, but the black power salute, and all it connoted, was to play a part in the internal turmoil that would grip the Army in the 1970s. Later, when I was in the midst of that turmoil, I often thought back to my first rather casual encounter with that sign of recognition between brothers.

A surprise awaited me at the squadron headquarters building at Bear Cat: the squadron had been ordered north to Danang, and three of the troops, along with the squadron command post, had already loaded on LSTs and shipped out by the time I arrived. While I had been gone, we had suddenly been directed to move north to the area just below the border between North and South Vietnam in response to a potential threat from North Vietnamese light tanks, which our intelligence people had gotten wind of. Though the threat did not materialize that spring, we were committed.

Only the headquarters troop was still at Bear Cat preparing to load, and I threw myself into the final preparations almost as soon as the jeep stopped in the squadron area. A small rear detachment and our air cavalry troop were staying behind. We had wangled four of our light observation helicopters to go north with us, but that was all that our division would reluctantly tolerate losing. The remainder of our air cavalry helicopters were simply too valuable to the rest of the division to be allowed to depart with us. For some reason, however, the four light observation helicopters we were taking had been directed to fly to Danang by stages instead of being shipped on the decks of the LSTs. The rationale was that the salt spray would ruin them, but in the end the long flight accomplished the same thing. We never did get all four back together and flying at the same time. Two fell out at various intermediate stopping points along the six-hundred-mile flight to Danang. By the time they made it up to the squadron, weeks later, one or the other of the two ships with the squadron was no longer flying.

While I coordinated the final preparations for moving the headquarters troop to port, I also made the necessary arrangements for providing administrative support to the squadron at its new location up north. Pay, mail, supplies, repair parts, and all the other supporting services that we took for granted while we operated within our division area would now have to be provided over a great distance. We would be working for the Marine Corps, initially, and that meant that most of our administrative and supply support would still have to come from our own parent Army division. I managed to work out a makeshift system for accomplishing all this before I saw the headquarters troop loaded aboard two LSTs moored in the Saigon River. I then took some tank engines and spare tank track and drove to Bien Hoa Air Base with a couple of trucks to promote a cargo aircraft ride to Danang. It was mid-February before I finally rejoined the squadron that I had left at Blackhorse to go on R & R.

The squadron had gone into bivouac outside the city of Danang as its successive ship loads had arrived, and it was now working for the Marine division that was headquartered there. The squadron now, however, temporarily consisted of only two of our three line troops. Immediately upon arrival, A Troop had been sent farther north to the city of Hue to join the fight to regain control of that imperial city from the North Vietnamese, who had taken it over at the beginning of Tet and who still clung tenaciously to large sections of it. A Troop was working under the control of an Army brigade, which was in turn working for the Marines, who were in overall charge of clearing Hue. The problems of supply and repair of vehicles that resulted were a nightmare for us. The Marines, by agreement, supplied us only with food and fuel. Our repair parts had to come from Army sources. The Army brigade, however, was an airmobile brigade and had no capability to support our heavy armored vehicles. To solve the problems inherent in this situation, I spent a lot of time arranging first to procure the parts that we needed from our own division, some of which were large and bulky and took up a lot of cargo airplane space, and then more time negotiating with the Air Force to transport the needed parts to Danang. From there I had to talk our repair parts onto the Navy landing craft that were used to resupply Hue. I was on the move continuously for almost ten days, doing the necessary arranging, catching rides south to Bien Hoa then back up to Danang, and conning landing craft captains into carrying tank parts.

Communication with our troop in Hue by the usual means was difficult. Its radios could barely reach us, and the more powerful Marine radio facilities were far too busy fighting the war for us to transact our supply business. So the squadron commander took to flying to Hue on alternate days to make contact in person with the A Troop commander. That way he could also deliver the mail that we brought up from our division while he was finding out what our troop needed for survival. These flights were always a bit nerve-racking. First, we used one of our own light observation helicopters that we had flown north and were keeping in the air on a shoestring. These ships had marginal navigation instrumentation because they were really not intended for anything but short flights in sight of the ground. Between us and Hue, however, lay the Hai Van pass, which rose to 3,900 feet, where it was shrouded in the northeast monsoon rain clouds. In fact, the pass seemed to hold back the monsoon from Danang, where the weather remained pleasant despite the clearly visible dark rain clouds hanging in the pass. In any event we could not fly our helicopters through those clouds. The alternative was to go around the base of the mountain mass and out over the South China Sea, which was also a nervous business in our single-engine helicopter. Nevertheless, that was our route to Hue, some fifty miles to the north of us. We would fly out over the ocean a little above the water and follow the coast to a point opposite Hue. Then we would pick up a little altitude and head inland through the shifting rain clouds, hoping that we would not "lose" the ground before we found our troop headquarters location. In that way, we kept in touch with its situation and found out what repair parts were needed to maintain operations.

Our helicopter link also became a medical evacuation link in those first grim weeks of the Hue operation because we were the only ones flying. Marine aviation was not willing to fly when the weather was below minimums, and on many days no Marine helicopters went in or out of Hue. Minimums did not bother our young warrant officer pilots, and our squadron commander felt a compulsion to make the every-other-day attempt to keep contact with our troop. Therefore, we launched whether we had minimums or not, and more often than not made it in and out on the same day. After word got around about our more-or-less regular flights, not a few wounded Marines owed their lives to an uncomfortable fifty-mile ride in a litter rigged to the skids on the outside of our little helicopters. Since then, whenever I hear criticism of Army aviation and our flying warrant officers, I think of those flights in and out of Hue on days when the more sophisticated Marine pilots, with their jet-aircraft and multiengine qualifications, would not leave the ground. Our guys did not know that they should not have been flying; they just flew.

To help us get the parts and other supplies we needed from our home base six hundred miles to the south, we experimented with setting up our very long range radios, which were part of a cavalry squadron's standard equipment, but for which we had rarely found a need in the relatively close confines of Vietnam. These radios used the principle of bouncing radio waves off clouds to communicate over extended distances. The first time we got the antennas set up and the radio in operation, we dialed in our assigned frequency and started trying to make contact with a similar radio rig that we had set up in the air cavalry troop's radio room back at Bear Cat. Nothing happened for a few minutes; then, through the squeal of the static, came a voice announcing that the SS "something or other" was receiving us loud and clear. Our first bounce had put us somewhere out in the Pacific Ocean on the way to Australia. We chatted for a few minutes with our friend on his ship then signed off to figure out what to do next.

Since the bounce was too long, the obvious answer was to cut down the frequency. Arbitrarily, we dialed in a frequency that was exactly half of our assigned frequency and spent the rest of the day trying to relay the word over various telephone systems between us and Bear Cat so that our rear detachment would know to do the same thing. The next day at the appointed time, we tried again. In a few minutes we were talking with the squadron rear detachment at Bear Cat. From the yells that went up at this feat, you would have thought that we had really contributed something significant to the war effort instead of merely having arranged to talk to another part of our squadron. Nevertheless, that radio link enabled us to stay supplied and repaired for the next several months and provided us with the only reliable connection with our parent division. No matter where we were sent in the northernmost provinces of Marine country, at a fixed time each day we talked with our rear detachment and arranged for the details of supply and administration to take place as though we were right next door.

One immediate result of our new radio arrangement was that I found out that three of our damaged ACAVs, which had been undergoing repair at the general support maintenance facility at Bear Cat, were now ready to be returned to us. I decided to hitch a ride back down once more in order to speed up getting those ACAVs and whatever other major engine assemblies I could find, into our hands at our encampment outside of Danang. So back I went to Danang Air Base and the routine of waiting to catch a ride. This time it took only half a day before I was headed south, sitting on the floor of a C123. A call from Bien Hoa Air Base at the other end brought a jeep from the squadron headquarters rear detachment, and I was back in the semideserted squadron area before dark.

I spent the next day looking for scarce parts and arranging with the Air Force at Bien Hoa to provide space on two C130s for my cargo. Within two days I had arranged to get the air transportation that I needed, and we moved the three ACAVs, together with the engines and track that I had gathered, to Bien Hoa. There we put the parts on pallets to facilitate loading them onto the aircraft and then drove our ACAVs into the cavernous bellies of the C130s. Two ACAVs fit into one plane, and the other one shared the cargo area of a second C130 with our pallets of repair parts. By midafternoon we were sitting on the active runway waiting to lift off.

We flew north and landed at dusk at the large air base at Tuy Hoa, which was on the coast about halfway to Danang. There I had a chance to check on the status of one of our light observation heli-copters that had been forced to set down there on its trip north. The needed repair parts had arrived, I discovered, and it appeared that it could be flown north to join us within the week. The next morning we were off early. By noon I was guiding our AVACs out of the C130s at Danang and forming a convoy to our bivouac area. One more long-distance supply run was complete, and a few more oper-ational vehicles had been added to our inventory.

While A Troop was fighting in Hue to help break enemy resis-tance in an environment that was particularly inhospitable to cavalry because of the restricted movement city streets impose, B and C troops were deployed to the south and west of Danang in the so-called rocket belt, the area from which any rocket attack would have to be launched on the heavy concentration of base camps that were grouped close around the busy Danang airfield. Their mission was to conduct mounted patrols during the day and outpost the high ground at night, from where they could detect movement in the valleys and could very quickly spot the flash from any mortar or rocket that was fired. Our actual contacts with the enemy were sparse, however, and the days tended to be long and uneventful. While the troops were running these rou-tine missions, however, they were also getting accustomed to the vastly different operating procedures used by the Marines. Everything from the method of obtaining clearance for supporting artillery fires that we requested to the criteria for obtaining scarce helicopter support was different from what we had been accustomed to. It was probably just as well that there was not much enemy contact during this break-in period because we had a lot to learn.

One evening I went out to spend the night with B Troop, which had been patrolling a valley in the rocket belt that day and which would occupy overwatch position located on the high ground that edged the valley during the late afternoon. I was going out to take a close look at their operation because it seemed to have more maintenance problems than average and a general inability to perform the normal support functions quite right.

I flew out and landed on the top of a barren, narrow ridge onto which the troop command post, maintenance section, and kitchen had been squeezed. Though this position was centrally located with regard to the surrounding platoon positions, it was open and not easily defended—and it was disorganized on the ground. In short it was a poorly selected position, all angles and slopes, that barely accommodated the vehicles and offered a very poor defensive potential in the event of an attack. By the time I had moved through the area with the troop commander and pointed out various improvements he might make, it was starting to get dark.

Somewhat concerned over the vulnerability of the position, I reminded the troop commander that he ought to make contact with the supporting Marine artillery in order to register in some defensive fires in case we were hit during the night. I listened as the troop commander made contact on the radio and made the routine request for registering artillery fire. Back came the answer that it was too dark to register artillery. We were practically speechless. Artillery fire is registered by use of map coordinates, and the flash of the striking shells is all the illumination that is needed to plot the necessary adjustments. Be that as it may, we could not convince our Marine artillery friends to fire into this free-fire zone—a zone in which there were no civilians and no restrictions on shooting. We had to content ourselves with substituting our own carefully registered heavy mortars, which were not needed on this night that remained quiet and uneventful. The next morning, after thoroughly raising hell about the poorly prepared breakfast and spending time trying to instill some order into the maintenance section's procedures, I flew back to the squadron to discuss with the squadron commander what I had found. We had to make a judgment on the capability of our B Troop commander, but the thing that really stuck in my mind was the lack of responsiveness of the Marine artillery. I wondered if it was an omen for future joint operations.

Our squadron headquarters was set up in a flat, sandy valley in the center of a ring of barren hills. Since the hills and the low land on the outer sides of those hills were occupied by our own troops and by Marine units, it was a relatively secure command post location. We lived and worked from our command post vehicles and a combination of tents and trailers with built-up sides and a roof that we had constructed. Since we were not on the move every few days, we followed the old Army dictum about continually improving your position. We put in a good perimeter fence of concertina wire to discourage unwanted visitors, and we constructed some amenities for ourselves. We rigged showers by hanging the canvas Australian shower buckets by a rope from a projecting vehicle corner or from a makeshift arm, then placed wood pallets—the kind rations are shipped on—underneath them as a flooring. These showers became a favorite gathering place for the local Vietnamese children who visited us, whenever we would let them inside the perimeter. It was clear that showering was one of their favorite sports.

The squadron staff members were kept busy during this period coordinating with the Marine division headquarters. After making these daily coordination visits, they would visit the troops to pass on the details of the next day's mission. They were also involved in making tentative plans for us to move further north, which was a rumored possibility.

One of the major problems in Danang soon turned out to be keeping the peace between the squadron's night foragers, who wanted to help me obtain parts, and our Marine hosts. Cavalrymen, left to their own devices, are inveterate "scroungers," and being isolated from our normal sources of supply simply served to reinforce that natural bent. The troop commanders wanted their vehicles to be operational, and their soldiers grew very clever at gaining entrance to one or another Marine vehicle park to strip off parts that looked like they might be useful. There were some pitfalls in this type of parts procurement, however. Though the Marines used the same types of tanks that we did, our troopers soon found out that the various fasteners used on the respective tanks were of a different size.

The big lug nuts that hold a tank's steel road wheels in place were, for instance, always in demand. One dark night several troopers painstakingly unscrewed a number of these lug nuts from parked Marine tanks and stealthily carried them back—only to find that they did not fit on our tanks. That episode, of course, left both the Marine tanks and our tanks without lug nuts and caused some understandable questioning by Marine authorities. Some of the early "borrowings" of the more sophisticated items had not been attributed to us at first because the Marines did not realize that we had radio repairmen assigned to our squadron and to each of our troops. Marines do not assign them so low in their organizations, so they did not connect us with the initial sudden and mysterious disappearance of radio equipment, equipment that required some technical skill to remove. Eventually, however, the connection was made, and we were barred from the Marine vehicle parks. Our headquarters was then asked to conduct a search to try to recover the borrowed items so that they could be returned to their rightful owners. All of this provided a diversion for many troopers, but it did not gain us any points with our hosts. It must have seemed to the Marines to be a little like inviting a horde of locusts to stay on your farm.

In late February we mounted the only significant offensive operation that we would run in the area close to Danang. At the instruction of the Marine division for which we were working, we sent our two line troops across a shallow river into a large, fairly isolated section of land that was completely enclosed by rivers and an estuary of the South China Sea. Though some foot operations had been conducted in this area before, no armored vehicles had ever penetrated the surrounding water barriers. For that reason the local Viet Cong soldiers who inhabited the area were totally unprepared for our heavy, tracked vehicles. We had success after success as the enemy, frightened by the unaccustomed sight of a tank or ACAV bearing down on him, surrendered or ran. The fire fights were brief, and the enemy never showed any of the tenaciousness for which he was so well known. By the end of the week, we had run up an impressive list of captured weapons, confiscated food caches, and enemy soldiers taken prisoner, with practically no damage or casualties suffered by us. My squadron commander asked to extend our operation to take advantage of the evident enemy surprise, but our Marine bosses had other plans for us. Reluctantly, we pulled back across the near river barrier and ended one of the most successful and least costly combat operations in which the squadron had ever been involved. The opportunity never came again. The next incursion with armor was conducted by Marine tanks, and by then the local Viet Cong had figured out what they had to do to oppose the tracked vehicles. They had obtained the mines and antitank rockets that made even mobile armor columns vulnerable. For a little while there had been an opportunity, but the planners had not been flexible enough to enable us to fully exploit it.

Unknown to us in our isolated Army enclave in Marine country, plans and strategies were changing in Vietnam. More Army presence was being ordered to this most northern section of Vietnam in answer to the same intelligence estimates that had brought us north originally.

The first indication that we received was the word, passed out at a briefing at the Marine division headquarters, that an Army division would be moving in to fill the gap in the sparsely settled territory that lay between the operational areas of the Marine division located at Danang and the Marine division located at Dong Ha, some one-hundred miles to the north. This Army division, which was the same one that had taken over my brigade's base camp the previous fall and with whom A Troop had fought the battle at Bien Hoa during Tet, was to be flown into Danang and would then move north on Highway 1 to occupy a new division base camp just south of the city of Hue. At the time the division's arrival meant little to us, and we took no particular note of it.

To orchestrate the newly increased Army presence in what had been primarily a Marine area, a provisional corps headquarters was established in the center of the new Army operational area. Suddenly, we had several headquarters with an interest in us. Though we were still nominally under the operational direction of the Marine division located in Danang, our one detached troop at Hue was working for an Army brigade, which had now been taken over by the new provisional corps. We became enmeshed in the works of this tangled chain of command because our armor represented the only Army armor in reach. Everybody wanted us. The troop in Hue was about finished with its mission, and what remained to be done was a job for foot soldiers working from house to house to clean out the last elements of resistance. Despite that fact, we could not seem to actually regain control of the troop, and the labyrinthine chain of command just referred to made it very hard to appeal to the right people. The clearing of Hue was almost over, but the commanders on the ground were reluctant to let go of our troop of armored vehicles.

Our opportunity came when we were directed to detach a troop to work for the new Army division. First, we very quickly decided that the troop selected for that duty should be the one that had worked with that division at Bien Hoa. That would give the troop commander an "in" with the division commander, who had decorated him and praised him so highly. That little bit of extra influence might protect our troop from being employed to its disadvantage by a staff that knew neither the troop commander nor the exact capabilities of the unit, and it would ensure that the troop commander would be consulted on proposed missions for his unit. Though A Troop was still committed to Hue, that fact just gave us added incentive to select it for the new attachment. What better way to get it out of Hue than to attach it to the newly introduced Army division and let the irascible division commander use his well-known force of personality to arrange for its prompt release to him. The general was certainly not one to brook interference if somebody was slow to give up to him assets that had been dedicated to his division.

Sure enough, our plan worked. We informed the provisional corps that A Troop was the troop to be put under the operational control of the Army division and that it would move as soon as we could obtain its release. A day or two went by, and there was no release. On the third day the Army division commander became impatient and made his impatience known. On the fourth day A Troop was released to join its new temporary parent. We all breathed a sigh of relief, and A Troop made plans to march south out of Hue along Highway 1 to the newly established base camp belonging to the Army division.

The bridges over the river that ran along the southern outskirts of Hue had been badly damaged during the fighting in the city, and the Highway 1 bridge was only barely intact. The center span almost touched the water, and vehicles drove gingerly down the incline formed by the weakened sections to the level center span then back up a similar incline to get off the bridge. Somebody should therefore have been very carefully monitoring the vehicles using that bridge, but nobody was paying much attention in the confusion that still attended the mopping-up operations in Hue. Our troop commander, in a hurry to leave the city that had hemmed him in for almost a month, chose to simply march out across that bridge and on down Highway 1 without checking with anybody.

Our squadron commander had flown up to overwatch the changeover of A Troop, and we were able to talk with him on our normal radios because of his altitude. Since the troop was not under our operational control, however, we had not been involved in the details, and we did not know until later that our troop commander's planned march route had not been coordinated with anybody. We therefore listened calmly to the squadron commander's radio reports as A Troop got under way and headed south. The ACAVs rolled smoothly across the bridge, we heard, and the tanks appeared to be making what is known as a "caution crossing" in view of the obviously weakened condition of the bridge. A caution crossing simply meant that only one tank would be on the bridge spans at a time, that there would be no shifting of gears or changing speed, and that a uniform ten-mile-per-hour speed would be maintained. That approach appeared to work just fine for the first two platoons, though our squadron commander remarked that he had some concerns about the sturdiness of the bridge.

Then the last platoon started across. As the last tank began its descent down the incline toward the weakened center span, the military police bridge guards, who probably should have kept us off the bridge completely, suddenly appeared at the back of the column. There was a good bit of commotion as they belatedly attempted to prevent the remaining vehicles in our column from using the weakened bridge. The last vehicle in the column, which was a tank, gunned its motor to get away from the perceived threat to its escape from Hue. As it gunned up the incline on the south side of the river to complete the crossing, its spinning tracks pushed the center span into the river, and a widening gap of water began to appear between the two bridge sections.

Undaunted, the tank kept moving up the inclined bridge section and on down the road after the remainder of the troop, leaving a broken bridge and some frustrated, gesturing military police in its wake. Highway 1, the main line of supply to Hue and north, had been cut by an "unidentified" tank that had broken through the only bridge intact at Hue. We decided that there was no need to volunteer the information as to whose tank it was. We were just thankful for several reasons that A Troop was out of Hue and not likely to return to that ruined city.

# VIII
# Marine Operations— Dong Ha

With the beginning of March came the first signs that the northeast monsoon would not last forever. Though the country north of the Hai Van pass was still shrouded in cloud, more of the pass itself was visible each day as the cloud line gradually started to lift. We had already received a warning order that our future operations would be in the area north of the Hai Van. Hue was now almost completely cleared of enemy, and additional Army units were moving into Quang Tri Province. The focus of attention was on the siege of Khe Sanh, and we could sense the increasing tempo of operations as we went about our routine patrols just south of Danang. Our A Troop was, of course, already very much a part of the new activity to the north of us.

Quang Tri Province begins about eighteen miles north of Hue and runs all the way to the Demilitarized Zone that divided North and South Vietnam. On a map it resembles a tropical miniature of the New Jersey coastal area. It is flat sand from the blue-green water of the South China Sea to National Highway 1, a two-lane blacktop version of the Jersey Turnpike that parallels the coast some eight miles inland. West of this national highway, which was heavily damaged during the Tet offensive, the land rises into craggy foothills that become progressively more rugged and more heavily wooded as they run farther west to the Ashau Valley and Khe Sanh. The Cua Viet River, flowing to the South China Sea on a course that parallels the Demilitarized Zone, cuts off the northern third of the province and makes a rough right angle with Highway 1 where it crosses it at Dong

Ha, some nine miles south of the Demilitarized Zone. In March this land is still in the grips of the northeast monsoon, which gradually lifts by early April. The northeast monsoon has none of the daily alternation of steamy sun and drenching downpour that marks the monsoon in the southern part of South Vietnam; instead, there are weeks on end of drizzle and low-hanging clouds that eventually convince you if you spend much time exposed to it, that the temperature is thirty degrees instead of the actual fifty. It was into this gray landscape, not yet fully recovered from the fierce fighting of Tet, that we were headed.

One warm, pleasant morning in mid-March, I climbed aboard a big twin-bladed Marine cargo helicopter at the Danang Air Base to make my first coordination trip to the Marine combat base at Dong Ha, which was to be our initial home when we moved north. We lifted off in bright sunlight, flew out to sea, and headed northwest over the sparkling water on a course that paralleled the coast about a half mile out. After almost an hour, we sighted a beacon and turned toward the surf line and mist that marked the shore below us. As we approached the shore, we increased our altitude and flew into a bank of gray, wet clouds that lay just in back of the coastline. From there to Camp Evans, our first port of call, we saw nothing but shifting gray fog below, above, and around us. Using instruments, and with the assist of a radio beacon, we flew through the murk to make a vertical descent onto the ridgetop dirt strip that was the center of Camp Evans. The ground came into view no more than one-hundred feet up. Once we landed, I looked around at what I could see of this advanced outpost while cargo and passengers were transferred. Everything was wet and gray; the makeshift shelters that the Marines had constructed looked drab and bleak among the small, knobby hills in wet scrub grass. Few troops were to be seen, and the clouds hovered low overhead. It did not look like a choice place to spend much time.

A half hour later we lifted straight up into the overcast sky and headed back toward the coast. Once we broke out into sunshine over the sea again, we turned northwest once more. Another thirty minutes and we were again turning inland. Before long we were settling down on the bustling airstrip in the center of Dong Ha. This busy airstrip was solidly built of pierced steel planking joined together, and even boasted its own low, wood-and-canvas terminal building. The helicopter hovered to a parking slot along the edge of the active runway, and I jumped off to walk to the terminal building. All the while there was a continuous stream of large C130 aircraft, the big four-engine assault cargo planes, coming in and going out. They did not stop for long, however, because this airstrip was in range of the North Vietnamese 130-millimeter guns located just on the other side of the Demilitarized Zone. To minimize the chance of losing one of these big planes, the C130s touched down with their rear cargo doors open and the big hydraulic rear ramp half down. They then taxied along at a moderate speed while pallets of supplies were pushed off the now almost fully lowered, roller-floored ramp. As soon as the last pallet had been pushed off, the C130s were ready to start their take-off roll and be airborne again. Forklifts quickly cleared the taxiway of the pallets so that the aircraft could take off and the next one could come in. Occasionally, one would stop for a few minutes to unload a vehicle or a gun that could not be pushed off while the aircraft was in motion, but the engines were never shut down, and the planes quickly lumbered back into the air.

What I could see of Dong Ha as I walked along the airstrip edge was as gray and desolate as Camp Evans had been, with the added disadvantage that the large population of troops and vehicles had worn off all the scrub grass and left a gummy mud surface in its place. Here, too, everything was damp and dank in the overcast, and that, in combination with the deep trenches sunk into the ground at intervals, made me think that I had walked onto the set for a World War I movie. The trenches soon symbolized Dong Ha to me. They were built under every building, many of which had holes cut into the floors so that you could dive into the protective earth at a moment's notice, and they bordered every facility from dining hall to latrine. It was obvious that this was a different kind of war than the one we were used to.

No more sporadic nighttime mortar or rocket attacks that placed a few rounds inside our perimeter at random—and allowed us to casually lay aside our flak vests and helmets when we were inside the perimeter. Instead, we heard the sharp crack of high-velocity guns hurling 130-millimeter shells down on us on a regular schedule. The shelling was so regular that the daily schedule at Dong Ha was synchronized to avoid the prime shelling time. Reveille was early enough so that breakfast and washing up were completed before the first incoming rounds of the day were expected, and the evening meal was served so that it ended before the normal evening shelling. Though the guns did not always adhere to a regular schedule, the accommodation of the daily routine seemed to work sufficiently well that casualties were relatively few in relation to the number of rounds that impacted within the base camp each day. It was very clear why none of the Marines was ever very far from his flak vest and steel helmet.

I spent the day hitching rides from point to point within Dong Ha and introducing myself to the Marine staff elements with whom we would be working. I found out how and where rations were picked up, where the fuel supply point was, and what ammunition was stocked at the local ammunition supply point. They found out how many tanks and armored personnel carriers we had, what our support requirements were, and how many troops we would be bringing in. Then I borrowed a jeep and drove out on the low hills on which the base camp had been built to get a feel for the interior roads and the terrain out by the perimeter, where we would be assigned space. I tentatively chose some likely looking positions, being careful to select hilly ground that would shelter our vehicles from the direct fire of those 130-millimeter guns and still give us fields of fire for defending the perimeter if need be.

I quit in time to eat the early supper meal and found a spare bunk in one of the tarpaper-and-wood buildings that had been designed as transient bachelor officers' quarters. The six cots in the small, unpartitioned building were arranged around the square hole in the floor that led to the trench below, and I am not sure whether the thought of the incoming shells or of accidently falling into the trench in the night bothered me more. In any event it was a quiet night, and it was not until I was almost finished shaving the next morning that I experienced my first shelling. Nothing hit close to me that morning, but I joined the general rush for the nearby trenches and waited it out in the damp ground with everybody else. After finishing my shaving, I made some final coordination checks with my various Marine contacts and then hitched a ride back to the airstrip. There I managed to find space on a departing C130 and fly directly back to Danang in the air-conditioned comfort of the crew compartment in less than half the time it had taken me to fly up by helicopter.

Shortly after that first trip to Dong Ha, we were alerted for the actual movement north, and almost simultaneously my squadron commander went on his long-awaited R & R leave to meet his wife in Hawaii. The move north therefore became my responsibility, and I was quickly swallowed up by the details of moving the squadron by Navy LST from Danang to the mouth of the Cua Viet River, from where we would be ferried up the river to the Dong Ha landing in one- or two-vehicle loads on the little landing craft—called "Mike" boats—that plied the river. Our preparations involved the meticulous space planning for loading on the LSTs and an all-out push to get as much of our equipment in top shape as we could before the move north to the very end of our repair parts supply line. Unfortunately, the latter effort gave rise to a renewed raiding of our neighbors' vehicle parks.

In the furor of this premove activity, the days slipped by in a blur, and it was suddenly time to break up our bivouac areas. One day we formed our columns in the predawn darkness in the order of our planned loading and moved to the port area—only to find that our LSTs had not arrived as scheduled. We pulled as far off the road as we could and relaxed for the first time in several days, knowing that nothing we could do was going to affect the deliberate pace with which our LSTs would make their way into Danang harbor and up the estuary to their assigned berths. I had been mildly surprised that nobody could tell us where the ships were at the moment, but it was made amply clear to me that Navy skippers did not call in checkpoints the way we did on the march and that until they were sighted entering the estuary we would simply not know how soon to expect them. Once that fact had been established, we resigned ourselves to relaxing in the sun and letting the day drift by. Toward late afternoon we received word that the ships were moving up the estuary, but it was fully dark by the time the first vehicles started to roll aboard under floodlights.

Just as the head of the column started to get under way, two Navy criminal investigators found me where I stood in the middle of my lined-up vehicles. They had been assigned to investigate recent reports of pilferage and wanted to know if I could provide any information on the subject. I assured them that we had thoroughly shaken down our troopers quite recently and that we had not found any new evidence of stolen parts or equipment. Our all-out effort to get everything working did not, however, make me feel very secure in my statement, and my insecurity was not lessened any by the sight of several troopers passing by in the semidarkness carrying what appeared to be radios in their arms. I was quite sure that the radios were not the result of the filling of any last-minute requisitions at the Danang depot. I cast a worried eye at the fenced vehicle park that adjoined the road. I knew beyond a doubt that the passing troopers were returning from a visit to the Marine amphibious vehicles that I could barely see outlined against the horizon inside that wire enclosure. The investigators did not, however, notice anything amiss, and I was not about to disrupt our embarkation by bringing up what I merely suspected.

I breathed a sigh of relief as the vehicles closer to me started their engines and began moving forward to the waiting LSTs, leaving the investigators little choice but to pursue their investigation elsewhere. When the last vehicles had been tied down, I took a small advance party and several of our command jeeps back to the Danang Air Base, where we bedded down before loading on a C130 at first light and flying north. Since the LSTs would take about eighteen hours to sail north, we would have time to lay out our positions at Dong Ha and be ready to meet the squadron as it came off the Mike boats at the Dong Ha landing. One of my first moves after I landed was to arrange for some Seabee bulldozers to gouge out a depression toward the top of a sandy hill that I had selected for our headquarters and then mound up the dirt so that our squadron command post would have a protected area on a good radio communications site in which to set up. Once the scraping was under way, I made the ten-minute helicopter flight to the mouth of the Cua Viet to oversee the disembarkation of the first troop from its LST.

B Troop came off the LST in good order and spread out over the sandy point to wait for the small landing craft that would ferry the troop up the river to Dong Ha. Before they could even begin to embark on these small Mike boats, we were mortared. Though the loading was disrupted while we hurriedly dispersed the vehicles and scurried to find what cover we could in the sand under the tanks, no damage was done. Still, it was disconcerting that the mortar attack was so well timed—as if some human eye, rather than some random pattern, were directing the shelling. In case there was any doubt on that subject, the additional mortar rounds that fell on us later at the Dong Ha landing convinced us that we were, in fact, the victims of observed fire that was being adjusted by somebody who could see us and talk to the gunners. Every time we moved north across the Highway 1 bridge at Dong Ha with our light vehicles, while our tanks were ferried across the Cua Viet River below, one or two mortar rounds were fired on us while we were near the bridge and the landing below it. Somebody kept a good watch from somewhere, and we were just lucky that the observers were not more accurate. We had some shrapnel wounds but never a direct hit.

As soon as B Troop started embarking for the twenty-mile trip up the Cua Viet, I flew back to Dong Ha. Headquarters and C Troop would disembark successively after B Troop had cleared the sand spit, but they would be staged ashore to match the availability of the Mike boats. The operation was paced by the availability of these little landing craft and by the daylight hours needed to make the two-hour trip upriver. The LSTs pulled back out to sea between unloadings, but some elements of B Troop camped out in the sand overnight that first night, and C Troop spent the following night on the beach.

Not far from the C Troop bivouac area were several brand-new Marine tanks, which had been off-loaded from a supply LST and were awaiting transportation to Dong Ha. They were sparkling new and still had all their accessories packed in the original wood packing cases that were banded to the tank decks—accessories that C Troop had long since lost or had damaged in combat. After dispersing their vehicles and digging shallow holes in the sand to protect themselves against a mortar attack, C Troop soldiers turned their attention to those brand-new tanks. They spent the next several hours sneaking up on the tanks without being observed by the Marine permanent party that manned this busy supply beach. Eventually, some troopers managed to get next to the tanks with wrenches and started carefully to unbolt the sides of the packing boxes on top of the tanks. It was tricky work in the dark because they could not afford to be spotted at their work by the Marines and because the bolts that held the boxes together squeaked as they turned against the damp plywood. Ever so slowly they backed out the bolts and slid the wood box tops off—only to find piles of rocks inside. B Troop had been there before them!

Our first operation after we settled in was to be a sweep up Highway 1 past the little Marine fire-support bases to just short of the Demilitarized Zone border in what we hoped would appear to be an armor thrust at the border. It was to be our shakedown operation in this new area of operations, but its main purpose was to divert the enemy's attention from the relief of Khe Sanh to the west of us. To control our operation, we would initially move a small command group five miles north of the Cua Viet River to a piece of ground just outside a fire support base known as "Charlie One." (All the artillery fire support bases were known by their map labels, which were a combination of letters and numbers; in this case, Charlie One stood phonetically for C1.) North of the Cua Viet River, on both sides of Highway 1, was an area inhabited only by the Marines who manned the fire support bases and the roving bands of North Vietnamese soldiers who were forever jabbing at them. The North Vietnamese shelled our combat and fire support bases, and the artillery at the fire support bases shelled the North Vietnamese guns. Charlie One took about twenty incoming rounds on a normal day under this regimen. Surrounding it was a sandy, cratered, lunar-landscape impact area for the artillery of both sides; here and there were the remnants of a church or a village that had long since been deserted by the rice farmers or fishermen who in the past had made the area their home.

I rode into this no-man's-land with one cavalry troop shortly before the start of our first operation. My purpose was to get an on-the-ground feel for the terrain and the dirt tracks that crisscrossed the area and to pick the precise location for our advance command post next to Charlie One. We took the expected rounds of mortar fire as we headed north across the Cua Viet River just outside the Dong Ha perimeter, but they were all misses that day. Once our ACAVs crossed, we spread out and stopped to wait for our tanks to be ferried across to join us. Then we continued north. We moved cautiously up Highway 1, staying widely dispersed, herringboning whenever we stopped. We halted our march frequently to send scout sections up the various side roads and gullies so that we could learn what was actually there, out of sight of the highway. After about an hour of this, the main part of our column started through a long-abandoned hamlet where there was a shattered church in its center right next to the highway. Suddenly, there was a large splash in the rice paddy to the left of the column. The noise of our vehicles on the move had drowned out the sound of the incoming round, but the splash left no doubt what was happening. Even before the first splash had entirely subsided, another round hit to the right.

We had been neatly bracketed by artillery fire in a way that I had often read about but had never before experienced in Vietnam. I quickly ordered the column to increase speed and move through the artillery fire, but the impacting rounds kept pace with us for several hundred yards before stopping as suddenly as they had started.

There had been no hits, but the capability that had been demonstrated gave us all pause for thought. We were accustomed to the relatively unsophisticated gunnery techniques that the Viet Cong had used down south. This was an entirely different thing: unless I missed my guess, the North Vietnamese gunners had been able to use the shattered steeple as a reference point and had then neatly bracketed our column while we were moving. They even had been able to adjust their fire to keep pace with our accelerated speed. Luck had prevented a direct hit this time, but the idea that we had been so effectively tracked was more than a little disquieting.

The shelling turned out to be the most exciting part of our foray. The rest of our trip to Charlie One was uneventful. We continued to move warily, and we continued to scout both flanks, but we encountered only drying sand. At Charlie One we looked over the possible command post locations, made some radio checks to test for the best radio reception, and coordinated with the commander of the fire support base about where we wanted to locate. The area was desolate, flat, sandy, and provided no cover. Once again it seemed that it would be prudent to dig in the command tracks for protection against the artillery fire from the north. I made a note to arrange for a bulldozer to accompany us for that purpose when we moved up; then we were ready to make the march back to Dong Ha.

My squadron commander returned prior to the actual operation, and I reverted to my position of second in command. The circumstances of his return, however, caused me a little embarrassment. The evening after our excursion north to Charlie One, I was getting ready to turn in after having gone over with our officers the details of placing the advance command post, when we would move it, and which vehicles and men it would consist of. By late evening my head was spinning and my cot looked very good. As I took off my jungle boots, I was interrupted by one of the enlisted men who manned our operations track. He said that we had just received a phone call from the headquarters of an Army artillery unit whose phone had been our initial contact point when we were moving in. They said that our squadron commander was on their outside phone line and was demanding to talk to me. Unfortunately, the outside call could not be transferred to the internal base phone lines. Reluctantly, I put my boots back on, woke my driver, and made the half-mile trip to the tents that served as the artillery headquarters. I kept wondering what could be so urgent that my boss was phoning at that late hour. I received the answer to that question very quickly after I picked up the field phone handset to the outside line.

My boss had arrived in Danang from his R & R to find no trace of his squadron. There had been no messages giving our new location, no instructions on how to reach us, and no information about what we were doing. He had returned to find that his command had disappeared without a trace. After describing his experiences in trying to locate us in somewhat scathing detail, he asked me why I had left him in that situation. The only answer that I could think of was the one that every plebe at the Military Academy masters: "No excuse, sir!" There was a moment of silence on the phone; then we began a more normal discussion of the general situation and how he would rejoin us. In truth I had been so busy with my immediate problems in moving the squadron and settling them in that I had not given a thought to how my commander would find out where we were. In later years he told me that my answer was the one answer that he had not been mentally prepared for—and the only one that could have quieted his righteous anger. He was sure, he later said, that he had thought of a retort for any excuse I could offer as he had tried to trace us through the labyrinth of the Marine headquarters and the marginal long-distance field phones from Danang Air Base. I obviously owed a vote of thanks to the upperclassmen who fifteen years earlier had drilled that response into me.

With the squadron commander back I turned my attention away from the operational aspects of our mission and concentrated once more on our supply and maintenance support. The sweep north proceeded without a hitch and with very little enemy contact, though there was a great deal of movement back and forth that raised dust and looked impressive. Other Army troops had been flown into Dong Ha over the past few weeks to further the aura of a major build-up, but what the opposition did not know—we hoped—was that they were the same soldiers being flown in over and over again. Shoulder patches had been taken off the soldiers' uniforms, and they were ostentatiously unloaded from their C130s, during the day; at night they quietly flew back to Danang in order to repeat the operation the next day. We hoped to create the illusion of a large build-up, a build-up that would combine with our noisy armor movement north, posing a threat to the North Vietnamese that would cause them to take their eyes off Khe Sanh long enough for our forces to break the stranglehold being placed around the Marine garrison there. Whether or not it had any effect on the successful outcome of the Khe Sanh relief operation, we never found out. All that we knew was that we encountered little resistance and that we found few enemy soldiers along the route north. Eventually, the troops reached a line even with Gio Linh, the last hamlet of any size south of the Demilitarized Zone border. There they halted and occupied positions that appeared to threaten the border itself.

One day I found that I had to transact certain business in person with the section of the squadron maintenance platoon that had accompanied the troops to their forward location. I decided to take advantage of the availability of one of our light observation helicopters, which was not needed for other operations that day. We obtained the necessary clearances from the Marines to fly north, and we were warned to stay below five hundred feet in order to avoid the artillery and mortar fire that went on almost ceaselessly overhead. With a mental image of the crisscrossing shells above us clearly in our heads, we lifted off and flew north, staying very close to the ground.

The flat, featureless terrain skimmed by below us, and my finger moved carefully along the map in my lap so that we would not overfly our troop positions. Though my finger had not yet reached the border marking boldly inscribed on my map, a river suddenly loomed up below us and rushed underneath. I knew very well that the only river north of the Cua Viet was the one that separated North and South Vietnam. We hurriedly made a climbing turn back in the direction from which we had come, busting the five-hundred-foot altitude limitation in our eagerness to reverse course as quickly as possible. We breathed a sigh of relief when the river once more passed beneath us. Sure enough, there was Gio Linh off to the left in front of us, and there were the squadron vehicles in their dispersed positions. Somehow we had veered off to the west too far in our flight north and had missed the village. I was delighted that our visit to North Vietnam had been as short as it was, and I learned a valuable lesson about map orientation during low-level flights. I also took a lot of kidding about being the only U.S. Army officer to mount a light observation helicopter attack on North Vietnam.

Whether or not our diversionary operation to the Demilitarized Zone border really served its intended purpose, the lifting of the siege of Khe Sanh was a success. The tightening stranglehold on that outpost was broken, and the Marine garrison was withdrawn. Thereafter, Marine and Army troops moved out that way and set up temporary fire support bases from time to time, but they never again invited the kind of siege that had just ended. The Marines occupied other, smaller strong points at Cam Lo and a place nicknamed "The Rockpile," but they never allowed themselves to get that tied down again. In addition, the steadily increasing Army strength in this northernmost province, with its accompanying helicopter mobility, ensured that there would be sufficient force available to move to meet any reasonable threat. It would be another three years before this area would be threatened again, and by that time the balance of strength would have shifted once more to the North Vietnamese. The rumored tanks that had brought us north would actually materialize out of the jungle border to overrun the little outpost just to the west of Khe Sanh, known as Lang Vei. There would be no American cavalry or tanks there to stop them then, but that was all in the future, and we could not foresee any of it.

For now, we had been successful, and the Army and Marine forces in the area set to work to capitalize on that success by increasing the intensity and aggressiveness of our effort to find and destroy the North Vietnamese forces that had been so recently engaged in besieging Khe Sanh. Our first participation in this new phase was to act as a blocking force against which Marines would try to push the ever-elusive bands of North Vietnamese soldiers. Our squadron faced to the west, moved a short distance into the low hills that lay that way, and began to slip slowly south while maintaining a screen on the edge of the first high ground. A Marine infantry force was operating farther inland still, and they were moving toward us in an attempt to flush out the bands of North Vietnamese that we knew must be lurking in the scrabbly foothills and gullies that lay between us. The object was to force these North Vietnamese soldiers out of their hiding places and make them move into our waiting screen of vehicles so that we could kill or capture them before they could infiltrate past us. Our cavalry troops stayed spread out in a line just behind the first ridge of the foothills, probing here and there and keeping to the lower ground so that they would not be too easily seen by an enemy force fleeing toward them.

The first several days were relatively uneventful. We kept track of the progress of the Marine force, encountered a stray shot here and there, and generally contended more against the heat, which was increasing as the monsoon season started to pass, than we did against any enemy. There was a little action. The North Vietnamese seemed able to elude the searching Marines, and we looked in vain for any activity in front of us. On the rare occasion that we did find a suspected target, we had to be very careful lest the range of our guns carry our rounds into the approaching Marines. After one incident in which our tanks fired their main guns at a suspected target, we were admonished about the proximity of Marine infantry. Though we had obtained clearance to fire, it had felt a little close at the other end. After that, we decided that we simply could not afford to fire our main guns at long-range targets. It was just too difficult to keep up with the precise location of the Marine infantry, and there was always the additional fear that a tank shell would take a bounce and skip into them. So we had to content ourselves with what was right in front of us within machine-gun and small-arms range. The days dragged by, and the nights were quiet except for the eternal background of artillery fire crisscrossing overhead and impacting near Charlie One as we sideslipped south a little each day toward Dong Ha.

On the fourth day of the operation, we finally got our action. A fairly large band of North Vietnamese was flushed out and pushed into our waiting line of armored vehicles. A brisk firefight developed as the North Vietnamese tried to penetrate our line, but it quickly became apparent to them that they could not fight through. They drew back a short distance into the scrub brush in front of our line, keeping up a sporadic fire to occupy us while they studied which way to move next. The troop commander in contact called for an extra platoon to reinforce his position so that he could extend his line and still maintain the same density of ACAVs. His object was to prevent the North Vietnamese from either going around him or slipping between the increased interval between vehicles that would have resulted from his trying to extend his line without reinforcement. A reserve platoon was soon moving toward the action from our command post area with our operations officer, who was also my bunkmate, guiding the new, young platoon leader from the command post location to the position assigned to him with the troop in contact.

The approach march was made without incident, and the platoon was soon integrated into the troop line. There was a lot of firing going on when the platoon arrived, with the heavy machine guns of our vehicles chopping into the brush immediately in front of our positions and a sporadic rifle and antitank rocket fire coming back at us. For all the noise neither side was inflicting very much damage on the other for the very good reason that neither side could clearly see its targets. We were firing at sliding shadows in the sparse undergrowth, and their fire was going high over us because they did not want to expose themselves long enough in one place to bring their aim down to where it could hit our vehicles, which loomed above them just behind the crest of the ridge. It was a standoff, and the operations officer stopped his ACAV to study the situation after releasing the new platoon to the troop in the hope that he could suggest some better way to pin down the North Vietnamese before they could escape us.

As he looked over the terrain from the top of his ACAV, a single rifle shot came out of the scrub and pierced his side at that vulnerable point where the two halves of the flak vest laced together. His crew applied immediate first aid to stop the bleeding, notified us that he had been hit and that he did not appear to be in too serious a condition, then called for a medical evacuation helicopter over the radio. His ACAV moved quickly to a safe location, sheltered from enemy fire, and in about five minutes the helicopter arrived. Our operations officer was conscious and smiling. He was two months short of his normal rotation out of Vietnam, and he knew that the wound would send him home to his family a little earlier than had been planned. While they carried him to the helicopter, he joked with his crew about the ticket home that he had just received, and he lifted his thumb in the traditional "okay" sign as he was lifted into the helicopter. Thirty minutes later he was dead from the internal bleeding that even modern battlefield medicine could not control.

He had been my bunkmate for three months in the close confines of the makeshift combination office and sleeping room that we had rigged out of plywood and canvas on an extra ammunition trailer. We had both been commissioned into armor branch from West Point, though he had been a year behind me, and we had both served in the same kinds of tank and cavalry units in Europe and the States. We knew the same people and had been through the same experiences. He had four kids and a wife back in Ohio who were anxiously waiting out the last two months of his Vietnam tour, and his own thoughts had already turned to his next assignment. We had been having long discussions as we prepared to turn in late at night about what type of next assignment would be most rewarding and what might be available for him. He was a smiling, black-haired Irishman who liked to joke and who liked a beer, and he had been a good bunkmate and a good operations officer. I packed up his belongings, wrote a letter to his wife, and closed out his life. As always in combat, death had come when it was least expected.

The round that had dealt the fatal wound to our operations officer turned out to be almost the last shot fired in the operation. The North Vietnamese slipped soundlessly north, and by dark we had completely lost contact. We remained on alert through the night, but there was no movement around us at all. In the morning we road marched the remaining short distance to Dong Ha along Highway 1. For the next few days we concentrated on doing some badly needed maintenance on our vehicles and restocked our supplies of fuel and ammunition. With only the long-range guns firing at us on schedule from up north, it was almost as if we were out of the war. We transferred our senior troop commander up to become the operations officer, conducted a memorial service, and made some other personnel adjustments to compensate for our loss. As the days went by, my new bunkmate and I adjusted to each other's habits and we stopped thinking about his predecessor. I put away his memory for a quieter time.

The following week we moved north across the Dong Ha bridge once more to search a section of the sand flats that lay between Highway 1 and the South China Sea. This flat, sandy area was still dotted with the remnants of the scattered hamlets and villages that had once contained peasant families making a living from their sparse gardens and paddies and from the sea. These now-deserted villages provided the only possible cover for the North Vietnamese soldiers moving through, and our mission was to search some of them to see what we could uncover. We would be accompanied on this mission by a South Vietnamese army unit that was garrisoned in the local area, and it would do the close-in searching. On the designated day we road marched north with B Troop and a small command group. We bivouacked next to Highway 1 and were joined by the South Vietnamese unit and its American advisor. With the help of interpreters, we went over our plans together and prepared for our joint operation. Early the following morning we moved out toward the first deserted village. Our armored vehicles, spread out in a slowly moving line, led the approach while the South Vietnamese infantry walked close behind and among our vehicles to protect us from the kind of tactics favored by the North Vietnamese in this type of situation: to wait in their daytime hiding places underground until the armored vehicles had passed over them and then to pop up to take them under fire from the rear.

As B Troop moved in close to the village, the South Vietnamese infantry seemed to slow and a gap developed between them and our vehicles. Whether they knew that we had stumbled into a fortified village or whether it was simply a lack of movement discipline, we never knew. What we did know all too quickly from the crackling radios in the command post was that B Troop had been taken under heavy antitank rocket fire from the ground that it had just passed over. There were North Vietnamese soldiers between our vehicles and our supporting infantry, and the infantry unaccountably had stopped. Before B Troop could fall back or regroup to meet the threat, three ACAVs were burning.

Then our tanks swung around, and the combined fire of the tank guns firing their own version of shotgun pellets and the concentrated machine-gun fire of the rapidly reversing ACAVs took effect. It was over in minutes, but we had lost three vehicles and nineteen men in those minutes, and we were not very kindly disposed toward our erstwhile allies. The burning of one of the ACAVs had been so intense that the crew, two of whom had been seen to have been wounded before the vehicle was enveloped in flames, had been incinerated inside it. The lieutenant, the son of a well-known California wine-growing family, the captain advisor to the Vietnamese unit, and two crew members were cremated in their vehicles to such an extent that there was no way to identify the individual remains. All four were eventually buried together in one of the rare joint graves in Arlington National Cemetery.

We ran one more large operation from Dong Ha, this time into the mountains to the west toward Khe Sanh. Our two cavalry troops and the squadron headquarters marched in over some narrow, winding, mountain switchback roads to an abandoned French plantation located on a high plateau. We searched the relatively open ground that surrounded it for several days, but we had no contacts. The most harrowing part of the operation turned out to be the road in and out. It wound up among canyons and over low hills so that it was an ambusher's dream. We were in constant fear of an ambush at the next hairpin turn, but it never came. Even our lightly protected resupply convoys went untouched in their daily runs between Dong Ha and the squadron forward location. By the end of the week, we knew that we would find nothing in the backcountry and we headed home to Dong Ha once more.

I had a special surprise waiting for the squadron when it pulled in. While they had been out in the bush, the squadron maintenance platoon and I had picked up our last big increment of new diesel ACAVs and had prepared them for issue. We had started getting the diesel ACAVs while we were still down south before Tet, but they had been issued only as replacements for unrepairable gasoline ACAVs. Since then, we had managed with a mixture of gasoline and diesel-fueled ACAVs. Now, however, we had been issued enough diesel vehicles to replace all of our gasoline burners. It was great to be getting new vehicles and to be eliminating the constant fear that we had of ruining engines by inadvertently mixing the two kinds of fuel, but the best part was the final elimination of the kind of fire hazard that had resulted in the cremation of the crew of that ACAV during our previous operation north of Dong Ha. The fuel tanks were located on both sides of the crew compartment between the inner and outer walls of the ACAV, and they were easily ignited when a round penetrated from either side. The low flashpoint of the gasoline caused it frequently to start burning too quickly and intensely for the crew to escape from a hit vehicle, especially if one of the crew was wounded. The diesel fuel would not ignite from an explosive hit, and the chances of surviving a direct hit on an ACAV increased significantly. That was about the best gift that could be given to a cavalry squadron.

By the time I had supervised the transferring of machine guns, gun shields, and accessories to our new vehicles and gotten the old vehicles ready for turn-in, it was April and we had a new mission. We were moving south toward Quang Tri City and away from the long-range North Vietnamese guns and the trench warfare atmosphere of Dong Ha. An independent mission in our own area of operations awaited us just outside Quang Tri City.

# IX

# Road Operations—
# Quang Tri City

The monsoon season had ended, and our tracks churned the broken surface of Highway 1 to dust as we moved south toward our new area of operation. The highway was still cratered and broken from the Tet assaults, and most of the highway bridges were still out. We forded some of the rivers with our tracked vehicles, while our wheeled vehicles gingerly crossed on temporary floating bridges. At other rivers the highway had been diverted to the parallel railroad tracks so that the shored-up railroad bridges could be used for crossing. Here and there we encountered abandoned jeeps and trucks that had been caught up in Tet; they stood beside the road in various stages of disrepair. The terrain around us was flat and sandy, though we could see the beginning of the hills off to our right as we drove toward Quang Tri City. Our initial destination was a plot of sand flat just off Highway 1 and just south of the outskirts of Quang Tri City. There we set up a temporary headquarters with one troop while the other troop and a tank company, which had been attached to our squadron, moved farther down the highway to secure a series of critical bridges.

We set up our squadron headquarters in the center of a triangular piece of the sand flat. The northern point of the triangle was a bridge. The legs were formed by Highway 1, which was built up above the sand flat, on the west and a sunken stream, which ran under the highway bridge and then southeast out into the sand flats that reached all the way to the South China Sea. Our presence provided protection for this key bridge, with its meager South Vietnamese guard. Our headquarters troop manned the apex of the triangle with its ACAVs, and our C Troop manned the rest of the perimeter, with one platoon set up across the deep stream to the east where it could move forward if need be. That platoon reached its position via a convenient ford that was within our perimeter. During the day, C Troop moved out on various missions, but it coiled back around us at night to provide protection. Our light observation helicopter also spent the night with us in the center of our perimeter, though it was maintained and fueled at an airstrip some ten minutes away. That base had been recently set up by a newly arrived Army aviation unit, which was part of an air cavalry brigade operating to the west of us in the foothills.

We soon settled into a routine that consisted of doing the things that cavalry had always done: we scoured the countryside for roving bands of North Vietnamese, we patrolled the road to secure it for the supply vehicles that used it, and we prevented the local guerrillas from mining Highway 1 in our sector by operating on it throughout the night. C Troop used the squadron headquarters location as its base of operation, and B Troop operated out of its own base camp along the highway to the south of us. From time to time, we also sealed off selected villages while the South Vietnamese militia and police searched for signs of the enemy, who moved and hit at night, hiding in the hamlets during the day. Occasionally we joined the infantry from the air cavalry brigade in its combat sweeps on the west side of Highway 1.

Our missions were assigned to us by the Marine regimental commander whose area we were operating in, and the pace was, for us, quite leisurely. We would receive a warning order in the evening, but no specifics. Early next morning the Marine colonel would fly out and brief us on the mission for the day; then the troops would move. The length of each mission was fairly short because it was midmorning before we had the mission briefed, and the cavalry platoons all had to be back to take up their highway security missions before dark. We soon began to feel pinned down and constricted by the short-range missions that we were running, and we began to feel vulnerable as the days extended into weeks while we remained sitting on the sand flat. We dug in our vehicles, built sandbag walls around the command post tracks, and constructed sandbagged culverts for personnel protection near the heavier concentrations of vehicles, but still we felt insecure.

As the Army presence in the area increased, traffic on Highway

1 became heavier. To control it, the air cavalry's military police started to assert control over the traffic. Clearances were needed for convoy movement, and the traffic flow was metered so that the long supply columns did not get tangled up with each other. Still, we were not under control of the air cavalry, and our missions from the Marines were given without any thought to road conditions. Inevitably, that brought our cavalry troops into conflict with the military police and the supply columns. Frequently, the highway was the route on which we started our various missions; increasingly, however, we were running into military police, who wanted us to conform to their convoy clearance procedures, and into supply columns, which continuously clogged the road. Despite the traditional prohibition about doubling a stopped column on a supply route, one young transportation lieutenant did just that one day, and C Troop found itself facing two solid lines of stopped supply trucks, which had completely choked off the road. Fortunately, we could get off the road and move parallel to it, but the time available for that day's mission was severely curtailed.

A few days later C Troop moved out on another search mission and was stopped on the road by a military police patrol. An aggressive military policeman pulled his jeep across the front of our column and demanded to see the convoy clearance for the troop. The troop commander patiently explained that he was on a combat mission, that he did not have a convoy clearance because he was not a convoy, and that he was losing valuable time as they talked. The military policeman was not to be moved. Finally, the captain ordered the lead vehicle to start forward, with the clear idea of making the military policeman move his jeep out of fear of being run over by the lead ACAV. No such luck. The jeep did not move, and the ACAV ground to a halt inches from it. The troop commander then got on the radio to ask the squadron commander what to do about the uncompromising military policeman. His radio transmission could be heard by the military policeman in his jeep because the captain's command track had a small loudspeaker bolted to its top deck that eliminated the need for earphones. Back came the laconic advice from the squadron commander. It was simply, "Shoot him!" The military policeman did not know what to do. His demand for convoy clearance had been spurned by the captain, his vehicle had almost been run over by an ACAV, and now the voice of authority over the radio was suggesting that he be shot if he continued to interfere with our mission. It was too much for him, and he backed out of the way. Nevertheless, it was an indication that our area of operations was getting too crowded.

Still we remained in our command post location, and daily we grew more nervous. There was a tree line within mortar range across some rice paddies on the other side of Highway 1 that we did not like, and there was too much slow-moving pedestrian traffic on the raised highway that could report on our exact positions on the sand flat. We were too exposed for comfort. The Marines, however, wanted us to stay put, where we could ensure the security of the supply line bridges, so we sat and waited and hoped that our fears were groundless.

Then one hot, dark morning all our fears were justified by the sound and feel and smell of mortar rounds slamming into our command post. The operations officer and I were instantly awake and grabbing for our equipment as we jumped from our cots inside our plywood trailer to the sandbagged culvert that we had constructed just below it for just this eventuality. Around us hatches banged down and radios crackled as the headquarters armored vehicles and the one cavalry troop circled around us, prepared to meet the attack. The small speaker that let us overhear the command radio in our trailer told us what was going on between the flash and concussion of the incoming rounds. We crouched in our little covered trench waiting for the situation to clarify itself. The commander had already made his way into the command post vehicles, and it did not seem prudent for all three of us to gather in there in case a round should drop on the two-vehicle complex. Then the half light of explosions and the violent orange-and-black gusher of an armored vehicle bursting into flame outlined shadowy figures running out by the perimeter, and it became apparent that the mortar rounds had been merely a prelude to a full-scale sapper attack on our position. Our guns were firing now, and the heavy machine guns mounted on top of the ACAVs and tanks poured diverging streams of tracers into the dark, while our own mortars threw up illumination rounds that swayed overhead on their tiny parachutes, giving an eerie glow to the whole scene. The wild noise of a full-blown firefight had by now drowned out the sound of individual explosions, and the only clue as to where the action was on the perimeter were the firefly muzzle blasts of small arms and the orange flare of exploding sapper charges.

In the midst of all this, I was amazed to see our light observation helicopter spiral up into the night sky among all the tracers. The pilot, who had been asleep next to his ship, had started the helicopter while keeping close to the ground next to it. When the blades were turning at full rpm's, he had jumped in and taken off in the middle of the firefight in a successful attempt to preserve it from damage. It was soon beating its way toward the airstrip, where it normally went for fuel and maintenance. That was a very brave act by a very brave pilot. Less than a month later, he was hit and forced down. He and his crew chief were killed defending their downed ship.

We had called for artillery support from the closest Marine artillery unit when we had first been hit. We wanted to put fire on the tree line that had been worrying us, but our own three mortars had their hands full just trying to keep illumination rounds in the air. Our fire request was transmitted over the right net, but there seemed to be an endless delay in getting a response. Eventually, some twenty minutes after we had called, we got the word that the first round was in the air. It landed inside our perimeter, where it fortunately did no damage. We immediately cancelled the fire request. Obviously, the lines of communication to the Marine artillery were too complicated for us to get accurate and responsive fire support, so we diverted two of our mortars to firing at the tree line outside the perimeter and kept the one remaining tube firing illumination rounds. It later turned out that the artillery problem had been a coordination problem caused by our being on the boundary between the Army air cavalry division sector of operation and the Marine area. That was small consolation. It was also small consolation to know that the air cavalry gunships were denied permission to enter the Marine sector and to come to our assistance even though they could see the firefight from their own base camp. We never did find out the reason for that one.

In the meantime rockets were whooshing over the command post vehicles, and the flash of explosions was continuing along the perimeter. Then the newly arrived platoon leader of the platoon across the sunken stream became frustrated by not being able to see his enemy and moved his ACAV forward in an attempt to get at his enemy. In doing so he immediately provided a better target by exposing the larger profile of the sides of his vehicle. Some waiting rocketeers took advantage of the situation. Before the ACAV had moved forward fifty feet, it had been hit twice. It shuddered to a burning stop. As if drawn by the flames, sappers dashed to the hole that had been left in the line by the ACAV and blew up the ACAVs on either side of the position the platoon leader's vehicle had just vacated. Fortunately, the typical sapper carried explosive charges and no weapons, so the danger to the crew members who managed to escape from their vehicles was not as great as it might have been. Still, there were enough armed enemy around to make it very uncomfortable.

At this moment the tanks from our attached tank company, which was camped further south on the highway and whose assistance had been requested by the squadron commander, arrived. One platoon moved across the sunken stream at a ford and moved in among the burning hulks of the ACAVs with machine guns going and the main guns firing the canister rounds that burst into hundreds of small shot at the muzzle of the gun. So close in was the fighting that one tank actually had a rocket pass through its main gun tube from one side to the other. At the same time the other reinforcing tank platoon from the attached tank company made a circuit of the outside of the perimeter on the Highway 1 side with all weapons firing. The noise rose to a violent crescendo then tapered off into an eerie silence as the predawn light revealed only a few running figures disappearing into the rice paddies across Highway 1. All was quiet.

I had moved to the part of the perimeter that was near the highway and had brought my jeep up so I could communicate with the command post and the rest of the perimeter while trying to organize the sector where I was. When the firing stopped, I jumped up onto the back of my jeep so that I could see better while still staying close to my two radios. As I stood up, I saw a lone figure rise out of the rice paddy with a weapon held over his head in a nonthreatening position. It appeared that he was trying to surrender, but I knew what was going to happen. Before I could even depress the transmit button on my microphone, the entire line of vehicles had opened up with heavy machine guns. By the time I had screamed "cease fire" into the microphone, it was all over. We would never know what the figure's true intentions were, and it was difficult to blame the keyed-up troopers who were manning their machine guns and who had been so recently fighting for their own survival. Still, it had not been pleasant to watch.

With that last burst of fire, we were left with only the crackling of burning vehicles. It was time to find out what our losses were.

The one platoon manning the perimeter across the sunken stream had borne the brunt of the attack. The perimeter had been broken at only one other place. There, at a point near the bridge, some sappers had blown up one of the headquarters troop ACAVs in the very first moments of the attack. Six sappers had crept through the smoldering dead spot that they had created and started toward the command post vehicles, which were the heart of the squadron headquarters, with their deadly little blocks of explosives. There were no fighting vehicles between them and the command post, and there were no fighting positions to stop them. Our sergeant major, a veteran of two wars, was very close to where the six came through. He had jumped into a nearby bunker when he was awakened by the first explosion, dressed only in his shorts and without his weapon. About the time he realized his circumstances, he sensed movement outside the bunker. When a sapper stuck his head in, the sergeant major tried to conceal his considerable bulk behind a sandbag. Apparently, he was successful because the sapper's head finally withdrew from the entrance to the bunker. The sergeant major later allowed that he had never felt quite that naked during any of his previous two wars.

The sappers made their way from there through the various administrative vehicles that were dispersed in the area until they reached our two water trailers, which stood in the kitchen area. That was as far as they got. Our cooks, who were lying under the kitchen trucks for protection, spotted them and killed them where they stood, using the old M14 rifles that we had never gotten around to replacing with the new, light M16s. The cooks were the heroes of the action, and those scruffy guys who dished out food in their dirty white undershirts were given a new respect when they served up breakfast a few hours later.

Our overwhelming response with machine guns had driven off the main attack before it had really gotten started. Apparently, the sapper unit that attacked us did not really know our capabilities, which was natural since there were no other cavalry units in the area. Their shock at the volume of return fire they had triggered had prevented a concentrated effort, and some luck with our cooks had made sure that the control of that firepower had remained intact. In fact, the volume of fire, kept up for almost an hour and a half, was the talk of the entire sector because many nearby units could see it from their positions on higher elevations.

Despite the damage to the platoon across the sunken stream, the sappers had been unable to penetrate much past the perimeter even there. We had lost four ACAVs, however, and paid a price in human lives. The panicked platoon leader, three weeks with our unit, had been severely burned over his entire body and was still unmercifully conscious. Remaining conscious was one of the added agonies of severe burn cases, and there was nothing to do about it. Thanks to our medical evacuation system, he was back at the Army's burn center in San Antonio, Texas, within forty-eight hours. In the end it was futile: we heard some two weeks later that he had died. His body had simply lost too much fluid to survive, despite the best efforts of military medicine. There were forty-seven others wounded and eleven dead, and the fighting had been particularly nasty out among the perimeter vehicles. There, in the dark of the first assault, our troopers, many of whom had been sleeping under their vehicles, awoke to face sappers creeping around the grounded bulldozer blade of an engineer tank or the track of an armored vehicle. That is a tough way to come awake.

The barely clad sapper bodies around the perimeter and the blood trails leading away showed clearly that the attackers had also paid a price. We gathered the enemy bodies on the edge of the highway so that we could go over them for possible intelligence information before having them carted off by the South Vietnamese authorities. We were in no hurry to get rid of the bodies because we wanted to be sure that the local villagers saw them on their way to market in Quang Tri City in the hope that it might discourage whoever had helped plot out our position for the sapper battalion.

About two hours after the attack had ended, while I was moving around our position supervising the clean-up and reorganization, I encountered one of our cavalry troopers dragging a sapper body toward the collection point on the road. He was dragging the body by one foot and was intentionally taking it over the roughest ground so that the head banged viciously against every rock and rut. We met at the end of the portable steel bridge that we had laid down temporarily to make it easier to cross the sunken stream to retrieve our burned vehicles. He had managed to hit every hole and hinge on the bridge as he dragged the body across. Each time the head bounced, the trooper swore and said something like, "Take that, you motherfucker!" I knew very well that he was not paying proper respect to the dead, and my instinct was to stop him. I did not, however. I walked on past as though I had not seen him, and he took no note of me as he continued moving toward the road with his head down, swearing at every lunge of the body. The trooper had lost two of his crewmates in the fierce perimeter fighting, and it seemed to me that this was as harmless a way as any to work out his grief. It may not have been strictly according to protocol, but this was one time when I was not going to try to impose abstracts of civilized conduct on a young man who had just come through a very uncivilized experience.

I took a little different tack a bit later when I found a group of troopers gathered on the highway, placing the collected bodies in grotesque positions then taking pictures of them. Placing cigarette butts in the bellybuttons of dead enemy soldiers and then taking pictures did not qualify as after-action therapy, and I sent the troopers on their way with a good chewing out. Such behavior may sound very bizarre when you consider it at a distance, but the relief after a fierce firefight in which men have been fighting for their lives affects them in strange ways. There is an almost hysterical release that allows them to do silly and cruel things without thinking about what they are doing. It is a time to enforce discipline, but only when you have a clear moral edge. They knew that posing the bodies was wrong, and there was no argument to my fairly severe criticism of what they were doing. I am not sure that I would have had the same moral edge if I had criticized the way the other trooper had chosen to transport the dead sapper body from his vehicle position to the road.

Still later that day another bizarre situation came to light, which led to the relief of the C Troop commander. It started out as a bit of gossip about the C Troop commander, who was claiming that his first sergeant owed him some money that had been blown up in the attack. The gossip passed around in a humorous way among the troopers, but it did not make sense to me. By the time I was through asking around, I had found out far more than I wanted to know. To start with, the troop commander had been paid, as we all had, on the day before the attack. He had then given a considerable portion of his pay, which was in military scrip, to his first sergeant to convert into American-dollar postal money orders on the following day. The sapper attack had intervened, and the troop command post tent, in which the money had been stored, had been hit by one of the first incoming mortar rounds. The money entrusted to the first sergeant had gone up in smoke, along with some other troop papers. To hold the first sergeant responsible for that accident of war was, of course, absurd.

When I hunted up the troop commander to ask him what was going on, I discovered that the story was even worse. It turned out that the money orders were for several crew members of his own command vehicle, from whom he had borrowed money. The money that he had borrowed was used to pay off gambling debts to other officers in the squadron—a vestigial remnant from the regime of the previous squadron commander. In the few weeks that I had served with the previous squadron commander, I had become aware that he liked to play poker and that he had gathered a group of headquarters officers from time to time for that purpose. In fact, that was one of the reasons that he had been living in a borrowed bungalow a long way from the command post the night that we had been ambushed south of Blackhorse on the last day of December: it was more convenient and private for his evening poker games than living near the command post would have been. In any event our C Troop commander had apparently run up several debts in the course of these games and had been hard pressed to pay them off. He had attempted to take care of the debts to his brother officers by borrowing from his own crew members, and now he had lost the means of paying them back—at least for a while.

There were more things wrong with this situation than you could count. First, it is strict Army policy that you never gamble with subordinates. Second, there is an even stricter Army prohibition against borrowing money from your subordinates. The fact that the previous squadron commander's love of poker had brought this about reflected poorly on his judgment, but the captain's judgment in borrowing money from enlisted members of his own command vehicle was even worse. He had created a kind of indebtedness that incapacitated him for further command, and he had compounded that bad judgment by attempting to hold his own first sergeant responsible for his current impossible situation. It became clear to the squadron commander that all this added up to a troop commander whose judgment could not be trusted with the lives of men and who had violated so many rules of leadership for a small, closely knit unit that he could no longer exercise effective command. The troop commander was relieved and sent back south to our parent division on the first available transportation, and that should have ended the situation.

It did not. Several days later, after we had moved to a new location and settled back into our routine, I flew south to deliver the mandatory relief efficiency report on the relieved captain to our division headquarters. I presented it to the division chief of staff, a colonel, and then went about my other business with our rear detachment. Shortly before I was to return north, I received a summons to the chief of staff's office. He asked me what I knew about the relief incident, and I told him. He then expressed the opinion that we had been unduly harsh on the captain and that his relief from command in combat would hurt his career more than his offense warranted. I made no reply except to indicate that my investigation appeared to support the decision of my squadron commander. He then handed me a letter for my squadron commander. I saluted and turned to leave. As I walked to the door, I glanced down at the letter and saw that it was not signed. I turned back and remarked, innocently, that the chief of staff had apparently forgotten to sign the letter. The chief of staff became quite angry as he took the letter back. He hesitated over signing it then gave it back to me unsigned with instructions to give it to my commander as a piece of friendly advice from him. It was only then that I realized that the colonel was trying to get around the fact that he was interfering in an illegal way with the efficiency report rating chain. Since the chief of staff was not my commander's rater, he had no business inserting himself into the chain. The unsigned letter was a gimmick to make it look as though it were an authoritative instruction without running the risk of being exposed to a charge of illegal interference. It had not worked in the desired way, and I was never forgiven for my unthinking attention to detail.

The letter and the accompanying efficiency report on the captain were duly handed over to my commnader, and the efficiency report was duly returned, unchanged, through channels to the division headquarters. Years later, when the captain appealed that report because it was hindering his career, I had the chance to see a copy of the completed form. The brigadier general, who had been the assistant division commander and my commander's rater at the time, stated in his portion of the report that though he had no knowledge of the people involved or the circumstances, he believed that the relief action had been an overreaction to the offense. In responding to the appeal, my ex-commander noted that though his own commander apparently did not believe that a sense of ethics and sound judgment were requirements for a commander in Vietnam, he believed that one could not command without them and that he would take the same action again given similar circumstances. He added, however, that he did not think that this one incident should be the basis for further adverse career action if it turned out to be an isolated one. He had made the same statement on the original relief efficiency report, but the system was no more capable of coping with that subtlety than the division headquarters had been in coping with an action motivated by the norms of ethical conduct. Given the eventual impact on the young captain, it is difficult to say who was right.

We had moved our squadron headquarters the day after the attack. Our new location was a temporary one on the southern edge of the town of Hai Lang, which was located about six miles south of Quang Tri City on Highway 1 at a point where a number of roads came together from the areas to the east and west of the highway.

It was a market town that served the fishing villages out on the beach and the farm hamlets that surrounded it. We found a flat area on the southwestern edge of town that might have served as the fairgrounds in better times. There was ample room for us to disperse; yet we were still within the cover of the town, with some abandoned buildings around us to shield us from the open country beyond. The highway was several blocks east of us, close enough that we could hear the convoys but far enough away that we could not be seen from it, and we were not bothered by the dust raised by the convoy traffic. The feeder road to the west ran by the edge of our location and on out to what had been the railroad that paralleled Highway 1 a mile and a half west of it. No trains had run for several years, however, and there was little traffic into town from that direction.

Our two cavalry troops and our attached tank company continued to operate along Highway 1 to the north and south of us. The tank company operated primarily along the highway and maintained a company command post to the south of us near a critical bridge crossing. One cavalry troop operated off the road with various airmobile infantry units, and the other troop set up at a small fire-support base on the feeder road that led toward the beach. From there it ran operations cross-country in the area that adjoined Highway 1, between it and the sand beaches.

We were told to be prepared to move onto the beach itself and

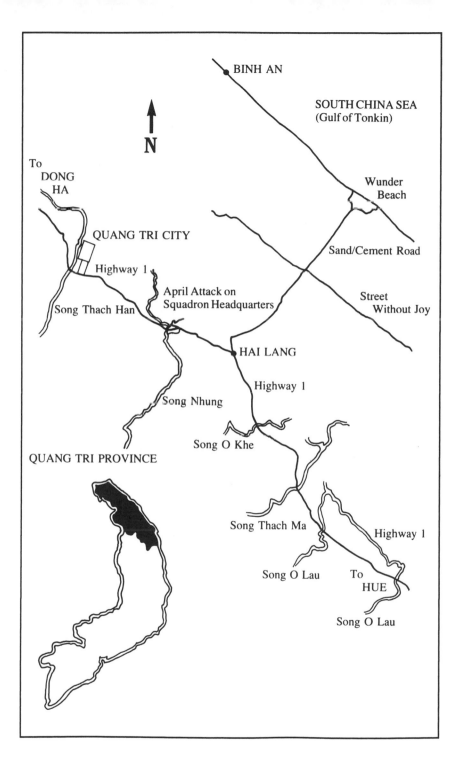

BINH AN

SOUTH CHINA SEA
(Gulf of Tonkin)

N

To
DONG
HA

QUANG TRI CITY

Wunder
Beach

Highway 1

Sand/Cement Road

April Attack on
Squadron Headquarters

Song Thach Han

Street
Without Joy

HAI LANG

Highway 1

Song Nhung

Song O Khe

QUANG TRI PROVINCE

Song Thach Ma

Highway 1

Song O Lau

To
HUE

Song O Lau

to take over a logistical port from the Marines, but it was not clear when the change of responsibility would take place. In the meantime we worked closely with the Marines who were securing the logistical port and the rough road that led to it. Almost simultaneously with the word that we would take over the beach area of operations, we were given an opportunity to bring A Troop back from its detached duty with the Army division just south of Hue. The tank company that had been working with us was better suited to the road mission into the Ashau Valley, which the division was now undertaking. We proposed to trade the tank company for our own cavalry troop, and the swap was approved. We would still be responsible for supporting the tanks, but they would be under the operational control of the Army division working toward the Ashau, and our troop would be released back to us to work in our new area of operations out by the beach.

To get ready for the switch, I made a number of trips to the Army division's base camp to find out what we needed in order to get our troop moving north. I also moved part of our maintenance platoon down there to give the troop the extra support it would need to be properly prepared for the road march to us. We obtained the proper clearances for the road march with the various controlling military police units along the route between the base camp and us because this truly would be an administrative move and we were well aware that a tank company and a full cavalry troop moving on the road could disrupt the supply convoys that filled the highway every day. The ever-increasing Army presence in this northern sector had put a severe burden on the two-lane highway that served as the only supply route into the area from the south aside from the water route.

Finally, all the arrangements were made, the march clearance was obtained, and the appointed day arrived. The tank company moved south without incident, and the next morning our troop was released to march north. As soon as we received word that the troop was moving from the Army base camp south of Hue, I went airborne in our light observation helicopter to fly column cover and attempt to ensure that nothing happened to snarl traffic on the way north. By the time I reached Hue from the north, the lead vehicles of the troop were approaching the bridge they had knocked down when they left Hue some two months before. By now the engineers had shored up the bridge so that a caution crossing could be made by our tanks without fear of damaging it further. Again, only one tank at a time could be on the damaged span, and it had to maintain a ten-mile-per-hour speed and not shift gears. The crossing was underway as I made my first pass over the bridge.

On the north side of the bridge, Highway 1 climbed out of the riverbed and ran parallel to the citadel of Hue in almost a straight line. The lead vehicles of the troop moved up this incline and then out along the straightaway until there was enough space for all of the troop vehicles to regroup into an uninterrupted march column before they moved on. There the lead vehicles stopped and waited for the slow bridge crossing to be completed by our tanks. In the meantime truck traffic piled up in back of the slowly moving tracked vehicles as it waited for the bridge to be clear.

From the air I could see the trucks stopped in a long line stretching south of the bridge even though it was still early in the day. There was no way, however, to speed up the one-tank-at-a-time crossing procedure, and we were progressing as rapidly as could be expected. Finally, the last of the troop vehicles was over the bridge and climbing the grade to the straightaway. As soon as the column was intact, the troop commander started it out to the north. The troop moved out smoothly, the vehicles picking up their march interval as they started, and soon the column was traveling at march speed. The line of trucks to the south also started to move, and I breathed a sigh of relief, knowing the impatience the supply column commanders would have been feeling at this delay in their routine—and knowing that they would be cursing our tanks for causing it.

There was some light Vietnamese civilian traffic moving south on the road, but it was not heavy enough to be a problem to us. Below me our column was moving at good speed. Then without warning a tank below me swerved to give more room to an oncoming Vietnamese bus. In trying to bring the tank back into line, the driver overcompensated for the speed at which he was traveling, causing the tank to move diagonally across the road to its left and to slide off into the steep culvert that lined the built-up roadbed of the highway. Behind it the column ground to a halt. I radioed down instructions to get the tank back on the road as quickly as possible so that we could resume the march, but I was told in reply that the tank had thrown its left track when it slid awkwardly into the culvert. That in itself would be a time-consuming repair, but then it turned out that the track had been thrown to the inside of the sprocket: it was jammed between the drive sprocket and the hull of the tank, which made it particularly difficult to get at to fix. The fact that the entire weight of the tank was on the thrown track did not help any. To leave the tank in place and move on without it would be to invite sure destruction once night came; to recover the tank and fix the track would block the main supply route for a couple of hours. There was no alternative. I directed the squadron maintenance platoon element that was with the troop to move up the halted column to the tank and begin recovery operations. Then, after reporting the problem to squadron headquarters and to the military police responsible for traffic on this section the highway, I landed to help ward off the fury of the blocked convoy commanders who were, no doubt, about to descend on the accident scene.

The only way to repair the tank track was to break it and then drag it out onto the highway and lay it out flat. With the track no longer jammed between the suspension system and the dirt bank of the culvert, it would be possible to drag the tank back up on the road, line it up with the track, pull the tank over the laid-out track, and put the track back together. That was going to take time, but there was no other way to do it. The squadron maintenance people and the tank crew set to work, and I tried to figure out what shortcuts might speed up the operation. I also tried to keep peace with the various officers from the blocked convoys, who were doubling our column in their jeeps to express their displeasure with the delay for which we were responsible. As I walked around the tank that was the cause of our predicament, I noticed that the road wheel lug nuts had telltale silver rings around them where the paint had been chipped off. The silver rings of bare metal were the result of loose nuts, which allowed the road wheel to vibrate against them. They were a sure indicator that the nuts had not been kept tight by the crew, and I began to have an idea of why the track had slid off. The road wheels were really two separate wheels bolted together at the hub to form a sandwich through which the center guides of the track ran. If they were loose, there was an increased chance for the center guides to slip out of the sandwich when under pressure such as that exerted when the tank slid into the culvert. Once the first set of center guides ran out of the sandwich, those guides would pull the rest out after them, and the track would be thrown. I stored away that observation for later and went back to doing what I could to speed up the recovery operation.

It took us about three hours to complete the job. That was pretty good time for the amount of work that had to be done on heavy equipment, but it had seemed like an eternity with all the gawkers and complainers surrounding us, impatient to get on with their own missions. We had blocked the main supply route into the northern sector of the country for the better part of the morning, and many schedules were fouled up because of it, but there had not seemed to be a better way around the situation. Nevertheless, I breathed a huge sigh of relief as the column started to move again and I once more went airborne in my helicopter. Later a fuller investigation into the maintenance of the suspension system on the tank showed that the tank commander had not been properly fulfilling his responsibility for maintenance. He was reduced one rank for his inattention. That was a tough way to rejoin the squadron, but the results of his negligence had been too great to pass over lightly.

With our three cavalry troops back under our control for the first time in three months, we were more than ready for our new mission when the order came to move. Our new area of operation centered on a supply base that had been set up on the beach. There, opposite deep water, a depot had been established from where Army amphibious vehicles, called LARCs and BARCs, could swim out to the supply ships, off-load their cargoes, and bring them back to the depot for storage and distribution. The official name for this kind of supply base was "Logistics over the Beach" base, or LOB, but it was known to all as "Wunder Beach," after the commander of the transportation battalion that operated the base. We were now given the responsibility for protecting this supply base, a large area of the beach to the north and south of it, and all the area between the water and Highway 1, some six miles inland. In addition, we were to continue our responsibility for Highway 1 within our sector. This new area of operations was a flat, hot, sandy area dotted with small fishing villages along the water and small farming hamlets between Highway 1 and a dirt road that carried the name "Street Without Joy." This road, which paralleled Highway 1 midway between the water and the highway, had been a center of guerrilla activity during the French Indo-China combat in the early 1950s, and it still was a haunt for the local Viet Cong. The name had been given to it by the French in an ironic tribute to the troubles they had encountered along the length of it. The sides of the road were honeycombed with bunkers and tunnels where both the North Vietnamese units from the nearby hills and the local guerrillas hid during the day. The beaches beyond were their main roads when they wished to avoid the bridges and towns, with their guard posts, as they traveled back and forth on their missions.

We moved the squadron headquarters and the headquarters troop the six miles to the depot on the beach in the last days of April and marked out terrain for the supply and maintenance elements of the squadron. We placed ourselves in the center of the supply base, which had a perimeter defense that was manned at night by the transportation unit and any other tenant units that came to stay at the base. Our cavalry troops would come in for refitting and to occupy parts of the perimeter as needed, but we already knew that we would ensure the security of the base by having the troops clear the area outside the perimeter and turn it into a neutral zone by their very presence. The Marine units from whom we took over the security mission had been infantry, and their patrols had been restricted to foot patrols that went no more than a mile or two in any direction. Our greater mobility would enable us to push back this defensive zone to a point where mortar shells could not reach the base.

With that plan in mind, we set about to make a permanent base for the squadron inside the perimeter. Initially, we moved the entire squadron into the base camp to clean up the area and clean out the bunkers. The Marines had not been very good at housekeeping, and the bivouac areas and the perimeter bunkers were a mess, so it took a few days to clean out old buried ammunition that had been left around carelessly, burn the trash that had been allowed to accumulate, put the perimeter bunkers and fence back into good order, and establish a routine for the security of the base. For some reason a few of the bunkers had been left booby-trapped, which was taking service rivalry to extremes. Fortunately, we found the wires before any harm was done.

We set up our squadron maintenance platoon and laid out a vehicle park area where maintenance could be done; we built a landing strip for our helicopters and the visiting command helicopters that we knew would be coming in; and we dug in our command tracks in a sparsely treed area where they would have a little shade and a lot of protection. This was as permanent a situation as we had been assigned to since leaving Blackhorse, and we settled in as well as we could.

We even set up our own wood latrines with honey pots of our own, which was the real sign of permanence. As a final touch, we strung a huge parachute from one of the trees and staked out its edges with rope so that the canopy provided shade. This improvised auditorium became the central gathering place for the troops for chapel services, meetings, and the rare movies that we were able to obtain when any one of the troops was in.

In the meantime the boundaries had been adjusted around us, and we found ourselves back working for the Army, which was a pleasure. It was good to be back with our own, and the mobility of the air cavalry brigade with which we were associated provided a good complement to our own capabilities. To free our cavalry troops for more mobile operations, we were given an infantry company to man our supply depot perimeter so that all of our troops could be used outside, either securing the camp or working Highway 1 or adding ground power to the airmobile infantry sweeps that the air cavalry was making. The perimeter duty was a good stand-down for the infantry company after sweep operations in the "boonies," and it relieved us of providing the troops for the perimeter guard requirement. Every few days a new infantry company would rotate in to perform guard duty and enjoy the relative civilization of the beach depot. It looked like the beginning of a very stable and productive period, and we all worked enthusiastically to get settled and to start spreading our influence over the area. We finally had a mission that would really use our capabilities in the best way, and we were eager to begin.

# X

# Base Camp at Wunder Beach

As soon as our base of operations was set up to our satisfaction, we went to work. We put one troop out on the highway to work the road and team up with the airmobile infantry, and we inserted the remaining two troops into the sandy area that surrounded Wunder Beach. They searched for rice and arms caches and tried to find and destroy bunker and tunnel complexes during the day. Then they ran night patrols to prevent the North Vietnamese from freely traversing our territory or picking up supplies.

Many of these patrols were run in connection with night ambushes. A squad of men would be dropped off from one of our moving ACAVs as a platoon made a last sweep across some piece of flat, sandy terrain in the fading light of day. The drop-off would be accomplished almost without halt near a growth of trees or a sand dune that lay along a suspected North Vietnamese or Viet Cong trail. From a distance it was impossible to detect the slight slowing as the squad jumped off the lowered rear ramp. For the rest of the night, the squad would lie in wait. Since all travel between hamlets by the local Vietnamese villagers was forbidden after dark, anybody moving at night was suspect. If the night travelers were carrying weapons and fell into one of our ambush sites, the squad lying in wait would open fire. At that, the remainder of the waiting platoon would quickly move from its lager area to the ambush site, reinforcing the ambush squad and dealing with any enemy band that might be too big for the ambush patrol. The two troops working the beach area each had such an ambush patrol operating on any given night. In addition, one or the other of them would also be responsible for running the road that led out to Highway 1 from our beach depot to ensure that it was not mined during the night. The distances were sufficiently short and the terrain sufficiently trafficable that all of our units were always within supporting distance of each other should they run into a problem.

There was a third group that we used for close-in ambushes to ensure that nobody got too near our supply depot at night. Our headquarters security platoon was not needed for its normal guard responsibilities inside the perimeter because of the infantry company that was under our operational control for perimeter defense. We therefore assigned the platoon the mission of putting out a small ambush fairly close to the perimeter on one of the many trails that ran near our base and connected the fishing villages to the north and south of us. They used the same technique as the troops farther out. On a routinely repeated dusk sweep around the outside of the perimeter, they would drop off a squad at a randomly selected trail intersection and continue on with hardly a halt. They would then return to their normal bivouac area just inside the entrance to the depot and remain alert in case they were needed to back up the ambush. With all of this activity going on outside our perimeter, and with the squadron's communications capability to keep us in touch instantly with it all, we felt pretty secure in our new base of operations.

Shortly after we settled into our new routine, the security platoon had a position come open for a vehicle commander. The young sergeant who ran our command post radios immediately volunteered for the job. He had come from the security platoon some months ago when we had needed a reliable man to head up our squadron operations center crew. He was one of those super noncommissioned officers who combines eager efficiency with a quick intelligence so that normally no detail escapes him. He had taken over the operations center crew that manned the radios and kept the maps posted in the command post tracks, and he had done a fine job of melding them into a team that could operate equally well on the move or in a base camp. Through it all, however, he had continued to miss the camaraderie and constantly changing routine of the security platoon. Reluctantly, we agreed that he could rejoin the platoon as a vehicle commander and squad leader. He had certainly earned the opportunity by his performance in the command post. Somehow he had managed to acquire a long-barreled .45 revolver, and he now made a great show of getting it ready for his new "field" position. There was a lot of good-natured kidding among the operations center crew about that and how he would do back in the "line." He responded by telling them that he was going to get a North Vietnamese rifle as a trophy before very long.

The sergeant went off to his new assignment, but he continued to drop by the operations center in the early evening when he was not running a mission to chat with his old crew and to tell them how he was coming with his new squad. After several days of running the last-light sweeps of the perimeter and taking his squad out on some short patrols, he was assigned to one of the routine night ambush missions.

It was a quiet night with no reported contact from our road-running platoons or our various ambush patrols, so those not actually needed to monitor the operations turned in early. As a rule it was quiet in the evening, so that was the time to get your rest; if anything was going to happen, it would be in the early morning hours, just before first light. This night was no exception. At about 3:00 A.M. we were all awakened by a sharp explosion fairly close to the perimeter, followed by the abrupt staccato of automatic weapons fire. I dashed for the nearby command post tracks to find out what the firing meant. As I entered the operations track, I heard the whispering voice of our recently reassigned sergeant coming over the radio speaker. His barely audible voice, pitched to make the least amount of noise at his ambush site, could not conceal his obvious elation with what he had just pulled off. He reported that his squad had just triggered a perfect ambush on a group of three armed men. The squad had waited quietly while the armed men moved down the trail and into the killing zone of the ambush. Then they had detonated a carefully sited claymore mine and opened fire. The combination of the exploding mine fragments and the deadly automatic weapons fire at close range had caught all three, the sergeant said, and he was now going out to get that North Vietnamese rifle that he had said he would bring in as a trophy.

I leaped for the radio microphone to try to stop him from going out into the ambush so quickly because it is never safe to approach your quarry without waiting to be sure that the action is really over. The sergeant's assistant started to answer my frantic radio call, but his words were blotted out by the sharp report of an explosion I heard simultaneously over the radio and outside. Then everything was quiet again. I had been too late with my warning. One of the enemy soldiers, though fatally wounded, had been able to arm and throw a hand grenade as the sergeant stepped out in search of his trophy rifle. We rushed out the standby reaction force from the security platoon, secured the area around the ambush site, and hurried the sergeant back to our aid station, but no doctor could fill the gaping hole that had been torn in his back. He died on the stretcher while we waited for a medical evacuation helicopter. If only he had not been so eager for a trophy and so elated over his first perfectly executed ambush.

Several days later a few of us were lounging outside the command post tracks in the early evening, musing over the death of the sergeant, when we were startled by M16 shots coming from the rapidly darkening vehicle park across the sand track from us. We all dived for cover, but there was no follow-on fire, and no rounds had actually hit near us. Puzzled, we dusted ourselves off and stood up as the headquarters troop commander appeared out of the dusk. He told us that one of his mechanics had run into the vehicle park with a loaded M16, believing he was being stalked by an undercover military police investigator looking for drug users. Apparently, the mechanic had become convinced over the last few days that he was the focus of a drug investigation. He had been talking about an alleged undercover agent who was tracking him, but nobody had paid much attention to his wild talk—except to give him a wide berth. The company commander was sure that the mechanic was one of a slowly growing group of drug users, but he had not been able to prove it. This evening the mechanic had grabbed a loaded rifle and headed off toward the vehicle park, yelling and shooting and claiming that he would not be taken. We had a very awkward situation on our hands: a soldier with a loaded weapon who had obviously become unstable, probably because of drug use, and no way to prevent him from hurting himself or others but to go out and disarm him.

We had to try to get to him before he did more damage than simply putting bullet holes in our vehicles. We were, as usual, all armed because we were never without our weapons, and there was not one of us who did not ponder for a moment the awful thought of having to use those weapons on a fellow soldier in self-defense if we could not safely disarm him. We split up after agreeing not to fire unless fired on and went out into the dark vehicle park. We slipped silently in and out of the rows of dark hulks of fuel tankers and supply trucks with our eyes and ears tuned for some hint of movement or sound that would pinpoint our quarry. It was tense work, none of us relishing what we were doing. After what seemed like hours, I heard a yell from a corner of the vehicle park. One of our sergeants had managed to come up behind the mechanic and grab him, pinning his arms so that he had to drop his rifle. Once disarmed, he seemed to slump into a daze. He was led back to the medic tent without resistance, and he kept muttering incoherently about the mysterious agents who were out to get him. We left him under guard, with the squadron surgeon trying to calm him, while I arranged to have him evacuated to a medical facility the next morning.

This strange incident was our first overt contact with the serious problems that stem from drug usage. Until then we had suspected one soldier or another of being high, but it had not been proved. The closest we had come was when a soldier turned in the marijuana of a crewmate. We would confront the guilty soldier, destroy the evidence, and administer a light punishment. The problem had been very low key. Settling into a base camp, however, had changed the situation by putting our troopers into contact with a drug source—either in the resident transportation battalion or among the Vietnamese peddlers who hung around the outside of the perimeter. We had entered the era of real drug-use problems. I encountered several more drug incidents in the remaining months of my tour, but worse was to come in the years that followed.

The days were now very hot, with ambient daytime temperatures approaching 140 degrees Fahrenheit, and the white sand reflecting the heat into everything. The armored vehicles became too hot to touch, and sleeves had to be kept rolled down to avoid actually getting burned from leaning on the hot metal skins. Operating out in the flat sand was hard on both men and vehicles. The sand grit got into everything.

Moving across an uninhabited beach area one day on a routine reconnaissance, the crewman on one of our ACAVs were startled to see a bamboo mat fly up from under the track of the vehicle in front. They called in the incident, and the column ground to a halt. To the absolute amazement of all involved, a little probing disclosed a trench lined with bamboo mats and filled with rice. The trench had been hidden with sand-covered bamboo mats, and only a freak of luck had enabled us to discover it. It was a great find. The rice in the trench would have fed a North Vietnamese regiment in the hills for a whole winter, and they would have no way of replacing it now. Without rice they would have to concentrate more on their own survival and less on combat operations. But what were we going to do with it?

The answer, of course, was to move it, but the loose rice obviously had to be put into some sort of containers if we were going to move it anywhere. Our various higher headquarters were delighted with our find, and all were very willing to allocate helicopters to us to lift out the rice, but nobody was forthcoming with ideas on how to prepare the rice for movement. We very quickly got the point that it was our problem. So we gathered up a large supply of the burlap bags that were normally used to make sandbags and delivered them to the troop that had made the discovery. A perimeter was set up around the area, and the troopers went to work in the hot, gritty sand, transferring the rice in the trench to the burlap sandbags. They worked with shovels and entrenching tools, and they placed the filled bags on big cargo nets that we spread out on the ground so that helicopters could haul the bags away when we were done. It was dusty, seemingly endless work, and it took our cavalrymen four days to ready the two to three tons of rice for evacuation. They secured the area from interference at night, and they shoveled rice during the day, while a few of them manned the heavy machine guns on top of a couple of ACAVs from where they could see a long way in all directions. It was a far cry from the traditional image of cavalry action, but it was as damaging to the enemy as any assault on a bunker complex would have been. The cavalrymen hated it!

So did the North Vietnamese. The night after we finally got the last of the rice bagged and lifted out by cargo helicopter, the North Vietnamese paid a visit to the farmers in the cluster of hovels nearest where the rice had been cached. These farmers had apparently been charged with the custody of the rice, which had no doubt been collected as a tax from them and from similar hamlets. The North Vietnamese terrorized the farmers, took what rice they had, and killed the hamlet's only cow as an object lesson, though the farmers had not had anything to do with our find and had in no way helped us. We had not even entered the hamlet in our single-minded concentration on getting the rice out of the area and getting back to our more normal reconnaissance routines.

When we heard about the trouble, we got some of the rice we had so painstakingly bagged and gave it to the farmers in the hamlet. We also managed to purchase a cow to replace the one that had been killed and presented it to the farmers. The incident, nevertheless, was instructive in terms of the limits of our ability to truly protect the hundreds of farm hamlets in our area. The farmers who lived in those hamlets recognized that limit and acted accordingly. They could not afford to be sympathetic toward us. It was not a matter of political preference; it was a matter of survival. They could not provoke the Viet Cong or North Vietnamese by their actions because we could not ensure their safety if they did. In fact, they frequently paid a price even when they had done nothing provocative, as was the case in this incident. The Viet Cong or North Vietnamese came and went into one hamlet or another on any given night, and the farmers had to live through it. Their major goal in life was to plant, harvest, and trade or eat, their rice before we tore up their rice paddies with our vehicles and ruined the crop or before others confiscated what rice they managed to harvest. It was not easy to be a farmer in Vietnam.

Our cavalry troops working the beach area within our boundaries frequently stayed out for several days at a time. They ran their patrols during the day, or they worked with the engineers at clearing the Street Without Joy of the foliage that provided hiding places for Viet Cong and North Vietnamese. Sometimes they assisted the local Vietnamese forces in searching a hamlet that might be suspected of harboring an enemy force. At night they simply moved out into the flat sand, away from any hamlets, and formed a big circle reminiscent of what the wagon trains did on their move west in our own country. They circled up with the vehicles all facing out. With the firepower they had and the flat, open space all around them, they were perfectly secure. The crew members of each armored vehicle would take turns manning the heavy machine guns from atop the vehicles, and the troopers would gather around small fires made of issued heat tabs within their circle of security to heat and eat their combat rations. If they were close enough, their rear detachment would run out a small resupply column in one of the tracked maintenance vehicles just before dark so that urgent maintenance could be performed at night. A hot supper prepared at the base camp went out also, along with the mail. The tracked vehicles that brought out the repair parts and the food would stay the night then run back to the base camp in the morning, secure in the knowledge that moving armored vehicles did not make much of a target in the open, unpopulated beach area during the day—or at least not the kind of target that somebody on foot would be much interested in taking on.

One quiet night an entire company of North Vietnamese literally walked into one of our cavalry troops that was circled up on the sand near the northernmost edge of our area of operations. The troop had put out a couple of ambush patrols along likely routes just at dark and had then settled in for a night of waiting and catching what rest they could. The armored vehicles were still, with only the occasional static crackle of a radio to break the silence—and that did not carry far. Even so, it seemed unbelievable that anybody could stumble into a group of thirty armored vehicles, tanks, and ACAVs spread out on the sand. That is exactly what happened, however, at about three o'clock the next morning. The troop lookouts saw them coming from their perches atop their vehicles and reported the progress of the slow-moving black shadows out in the sand. A quiet radio check ensured that it was not our own ambush patrols that had somehow decided to move instead of stay in place. All of the patrols assured us that they were in place and could see no movement around them. The troop waited and quietly brought around all its guns that could bear to point at the oncoming shadows.

No vehicles were moved, no engines started, and no noise made. On they came. They were within a football field of the perimeter before they realized we were there. By then it was far too late, and the heavy machine guns did their pitiless work. Some were killed, some scuttled off into the darkness and the folds of the sand dunes, and a few wounded were captured. One of the wounded prisoners was a lieutenant. Through our interpreter, he expressed amazement that we were in this area. We had apparently crossed the invisible district boundary that ran east and west through the sand to the south of the troop's location and were operating in a district where government troops had never operated before. Previously, the lieutenant said, he and his men had moved at will north of that district line, relaxing in the fishing villages after their missions along Highway 1, secure in their knowledge that government troops never ventured north of that district boundary. We marked off one more refuge area that would not be used again with impunity and one more unit that would not endanger our area of operations for a long time to come.

Our cavalry troops took turns at the slow business of clearing foliage away from the sides of the Street Without Joy and leveling the ruined foundations and unused rice paddy dikes that bordered the road. The objective was to deprive transient North Vietnamese units and the local Viet Cong of likely hiding places. They had been using these facilities for a long time, however, and the challenge to our patience and skill was great. Like the bagging of rice, this work was slow and hot, and it carried with it the added danger of plentiful booby traps and sudden sniper assaults as the enemy tried to make us pay for destroying his twenty-year-old sanctuary. We suffered a casualty almost every day from the booby traps, no matter how careful our troopers were, and there were sporadic deadly encounters between our troopers and the enemy as our soldiers moved into the foliage or foundations, where our vehicles could not go, to secure the engineer bulldozers that would level the area for us. These encounters more often than not were matters of mutual surprise, fought at pistol range as the men moved through the heavy foliage and the overgrown, deserted buildings. But the work went on and the area of sanctuary became smaller. As a result, the fishermen and farmers started to use the cleared parts of the road to take their fish and rice to the local market to trade. Once the hiding places were gone, they understood that they could go to the markets without being held up for a passage tax on their way to or from the market towns. Once that happened, the roads were in such constant use that it was difficult for the enemy to further mine them during the day.

In mid-May one of the engineer bulldozers, working at leveling a dike while our ACAVs stood watch from the road nearby, lunged unexpectedly forward and down as it pushed against what had appeared to be a solid section of dike. Four figures tumbled out of the suddenly exposed tunnel in front of the bulldozer blade. They were dazed by the sudden blinding light of day, and our troopers were too startled by what had happened to do anything for a moment. Then, to the surprise of the watching troopers, one of the figures raised that rarest of all weapons among our opposition, a pistol, and fired at them. That broke their temporary immobilization, and the return fire was overwhelming and final. Still, it had been an event! A pistol in the hands of a local guerrilla or a North Vietnamese soldier signified a very special catch. Only the highest-ranking officers were given such a weapon.

The troopers quickly moved forward to search the area and the bodies. Papers found on the bodies and books found in the tunnel bore out the significance of the pistol. We had stumbled on a tax collector for the Viet Cong, the local Viet Cong agricultural administrator, and two assistants. The books and papers would give the province government a good picture of the local Viet Cong organization, which could not be obtained from any other source, and that organization would be irreparably hurt by our chance encounter. Among the papers of the one who had fired his pistol was a picture of himself taken in front of the Ministry of Agriculture in Moscow. Quite by accident we had eliminated an expert administrator, schooled in Russia, who had been infiltrated south to organize the local farmers. His modern ideas on agriculture would have made him a respected figure among the local farmers, who still followed their traditional primitive practices, and he would have had the ideal entrée to then organize them for his own purposes. A bulldozer blade had wiped out fifteen years of work. Soldiers were not hard to recruit or coerce into service, but neither the North Vietnamese nor the Viet Cong had an inexhaustible supply of trained organizers who fitted into the local community and who knew the local people.

As the first weeks of May passed, the dust from our moving tracked vehicles rose higher, the rice paddies got harder, and the heat became almost unbearable inside the steel vehicles. Our cavalry troops took to moving down to the water's edge for an hour or two in the late afternoon so that the men could swim and cool off while they performed the necessary maintenance on their vehicles and weapons and cleaned up prior to another night of ambush patrols and relief of outposts that came under attack on Highway 1. But these attacks had become less frequent, and our ambushes had fewer and fewer contacts. It had become progressively more difficult and more expensive for the enemy to move through our area because of our continual patrolling and the omnipresence of our cavalry troops. Though we still cleared the road connecting our supply depot with Highway 1 every morning, we had found no new mines in a week or two. The sector was becoming quiet thanks to our ability to appear to be everywhere at once.

From time to time, we were called upon to seal off an isolated hamlet, or a cluster of hamlets, in order that the Vietnamese Regional Forces troops could search them for the caches of food, hidden stores of weapons, or other evidence that would indicate that the Viet Cong or North Vietnamese were using the hamlets as a supply base. The Regional Forces were really a kind of militia who were primarily employed in guarding the villages and bridges in government-controlled areas, and they were far from being an effective combat force. They were a combination of police and light infantry, and they frequently had an American advisor who was versed in civil government and paramilitary operations. Organized as they were as a static defense force, they lacked the confidence or will to venture into the far reaches of our area of operations without back-up forces to protect them in the event that they stumbled on an enemy combat force disposed to fight. We therefore acted as a security force for their search operations.

One day in mid-May we were directed to provide a troop to act as security for this type of search mission in a particularly isolated northern section of our area, close to where the North Vietnamese company had wandered into our circled-up troop a week or so before. The operation was intended to assert a government presence in that particular district, which was hostile toward the government and provided a sanctuary for the local Viet Cong forces. Our cavalry troop moved from its night bivouac position in the early morning hours and threw a large circle around the two or three clusters of shacks that constituted the target hamlet. They were in place well before any of the inhabitants were ready to go out to their rice paddies, so nobody who had spent the night could get through the armored vehicles encircling the village on the flat sand. From the top of their ACAVs, the troopers could watch everything: nothing could come or go without being observed. And nobody made the attempt.

About seven o'clock that morning a cargo helicopter swirled down inside our protective ring of vehicles and delivered the Regional Forces searchers, complete with their American advisor. They were a ragtag group as they straggled off the rear ramp of the U.S. Army helicopter in their individualized field uniforms and gathered in a group to await their instructions. The helicopter lifted off to go about its other transporting missions, and their advisor detached himself from his charges to find our troop commander and coordinate the operation with him. The advisor told him that his Regional Forces were going to search the shacks for any evidence of Viet Cong presence and that, in addition, they would check the identity cards of all inhabitants and segregate for questioning any suspicious members of the hamlet. That sounded simple enough, and the troop commander simply nodded assent. They traded radio frequencies so that each could contact the other if necessary; then the advisor went off to help his counterpart get the operation going so that they could finish in time for the prearranged return of the cargo helicopter later in the day. Having seen no evidence of any armed enemy, our troopers were settling down to overwatching the scene in a relaxed fashion that would help them to cope with the growing heat and glare of the day. It was shaping up to be a dull, uncomfortable day as the armored vehicles grew hotter and hotter to the touch. Still, it would not do to become too relaxed in that hostile environment.

The troopers watched as the Regional Forces split into two groups. The larger group spread out and started toward the near edge of the hamlet, while a smaller group set up a command post and a temporary detention area between us and the edge of the hamlet. They could see figures moving in and out of the shacks, but there seemed to be no excitement or commotion. From time to time, some of the searchers would come out to bring small groups of people to the detention area, but there was no resistance to this and everything seemed to be running quietly and methodically. Then the vehicle commander of an ACAV close to the detention area called the troop commander to remark that it seemed that only women and children were being brought to the detention area. The troop commander contacted the Regional Forces advisor and asked in a mildly curious way what was going on. The advisor explained that they were finding no men in the hamlet, which was a good indicator that the inhabitants of the hamlet were Viet Cong supporters—and, in fact, that the men might be off doing something far more deadly than farming. As a result, they were detaining some of the women for questioning. Still, nothing about the situation seemed unusual for an "enemy" hamlet in a hostile area.

Next the troop radio net came alive with several simultaneous reports from the vehicles nearest the detention area that the Regional Forces interrogators were physically abusing some of the women and appeared to be sexually molesting them. Our troop commander immediately contacted the advisor on the radio and demanded that he intervene. The advisor responded to him that it was not our business, that it was a Regional Forces operation, and that this was an enemy hamlet. At that our troop commander radioed to squadron headquarters to outline the situation and ask for guidance. The squadron commander monitored the radio transmission from his helicopter, in which he had been making the rounds of our various troop operations, and headed for the hamlet. Upon arrival he asked the advisor to meet with him and give him an explanation for the conduct of the interrogators. The explanation was the same: this was the way the Regional Forces operated in an enemy village, and it was not our business to interfere.

Our squadron commander was quiet for a moment then explained in a tightly controlled voice that either the advisor would ensure that the abuse of the women stopped or we would pull out and leave him and his Regional Forces to fend for themselves. The advisor responded that it was out of his hands and that we were obligated to remain and support him. Our commander turned to our troop commander and told him to move out. With that he walked back to his helicopter, while the American advisor threatened us with all sorts of dire consequences when he reported our pulling out to his superiors in the American advisory chain of command.

As our command helicopter lifted off, the engines on our armored vehicles were already turning and the troop was starting to unwind into a march column. The sound of the engines and the movement of our vehicles got the immediate attention of the Regional Forces soldiers in the detention area, and they stopped what they had been doing to watch our departure. We never heard what happened after we pulled out, but our guess was that their fear that the men from the hamlet would return before their helicopter came back to collect them from what had suddenly become a very isolated and hostile environment would overcome their desire to brutalize defenseless farm women. We never heard a word about our pulling out either.

While we had been settling into our new area of operations, the sources for our repair parts support had been changing. The increased Army presence in the northern part of the country had finally brought a much-enlarged Army logistical base to Danang. No longer did we have to depend entirely on our tenuous contact with our own division south of Saigon. Now we had Army supply and maintenance facilities in Danang itself and forward contact elements in the Army base camps along Highway 1 between us and Danang. I had made contact with these forward elements already, but I had not had the chance to make the rounds of their headquarters and depots in the Danang area. Our urgent need for replacement tank engines and some other unique major repair parts made it necessary that I go to Danang to try to speed up the pace at which we were getting these critical items. In order to make the rounds, however, I would need transportation, so I decided to drive down to Danang in my jeep. The road was more or less clear, and it seemed not too risky a prospect for my driver and myself to make the trip if we started early enough in the day to get into Danang well before dark.

One hot May morning we checked the jeep over very carefully, stowed more M16 ammunition than either my driver or I usually carried in the back of the jeep, and headed through the gate of our supply depot for Highway 1. The road out had been through its morning clearing for mines and ran on ground that was crisscrossed by our cavalry troops, so there was no real threat there. We were in radio contact with all the squadron elements; besides, single vehicles frequently made a run over our sand-and-cement road without incident, so we moved along without much worry of any danger. About halfway out we started passing the small truck convoys that came in each day to shuttle supplies out to the various base camps from which the air cavalry division elements operated. From there on we had plenty of company. Once we came to the junction of Highway 1 at Hai Lang, we were on the main supply route, with military police checkpoints and patrols plus the endless long convoys of trucks that ran up and down the highway, feeding the Army and Marine units with the supplies that could not be easily brought in over the beach at our supply depot. Driving south to Hue was similar to being on the roads around Saigon: we were rarely out of sight of either a convoy or a military police patrol or a guarded bridge. The bridges themselves were showing a remarkable degree of repair in the four weeks since I had flown over this section of road, and some of the road itself was actually being covered with asphalt. Soon we were out of radio range of the squadron and on our own completely. We passed Hue in the late morning and drove across the highway bridge that we had been so involved with on previous trips. It, too, seemed to be much more sturdily reinforced now. There was a lot of Vietnamese civilian traffic close to Hue, and it appeared that life was returning to normal despite the ruined and shell-pocked buildings that made Hue resemble pictures I had seen of bombed-out European cities during World War II.

South of Hue we encountered heavy military traffic as we moved into the area that contained the headquarters for the provisional corps, which now commanded all Army elements in this northern part of Vietnam, and the headquarters of the Army division to which our tank company was attached. But as we moved farther south, past Phu Bai, the traffic started to thin out noticeably, and we traveled for some distance without passing outposts or U.S. Army traffic. The road ran flat and straight here, with marsh and sand on the left between us and the South China Sea and flat land on our right that gradually rose into the foothills in the distance. Though it was open country, it suddenly felt very lonely.

After about an hour of this nervous driving, we approached a large inlet from the South China Sea that came almost to the road's edge. Ahead of us was the town of Da Bac, which showed on my map as a Vietnamese military outpost. That was reassuring to us, but as we approached, we heard the unmistakable sound of incoming mortar shells. Despite the flatness of the land, we could not see where the action was, so we continued warily down the now-deserted highway. Off to our left I spotted the flash of impacting shells on a tongue of land that ran out into the water below the level of the road. A group of Vietnamese military vehicles was lined up on the flat ground and had been taken under fire by mortars that must have been firing from off to the right of the road. I could see the soldiers moving quickly in and out of the vehicles as they tried to find cover. We moved to the side of the road and eased the jeep partially into the culvert while we watched to see what might develop. Both of us had our weapons out and loaded as we sized up the terrain around us and tried to spot some indication of movement that would mean enemy soldiers. We were feeling very exposed, and a trifle stupid for having put ourselves into this position.

As we watched, one of the trucks took a direct hit and started to burn. That seemed to decide the unit on what to do, and the soldiers ran for their vehicles, started them up, and moved out onto the road and away to the south at top speed. In a moment there was nothing left but the dust of their departure and the burning truck. We waited to see what might happen next, but the incoming mortar rounds stopped, and there was no movement anywhere that we could see. We waited another ten minutes to be sure that no enemy soldiers were going to come down to check out the damage that they had done, but when all remained quiet, we decided to move on. We slowly brought the jeep back onto the highway. I was standing up to see if the extra height provided by being up on the built-up roadbed would disclose anything threatening off to our right. I could see no movement anywhere, however, and we decided that the best thing to do was to simply floor it and get out of the area. We picked up speed quickly and, with my eyes and M16 focused on the right side of the road, dashed past the piece of flat ground with its burning truck and drove on. The road remained deserted until we started the climb up to the Hai Van pass forty minutes later, but we encountered no further incidents.

As we began to climb, we came on an Army engineer unit working on improving the road. They had security out, and their heavy dump trucks and scrapers were moving back and forth, dumping gravel and leveling it prior to putting down a stabilizing surface. It felt very good to be back with U.S. Army units as we drove along, stopping now and then because of the road work. As we climbed higher among our new-found security, we started to look beyond the road fringes again and to appreciate the view that we were getting of the coastal beaches to the north of us on this bright, sunny day. At each climbing turn on the road up, we could see sand beaches spread out below us to the north for miles, and from this distance they were both beautiful and peaceful—the perfect location for a resort. It was some contrast to the shelling we had encountered down there just an hour earlier.

At the top of the pass, we found a fairly large Vietnamese military outpost and a helicopter landing pad; then we were headed down toward the bay that ran from the base of Hai Van mountain around to Danang. We were back in civilization. Ahead of us were the bright ESSO signs on some huge oil-storage tanks that made the scene look almost like home. The road now turned to solid pavement and ran through a combination of shantytowns and industrial buildings that marked the outskirts of Danang on the north. Both military and civilian traffic became heavy, and we carefully unloaded our M16s as we drove into the city and started our search for the newly arrived Army logistical support elements. Eventually, we wound through the city to the area from which we had embarked on our LSTs for the trip to Cua Viet several months before. Across the bridge I found newly posted directional signs that indicated where the units I was looking for were located. For the remainder of the afternoon, we dropped in and out of various supply and maintenance headquarters, establishing or verifying our account with the staffs, checking on the status of parts and major vehicle components that were on order, and determining when we might expect to receive replacement vehicles for those that had been damaged beyond repair. A surprising degree of sophistication had been introduced since we had moved north, and I was able to find out where in the supply system reaching back to Saigon and Long Binh our various needs were located and when I might reasonably expect delivery to the direct support units that were working with us near our base camp.

As evening came on, we headed toward the headquarters for the Marine amphibious force because we knew that we could get overnight accommodations there in a secure area and be able to take advantage of the amenities that went with a senior headquarters. We found a secure place to park our jeep, a barracks room for my driver, and a visiting officer quarters room for me. Agreeing to meet at seven o'clock the next morning, my driver and I split. I went to my room, enjoyed my first real shower in three months, then went down to the officers' club for a meal eaten on china with silverware, the first in a long time. I then took advantage of the nightly movie and turned in, secure in the knowledge that I was not responsible for anything going on around me and that the headquarters was both amply protected on the ground and so placed that it was not a normal mortar target. It was an unusually pleasant and restful night, and I was more than ready to get on with our business when I met my driver the next morning after another "luxury" meal with all the niceties that go with a fixed dining hall at a large headquarters.

I spent the morning making my rounds and introducing myself to additional staff officers who controlled the fate of our supplies and repair parts. The emphasis, as always, was on the vehicles. Our other supplies were common to all units and came without much special hand massaging. Our problems were always with ammunition for our tanks and for the parts to keep our vehicles running. Since we were the only cavalry unit assigned to the area, those parts were unique to us and not nearly as plentiful in the supply system. Under those circumstances it did not hurt to have my face and name associated with a supply account number in the minds of the system operators, and it certainly helped me to have a name and phone number to use when I needed assistance in obtaining a critical part. By noon we had made all the visits we could make, and we returned to the Marine headquarters to have one more civilized meal before making our way north. I had decided that I would rather not drive the road again, so we made our way down to the docking area for the Army transportation boat units and the Navy coastal shipping that sailed between Danang and Cua Viet. Without too much trouble we found an LST that was sailing for Cua Viet later in the afternoon and had room for us and our jeep. We made a quick visit to the large post exchange that had blossomed along with the other support activities and then loaded our jeep onto the LST.

The trip north was pleasant. We sailed out of the Danang harbor about sunset and moved out to sea past a German hospital ship that lay anchored in the harbor to help Vietnamese civilians. We passed the fishing nets and the sampans and finally sailed through the harbor entrance and out into the open sea. We turned northwest, parallel to the coast about three miles out, and headed for Cua Viet. The accommodations were fine and the trip was relaxing. Though the LST is not a big ship, it still had its complement of linen and silver, so it was a real luxury cruise to me. The night passed quickly, and we were off Cua Viet by early morning. It was midmorning by the time we could run up to the shore to off-load, but we drove our jeep off quickly and found an LCM that was leaving for Dong Ha that had room for us. From Dong Ha we drove south past Quang Tri City and past the site of the attack on the squadron command post; then we turned onto our own sand-and-cement road to Wunder Beach. We arrived in late afternoon without incident to find that the chaplain had driven over a mine on the shoulder of Highway 1 in our absence. His driver had allowed the wheels to get off the road, and they had hit a hidden mine that had blown up the back of the jeep while blowing the chaplain and his driver clear. They both had bad headaches but were otherwise unharmed. The event, however, reinforced my thought that driving to Danang had not been the smartest course of action and was not to be repeated.

# XI
# Local Affairs

In early June the list of those selected to attend the course of instruction for the following year at the Army's Command and General Staff College was published. The special significance of the list for me that year was that I was selected, and that meant leaving Vietnam early. Since the course began in early August, I would have to depart in June in order to allow for travel time and leave. While an early departure was very appealing to me while I was out on the sands of a Quang Tri Province beach, the Army required a commitment to an additional two years of service upon completion of the course. Such a commitment to additional service was usual with any Army course lasting longer than nine months; I had just never given any thought to it previously. Now, however, after twelve years of service, I found myself reluctant to make the commitment without thinking about it, and I was unable to think about it objectively in the midst of the nighttime ambushes, sudden firefights, and the general pressure of day-to-day life in a combat zone.

The questions that needed resolution before I committed myself to additional service were not, however, the questions that were the focus of the media and the protestors; my questions had nothing to do with the morality or the rightness of our cause. They had to do with the way in which the Army conducted its business in Vietnam. Though I was more than content with my current position and situation, where we had the latitude and authority to fulfill properly our responsibilities as leaders, I could not forget the overcontrol I had witnessed during the earlier part of my tour in my previous division.

Nor could I forget the unnatural concentration on awards and decorations that had permeated the senior ranks in that organization.

Command of a battalion or, eventually, a brigade was the goal of every combat arms officer, yet I had seen incumbents of those positions reduced to messenger boys by the overweening interference of general officers hovering twelve hundred feet above the action in their command and control helicopters. I had seen that interference, in turn, lead to a paralysis that could cost lives while the generals flew back to their air-conditioned trailers to be briefed on the next day's activities—and deliberate on what they would next try to influence from the air. Philosophically, I knew that the relatively small scope of our combat activities caused this overcontrol by not providing enough challenge to occupy the minds and energies of our generals, but that did not make it any easier to tolerate the situation. The fact still remained that battalion and brigade command had been robbed of its mystique in my eyes. If, then, those commands were the goal of my combat arms service, what was the point? My current situation contained none of the elements that bothered me so much, but I knew beyond a doubt the potential for that to change overnight with the introduction of new personalities into my chain of command.

While the outside world had doubts about the morality of what was taking place in Vietnam, I had doubts about the professionalism of the Army. I was not alone in these doubts, and a lot of regular Army officers of my generation spent a good deal of time pondering them. Those who were involved in the advisory effort had, in addition, to contend with the politics of the complex combination of advising and attempting to show progress as a result of that advising, while not being actually in control. It all made me wonder if I wanted to invest more years, and I needed time to resolve those doubts before I made a further commitment to service.

I decided to ask to defer attending the Command and General Staff College. Since the need for officers to serve in Vietnam was draining them from stateside assignments, it was not difficult to volunteer to return to the Military Academy for an additional year as an assistant professor. And since it was in the overall interest of the service to free up another officer for assignment to Vietnam, I did not have to discuss my doubts to justify my request. If I decided to stay in the Army after I had had time to think about it in an environment more conducive to cool consideration, I was sure I could successfully compete for the Command and General Staff College the following year. My request was quickly approved, and my shortened tour went by the way while I settled in for the remaining weeks of a normal twelve-month tour.

One day in early June the local district advisor, a worn-looking American artillery major, and the dapper Vietnamese major who was the district commander, paid an unexpected visit to our command post. This unannounced visit was also their first such visit, so when we were told that they were at the gate to our supply base, we were a bit curious as to what was to come. While their little convoy of security vehicles was being escorted to our command post, we scurried around to arrange some chairs in the partially shaded space in front of the command post tracks and to have some coffee and cake brought up from the kitchen area. When they arrived, we made the two majors comfortable and waited for the purpose of the visit to emerge.

The conversation eventually moved to the lessening enemy activity in the district. The advisor, speaking for the district commander, made some complimentary remarks about the impact our presence had made in his district. He went on to comment on what a great success our sand-and-cement road was. This road, laid out by the Army engineer battalion that lived with us on the supply base, was the truck route between the beach and Highway 1. It was merely a graded track in the sand that had been partially stabilized by spreading huge quantities of dry cement over the graded sand. Evening moisture provided enough water to bond the mixture, and the engineer rollers and the heavy truck traffic compacted it into a reasonably hard surface. The advisor stressed that it provided a critical link between the farm and fishing villages and the market town of Hai Lang, out on Highway 1, where the district headquarters was located. It was, he said, revitalizing local trade. He kept repeating that there was a lot of traffic on that road, both military vehicle traffic and civilian foot traffic, and that it certainly was nice to know that the road was secure from the enemy. The Vietnamese district commander smiled and nodded while all this was being said.

There was a little silence following this speech, and we all sipped our coffee and waited. Then the American advisor asked how we would feel about having a roadside store built at the point where several trails from villages joined the road. My commander replied that he really did not see the need for such an enterprise, knowing full well that it would be aimed at attracting our soldiers rather than the villagers who passed by and, as such, could provide a good intelligence-gathering source for the enemy. The discussion of the merits and demerits of a store on our turf went on for several minutes, until it became obvious that we were not going to support such an endeavor. As the discussion progressed, the district commander became less and less jovial and the advisor became more and more aggressive about the obvious economic and pacification advantages of what he was proposing. Without our support, however, a store could not survive, and all the parties to the conversation knew it.

Eventually, the advisor gave up, and he and his Vietnamese counterpart prepared to leave. They were both obviously upset with our obstinancy. As we walked to their waiting vehicles and security squad, my commander went ahead with the district commander. The advisor stayed back with me to make one more plea. The store, he said, would be run by the district commander's brother-in-law, and the commander would be very pleased if we would make it possible. I just smiled, and as they drove off, I thought how lucky I was not to be enmeshed in the politics of the advisory effort. We never did have a store on our road, and the enemy never did manage to get advanced information of what we were doing—at least not that they used to any advantage against us. And I decided that the complications of my job were nothing compared to those of being an advisor. There was no doubt in my mind that being with an American combat unit was the best of the possible situations.

In April, when we had first moved south from Dong Ha, we had been among the first units to return to the Quang Tri City area and to start using the roads after the fierce fighting of the Tet offensive. Those roads had still been spotted with vehicles that had been caught out on the road when Tet began. Some had been abandoned because the roads had been blocked, and some had been left where their occupants had been killed or wounded in an ambush. All of the vehicles were damaged, but most were repairable. The potential for repair was all too obvious to our mechanically-minded troopers, and the temptation was too much to pass up. We soon found that we were acquiring vehicles at a great rate. It was just too easy to get the use of one of our recovery vehicles, and the extra jeep or light truck that resulted was just too convenient for administrative use around the camp or between the troop bivouac area and the various support facilities, for any right-minded trooper to pass up the opportunity.

For a while barely repaired jeeps actually became a trading item. One of our troopers even went so far as to trade a jeep for a prized Russian pistol when he found a passing Marine who believed that motorized transportation was more important than a war trophy that could not be taken out of the country. Unfortunately for the Marine, the jeep died of a broken transmission a few hours after the trade.

Sometime during this period, our support platoon—the headquarters element that provided the truck transportation for our fuel and supplies—acquired a five-ton tractor of the type used to pull the big cargo trailers. They found it on its side off the road, and they used one of our recovery vehicles to right it and pull it to the maintenance area. Throughout May the support platoon truckers, and any mechanics they could lure into the project, had gathered around it after supper and worked on putting it in running shape. With all that talent they had it purring by the end of May. The next step was to paint it and put our unit markings on it, and there it sat in the support platoon vehicle park in all its pristine splendor. Just looking at the handiwork, however, was not enough to satisfy real truckers' souls for long; they had to figure out a way to use it! To do that, they had to find something to pull, and nothing authorized as equipment for a cavalry squadron came near to filling the bill. Then some of the support platoon drivers got to remembering the Marine supply yard at Dong Ha where they went to pick up some of our bulkier supplies. The supplies were delivered to that supply yard on flatbed trailers, which were left in the yard until empty. They were then switched for arriving loaded ones and convoyed back down to Danang to be reloaded. There always seemed to be several empty ones parked and waiting to be picked up.

One morning two of our more adventurous truck drivers simply drove up to Dong Ha, waved to the Marine in charge of the supply yard, and backed up to an empty flatbed trailer. They casually dismounted from the tractor, hooked up the cables and hoses, and drove off, with another wave to the watching Marine, as though it were a routine job. There was no fuss, and no complaint followed. They had gotten away clean. Thereafter, whenever possible, the support platoon used its prize for hauling bulky supplies. Instead of sending two of our own trucks to do the hauling, the tractor and trailer were sent, and the drivers competed for the privilege of driving this "real" truck. Of course, the whole idea verged on misappropriation of government property, but the equipment was still in government service, and it was so obviously good for support platoon morale that we chose to take no judicial notice of what was going on.

The proliferation of extra jeeps in our cavalry troops was not so easy to overlook because they made our troopers too mobile. It became difficult to know where our off-duty troopers were going to turn up in their rare moments of free time. After several incidents of finding our people in locations where they definitely did not belong, we decided that we could no longer afford to humor our shadow jeep fleet. The word went out to troop commanders to turn in the extra jeeps. The troop commanders, however, were as reluctant to come down hard on their extra jeep owners as we were to make our support platoon get rid of its tractor and trailer. A good-natured game of "hide-the-jeep" followed.

The squadron commander and I were both assured that action was being taken to get rid of extra vehicles, but we knew better. We waited to catch our troopers driving in their illicit vehicles; then we confiscated them on the spot. The troopers' response was to change the unit markings on the bumpers so that it became difficult to know whether we were looking at our own authorized equipment or that which had been acquired from the countryside. When we passed a jeep on the road, there was no way of telling whether it was a legal or an illegal vehicle. Sooner or later, however, we would encounter two jeeps with the same bumper markings, and one more extra jeep would be eliminated. We probably didn't find all of them, but the diversion provided was a good relief from the grimmer routine duties of the squadron. Also, we knew that when we shipped back south we could inventory our equipment as we loaded it on the ships and cut out all the extras before we returned to the more legalistic operated environment of our parent division.

One or another of our cavalry troops had been operating in the extreme south of our operational area since we moved to the beach. We rotated the troop assigned the task, but the mission remained much the same. It operated along Highway 1 in cooperation with the airmobile infantry units that were continually sweeping the gently rolling terrain on both sides of the highway. They performed nighttime road-running operations that kept the highway from being mined and were available to assist in protecting the key bridges. Frequently, the bridges were protected simply because the troop bivouacked next to one or another of them and used those locations as bases of operations for its road running.

A platoon from this troop was working with an infantry company in mid-June on a sweep of the dried rice paddy land that lay between Highway 1 and the South China Sea to the east. Late in the afternoon the troopers ran into sudden, intense enemy fire. The action started when one of the platoon tanks was hit by an antitank rocket fired from behind a low dike surrounding a dry rice paddy. The hit caused an explosion in the tank, and the crew quickly evacuated the heavily smoking vehicle under a hail of small arms and automatic weapons fire coming from the same dike. They were picked up by the nearest ACAV, and the combined cavalry-infantry team then dropped back one hundred yards to reorganize and see what they were up against. Our platoon spread out its vehicles and faced the dike from which it was receiving fire, with the infantry troops dispersed between them along another old dike, and the action settled down to the two opposing lines facing each other about three hundred yards apart. The enemy fired on our vehicles, which loomed above the flat terrain, and our troopers fired back at the puff of smoke or the moving grass that indicated the probable origin of fire. The reluctance of the enemy force to expose itself to our fire prevented it from being able to hit our vehicles at the same time that it prevented our troopers from hitting the enemy. It was a standoff for the moment, with no great danger to either side and covering darkness coming on. The damaged tank remained halfway between the lines, smoking lightly.

The report of the action and of our damaged tank came to us on our radios almost immediately, and the squadron commander decided to use what light remained in the day to fly out to the scene of the action and look over the situation for himself. He landed some distance in back of the line of armored vehicles and infantry and walked up to our platoon, being careful to stay in line behind one of our vehicles so that his movement was masked from the enemy. The position that we had taken along the old dike gave cover for the infantrymen if they lay flat, and our commander dropped down among them to see what was happening. He beckoned for our platoon leader, who had seen him arrive, to join him; then he turned his attention to the scene in front.

There was a lull in the firing at the moment, and in the resulting quiet, our commander heard the distinct sound of the damaged tank's engine. Incredulous, he confronted the platoon leader. The platoon leader had no explanation. The crew was sent for and soon joined the two officers who were hunched down behind the low dike. After a few moments of questioning, it became clear that they had evacuated the tank when it was first hit and the crew compartment had filled with smoke, assuming that it was about to go up in flames. They had not waited to determine the extent of the damage, which was partially understandable under the circumstances. It was equally clear, however, that in their panic they had left a "live" tank in no-man's-land just waiting to be driven off—by anyone. Nobody had ever heard of our forces losing a working tank to the enemy, and we certainly had no intention of being the first.

Under a good covering fire from the overwatching vehicles and the protection afforded by the rapidly fading light, the chagrined platoon leader led the embarrassed crew back to their tank, urged on by some fairly unkind words from our squadron commander. In a moment they had covered the ground to the tank and were up on it. In another moment the tank was moving back to our line, scarred but completely operational. The antitank rocket had impacted on the turret and set fire to the gear carried on the outside, but it had not penetrated into the crew compartment, and no real damage had been done. In the excitement of the moment, the men had not stopped to look. They had panicked at the sound of the exploding rocket and the resulting heavy smoke from the burning gear and had nearly lost their tank. Our commander returned to our command post later that evening shaking his head. The tank crew and the platoon leader took a lot of kidding over the next few weeks, but the potential damage of panicky actions in combat was clear for all to see—and the lesson had not been too costly.

One afternoon a young Vietnamese boy was brought in to our medical aid station. Our troopers had found him at the edge of a hamlet after a short firefight with some enemy soldiers. The troop had been on a routine sweep and had been taken under fire as it approached a small farm hamlet clustered under some sparse trees. The troopers immediately returned fire with their heavy machine guns from the tops of their ACAVs and deployed on line. They then charged the hamlet. Their heavy return firepower and the shock of their charging armored vehicles apparently were more than the enemy was prepared to deal with. There was no more firing. The hamlet was searched by our dismounted troopers under the watchful eyes of the ACAV gunners, but the enemy had either melted away or had simply hidden their weapons and melded into the family groups that were hunkered down in the shallow bunkers that all of the farmers in this area routinely dug under their shacks. The troopers found no weapons or ammunition.

The young boy had been discovered lying behind a tree on the near edge of the hamlet; he had been watching the action with a boy's normal curiosity. While watching, he had been brushed by a stray round from one of our .50-caliber heavy machine guns. The .50-caliber round, designed to penetrate light armor, is a formidable thing. The bullet, which is as big around as a nickel, had touched the boy's leg lightly in passing and had taken off the better part of his calf muscle. The troopers who discovered him gave him immediate first aid then brought him directly back to our surgeon.

We felt terrible about it, and the troopers involved in the action felt worse. But there was no sure way to avoid this sort of accident of war. We could not take fire without returning it or we unnecessarily exposed our troops by rendering them defenseless and you could never be sure where each machine-gun round would go in a melee. Survival of an ambush, as we all knew too well, depended on an immediate and overwhelming response of fire. While nobody had wanted to harm this thin young boy, neither had anybody been able to tell at the outset whether it was a well-planned ambush backed by a strong force or only a passing bit of harassment. We refused to allow our tanks to use their main guns to fire on a village without authorization from the command post, which was granted only after a thorough probing of the situation over the radio, but we could not sensibly impose the same restriction on machine-gun fire. That would render our troopers defenseless. In this case the tanks had not fired at all. They had stayed back, prepared to assist, if needed. None of this helped the boy now lying in front of the surgeon. Our remorse was small comfort to a kid who would forever have a deformed leg. We arranged to have him evacuated to a surgical hospital where whatever was possible would be done to repair the leg, but nobody felt very good about the day's work.

One of the advantages of being close to the South China Sea was the availability of naval gunfire to support our efforts. When we had first occupied our beach area, we had been impressed by the huge depressions we had found out in the sand; they represented the points of impact of sixteen-inch shells lobbed from the guns of our single operating battleship, the USS *New Jersey*. At night we could hear the big shells hurtling overhead. The sound was distinctive, to say the least: a combination of the sound of a low-flying jet and an airborne locomotive. Having seen the size of the shell hole that a sixteen-inch shell made, it was vaguely disconcerting to hear them lumbering by. You could not help wondering about the potential for one to impact short of its target. The reassuring thought to counter that unpleasant possibility was that we had all been taught in the various service schools through the years that naval gunfire was the most accurate form of indirect fire support available. It was almost an article of faith.

Our growing familiarity with the subject soon disabused us of that piece of lore. One day we tried to take advantage of the sixteen-inchers to flush out a particularly persistent group of dug-in enemy. We called for the Navy fire support on the appropriate radio channel. Back came a question about how close our troops were to the target. We responded that they were about three hundred yards from the target. The detached voice on the radio replied that they could not fire our requested mission with sixteen-inch guns if the friendly troops were closer than four thousand yards to the target. We politely thanked the Navy and went back about our business of getting at our opponents with more pedestrian means. To pull back four thousand yards would be to lose contact with the enemy forever. It turned out that what we all had been taught about the accuracy of naval gunfire was true—once the guns were registered on their targets; before that, the probable error was plus or minus four thousand yards for the sixteen-inch guns. That made sense when you stopped to think about a ship bobbing in the ocean, no matter how large it was, trying to correlate its position in the open sea, fixed by longitude and latitude, with a land position, fixed by a one-hundred-yard grid square on a topographic map. Given that, and the tremendous explosive power of that sixteen-inch shell, a four-thousand-yard buffer zone was none too much.

The demolishing of that article of faith, however, did nothing for our peace of mind when we heard the sixteen-inch shells passing overhead at night.

For most of the month of June, one of our cavalry troops had been assigned back up north to work for the Marines in their operations around the supply beach at the mouth of the Cua Viet River, which was the point at which we had disembarked when we had first come to Quang Tri Province from Danang. It still was the reception point for many of the supplies and replacement equipment destined for Dong Ha. The troop was kept busy probing the beach area and scrub dunes that surrounded the supply beach. Occasionally, it was ferried across the Cua Viet River to extend the probes to the north. The idea was to keep the North Vietnamese bands at a distance from the supply beach and to prevent them from getting in close enough to disrupt the supply operations by either a ground attack or a mortar or rocket shelling. We were simply applying the same principles that worked so well at our own Wunder Beach: keep the enemy off balance by making it so that he never knows when our armored vehicles will show up to pounce on him.

It was a good independent mission for our troop commanders, and the experience of planning the relief and the movement to and from the Cua Viet was good practice, so we rotated the three line troops through the mission. Since the maintenance capability for our heavy vehicles was practically nonexistent at the supply beach, we found that a week was the limit for a troop to sustain itself. After that we would either have had to move too much of the squadron base up for support in an already overcrowded and confined area or the troop's vehicle availability rate would start to fall off sharply. It was most efficient, therefore, to the overall mission to simply switch troops after about a week.

A fresh cavalry troop would march up the eleven miles of hard sand at the water's edge and arrive in time to take over while the day was still young. That part of the exercise was a simple tactical march in column, but it did give the troop commander some good practice in planning for his supply and maintenance support on an independent mission, and he had to make the necessary coordination for the smooth assumption of the operations at Cua Viet. The returning troop commander, however, had a project that was a little more challenging.

He was always directed to make an area reconnaissance over the eleven-mile stretch of beach and sand dunes, sometimes concentrating his efforts on the sparsely populated dunes that gradually ran into rice paddies farther inland and sometimes concentrating on the fishing villages that dotted the beach. In this way we managed to sweep the area between Cua Viet and our own supply depot every week or so. We looked for signs of unusual activity or for the uncommonly large quantities of stockpiled rice or dried fish that might indicate that something was going on. We knew that this northern area of our sector was a favorite resting place for transiting North Vietnamese battalions, but our sweeps had not produced any enemy contact. Nevertheless, the mission was good practice, and it did keep the inhabitants of the fishing villages honest—or so we thought.

Toward the end of June, we conducted one of these troop rotations. The returning cavalry troop got off to a good start in mid-morning and moved off down the coast. The axis for the reconnaissance this time lay just inland of the beach and the fishing villages so that any enemy encountered would be caught between the troop and the South China Sea. It was a routine, uneventful operation until the lead tank of the troop came within about 150 yards of the village of Binh An, midway between Cua Viet and Wunder Beach. Then there was a burst of small arms fire, and an antitank rocket slammed into the lead tank.

The troop quickly deployed and returned fire on the enemy, while elements of its unengaged platoons moved quickly to the north and south of the village to seal it off. So quickly did the troop deploy that it managed to cut off the three North Vietnamese soldiers who had fired on the column and who were trying to withdraw into the village. Simultaneously, the squadron radios at Wunder Beach crackled with the news of the firefight, and we quickly launched our light observation helicopter to get a better look at the situation. The pilot's report a few minutes later added to our surprise and indicated that this contact was not going to be a quick skirmish. He radioed back that he was observing large numbers of villagers fleeing south with what possessions they were able to carry. Such an exodus was almost always a sign that we were in for a serious fight because only the most extreme fear would cause the Vietnamese fishermen or farmers to leave their home villages or fields. A little later our suspicions were confirmed. One of the North Vietnamese soldiers just captured on the outskirts of Binh An admitted under interrogation that his battalion of about three hundred men was dug in inside of Binh An.

Our squadron commander ordered our other cavalry troop to break off its routine mission for the day and move to reinforce the troop in contact. That troop had already deployed in a rough semicircle facing southeast, and its sister troop marching up from the south joined it to form a horseshoe-shaped cordon around Binh An. The South China Sea blocked escape to the east, and we had already asked the Navy to position patrol boats offshore to seal off any seaward escape routes. Knowing that we had trapped a battalion of dug-in North Vietnamese inside our cordon, we adopted a very deliberate and methodical approach. The sporadic fire coming from Binh An indicated that there was a lot of fight left in the enemy, so our squadron commander requested supporting artillery fire from nearby Army units and from a Navy cruiser and two destroyers that took station offshore. The cordon was set far enough back to allow for the registration of the five- and eight-inch Navy guns on these ships. The order to commence firing brought a shattering avalanche of high explosives down on the village. This fire was kept up for the better part of the afternoon and was lifted only long enough for us to bring in a loudspeaker team to urge the North Vietnamese soldiers in Binh An to give up. There was no response to this Vietnamese-language request, and the bombardment was resumed. In the meantime our squadron commander had requested two reinforcing infantry companies to ensure that our cordon line was solid enough to contain our quarry. They arrived during the early afternoon and took up positions interspersed among our two cavalry troops.

As the afternoon wore on, we became concerned that the North Vietnamese might make a mass attempt to break out of the cordon after dark. To disrupt any such plan, we moved in on the village in the late afternoon. One troop tried to attack from the west of the village toward the sea, but its assault was stopped at the very edge of the village by a drainage ditch, which could not be crossed by our armored vehicles, and by the fairly heavy enemy fire that covered the ditch. They pulled back, and the northern edge of our cordon, reinforced by the recently arrived infantry company interspersed between our vehicles, assaulted toward the south. The vehicles on the south side of the cordon buttoned up their hatches so that the assaulting troop could use its machine guns without fear of hurting our own troops. The assaulting troopers moved through the village until their small arms and machine-gun fire was bouncing off the vehicles on the southern cordon line. Then they turned around and fought back to their original positions. As soon as they were clear, the shelling was resumed.

Our troopers then settled into their positions and prepared to spend a night of watchfulness. There was sporadic small arms fire as darkness came on. The artillery shells continued to explode in the village, though the rate of fire had been decreased. Our tanks used their searchlights to light up the beach area, and the troopers manning the cordon on the inland side used night-vision devices to augment the flares that were fired at regular intervals to illuminate the area. In this way individual North Vietnamese soldiers and occasional small groups of the besieged enemy were spotted as they tried to grope their way out in the dark. Most of them were stopped or turned back by our small arms and machine-gun fire. Some were captured. At first light we requested an increase in the shelling. After about an hour, the fire from the supporting guns was lifted. In the silence that followed, the cordon started to tighten around Binh An.

The northern and southern sides of the cordon moved toward each other with their vehicles buttoned up, while the western portion of the cordon remained watchfully in place to ensure that no enemy squeezed out in that direction. The two troops met only light resistance as they moved toward each other, stopping when their machine-gun bullets were bouncing off each other's vehicles. Then they pulled back. A second assault was now made, with the infantry accompanying our vehicles. We were careful to direct our fire down because this time our infantry was exposed to the fire from the opposite side of the cordon. Stunned North Vietnamese now began to appear and stumble toward our vehicles, their hands over their heads. The battle was over.

In the clean-up operations that followed, we recovered 233 bodies and a considerable number of crew-served and individual weapons. In addition, 44 enemy had surrendered to our troopers, the bulk of them during the previous night when it must have become apparent to some of them that they were in fact locked into an impossible situation. The remainder of the prisoners had surrendered to us during the final assault. Among the dead were the battalion commander, his staff, and all of his company commanders. We had suffered 1 dead and 9 wounded, and all 9 were returned to duty the following day.

Obviously, Binh An had been a resting place for North Vietnamese units moving across the area en route to or from the foothills that ran inland from Highway 1. Its location in a relatively unpopulated beach area that lay at the outer edge of our squadron's operational sector had made the North Vietnamese feel secure in the village. We had stumbled into them and had been able to turn the situation to our advantage, but it was more than stumbling, and it was not merely luck that was bringing us success in depriving the enemy of his local sanctuaries. It was men in hot steel vehicles, out in the glaring sand, looking and poking until the enemy, North Vietnamese and Viet Cong alike, never knew exactly when or where an armored column might crop up next. It was casualties from booby traps and hours of boredom and minutes of terror when only the skill of the driver or the gunner really mattered. And the results, as June turned into July, were quiet nights, infrequent contact with the enemy, and clear roads in an area that had been hostile territory for years. Highway 1 was now solid, uncratered blacktop from Danang north to Dong Ha, the Seabees and Army engineers had put in new bridges to replace the destroyed and shaky ones that had carried us in early April, and local farmers and fishermen were out traveling those roads and bridges to market as they had not been able to do a year before. Our cavalry squadron had a part in that, along with the other Army units that moved into Quang Tri Province to flesh out the Marine effort in that northernmost corner of Vietnam. And that was one accomplishment that could actually be seen and touched in a war where progress was not always easy to quantify.

# XII

# Changing of the Guard

With July came planning for welcoming our new squadron commander. The six months since the January ambush had passed very quickly, and it was time for my current commander to leave. The new commander had been designated and was to do his in-processing through division during the first days of July. We decided that I should make the trip south once more to help him with his processing and to familiarize him with the terrain on which we would operate when we moved south again to rejoin our parent division. It seemed like a good idea to show him the road nets in what would likely be our area of operation, to familiarize him with the port area where we would disembark outside of Saigon, and to give him a feel for the general lay of the land around Bear Cat against the time when he would have to plan for our reintroduction into the Saigon area. In addition, I would introduce him to our air cavalry troop and our rear detachment before he came north and became enmeshed in our combat operations, which would quickly occupy his energy and leave little for the rear area. The result of these efforts, we hoped, would be an easy transition for a fully oriented new commander.

I flew south. Nothing had changed at Bien Hoa Air Base, or on the dusty road to Bear Cat, but the squadron area looked even more dreary and rundown as a result of our four-month absence: only the headquarters building, with its small rear detachment, and the air cavalry troop area looked alive and well maintained. The rest of the squadron area looked like a ghost town. The wood frames of the troop tents were loose, the wood floors had warped in the dry heat, and the canvas flapped dustily among the weeds along the sides of the tents. The rest of Bear Cat also seemed to have a lowered level of activity this time. The division was focused more and more on the Delta to the south, and an alternate division base camp was being built out of the swamps down there. The locus of the division was moving ever farther south while we continued to operate completely out of its orbit to the north.

The new squadron commander arrived the next day, and I escorted him through his initial in-processing and briefings. After the first flurry of briefings and visits, we started to have time to get out on the roads, but he showed no interest. Instead, he wanted to go to the headquarters at Long Binh so that he could visit a friend on the staff and look over the goods in the large post exchange that was located in the sprawling headquarters base camp. The "friends" turned out to be a well-known armor colonel who was serving out his time on the operations staff of the headquarters, U.S. Army, Vietnam, awaiting his moment to take up command of the cavalry regiment for which he had already been designated.

Our plan to orient the new commander on the local terrain and road nets went by the board, and I arranged for a trip to Long Binh instead. We drove up one morning and wandered around the post exchange, killing time until our appointment with the new commander's friend. After a quick lunch at the post exchange snack bar, we drove over to the headquarters of U.S. Army, Vietnam, and found our way to the plans and operations section. I was invited to sit in on their conversation, so I was able to listen as the friend passed on his thoughts on cavalry operations, armored vehicle maintenance problems, and air cavalry flying techniques. I decided that he was extremely well prepared for his forthcoming command. He already had a notebook filled with items that it had taken me eight months to learn the hard way. He talked knowingly about the tendency of cavalry units to get sloppy, to pay insufficient attention to maintenance, and to be too slow to respond—all tendencies that we fought daily. He also talked accurately about valid helicopter availability rates and about the low altitude and slow speeds at which scout helicopters must fly to do any real good. Obviously, his previous tours in Vietnam and his personal intelligence system had provided him with some very perceptive insights into the operational problems of cavalry. I wondered if my new commander appreciated the value of what he was hearing. I also wondered, briefly, why he had not secured a squadron command in the colonel's new regiment if they were such good friends.

After a bit more discussion, our host took us on a tour of the headquarters war room. The tour was accompanied by pungent comments about enemy movement and the combat records of various of our own units. It was interesting to see the view of our operations from the other end, as it was portrayed here on backlighted maps that displayed the disposition and movement of combat units with brightly colored symbols and lines neatly laid out. Here the focus was on percent of vehicles available and percent of troops actually in the field. It was difficult to equate this hushed, air-conditioned display of data with the hot, dusty, dirty, dangerous activity that it represented. As always, the headquarters view of combat, necessary as it is in its own right, was far different from the reality of the troopers in their hot vehicles in the sand. After looking over some more of the headquarters command and control apparatus and after my commander and our host traded a few more stories about their previous tour together in Washington, we said goodby. In short order we were passing the gates and entering the stream of military traffic headed south toward Bear Cat.

The next day I gave our new commander over to the D Troop aviators. They briefed him on their operations, their helicopter availability rate, and their maintenance problems; then they flew him off to the Delta to the south of Bear Cat so that he could get an appreciation for the combat activity in that water-filled swamp, where so much of the division's resources were now centered. I took advantage of the free time to go for an orientation ride in one of our brand-new Cobra gunships. This slim, sleek helicopter, designed from the start to be an assault vehicle, was a different experience entirely from the standard Huey gunship. It climbed and dived like a fighter plane, and the weapons system and sighting apparatus were something to behold. It was very clear that this new piece of equipment was going to make a vast difference in the effectiveness of our aerial gunnery. It was a fantastic ship and a fantastic experience. I came back to earth figuratively and actually in time to meet my new commander and to take him off to his final round of briefings at the division headquarters before we headed north to join the squadron.

The change of command came a week after we arrived back at Wunder Beach and was performed with a degree of military precision that was somewhat amazing for an organization that had taken no interest in marching or drill and ceremonies in months. We even managed a mimeographed facsimile of a formal invitation for the ceremony. Both our own division commander and the local division commander, under whom we operated, participated in handing over the colors to the new commander, amid some barbed comments back and forth regarding to whom we really belonged. The troopers did themselves proud, and we were duly complimented by the generals and the other ranking officer guests who had found their way out to our headquarters in response to our invitations. Then the commander with whom I had rebuilt the squadron after our deadly ambush on the last day of December was gone, and I was left to adjust to a new commander who had not been through all that with me. Since he had no real understanding of where we had been and what we had done to arrive at the stage in which he found us, he could not understand why we were not better than we were. Unfortunately, his desire to make us better focused on some things that had remained singularly unimportant to us as we were conducting our combat operations and surviving in Quang Tri Province.

For example, he found that saluting was lax. That meant that there was not enough saluting going on in the headquarters area, because our troopers really were punctilious about saluting out on the road as our vehicles passed or when they reported to us on some official business. It was true that we had not paid a lot of attention to saluting in the command post area, where enlisted and officer staff passed each other dozens of times a day. Also, we had not been particularly concerned whether the headquarters clerks jumped up from their radios or field desks and reporting when we went to conduct supply or maintenance business at the command tracks that constituted our logistical center. Now all that changed. Everybody saluted everybody, and I was startled to have my ex-driver, newly promoted to supply clerk, jump up from his desk, announce his name and rank, and go through the formal reporting procedure when I came to check on our supply requisitions. Formal reporting to a visiting officer has its place, but

I wondered if it was useful when officer and enlisted man had spent as many hours sitting next to each other as we had. It all seemed a little too much for a workaday fighting team that had never ignored military courtesy, but which also had never attempted to make a fetish out of spit and polish. All things change, but it was hard to gather a whole lot of enthusiasm for this particular program after what the squadron's energies had been devoted to for the last six months.

Other things were changing also—and had been changing for some time. The new lieutenants who were coming in as replacements lacked the benefit of the experience in the peacetime Army that their predecessors had possessed. We had run through the crop of lieutenants who had served a couple of years in Germany or the States before being assigned to Vietnam—in fact, the Army had speeded up promotions to meet shortages so that lieutenants were being promoted to captain in only two years. There was an additional problem that was even more worrisome than simple lack of experience. Too many of our new lieutenants seemed to be not quite as bright or mature as their predecessors had been. No longer were they college graduates, or even college dropouts. Now the minimum requirement for a commission was a high school education or equivalency. Then there was a preshipment requirement of four months' service in the States after officer candidate school and branch training. That four months was supposed to give them some seasoning after their schooling, but it seemed to have the opposite effect. After having been immersed in tanks and ACAVs at their branch training school, they were frequently sent out to serve in basic training assignments where they spent the four months teaching drill or rifle marksmanship. By the end of it, many had forgotten what they had learned about armor and cavalry. Though we still occasionally received a regular Army lieutenant with a college or Military Academy background, most simply were not up to those standards. Bright, talented college graduates had other goals than to be officers in the U.S. Army.

An extreme case of what could result from this situation occurred one morning in the sandy, temporary vehicle park of our C Troop. A platoon was getting ready to move out on a routine operation to sweep the road between our beach and Highway 1 when I arrived to check the readiness of the platoon, which was already lined up for the start, with its vehicle engines idling quietly. The new lieutenant in charge, on the verge of his first mission, reported to me and led me along his waiting column. As we walked beside his lead tank, my eye was caught by a large hunk of white cloth wrapped around a track-support roller. The normal, well-maintained support roller consists of a pair of rubber-rimmed wheels bolted together at the end of a shaft that extends out from the hull. The track runs over the turning support rollers as it makes its way back to the drive sprocket and then down to the ground. There are three rollers spread out under the top of the track to support it. In this case there were only two—and the cloth-covered stub of a shaft.

I asked the lieutenant about the cloth. He told me that the support roller had broken off its shaft and that the cloth was to protect the shaft. I pointed out that the track was going to drag the cloth off the shaft the moment he started moving and that, more important, we did not move tanks without their support rollers—unless there was some unavoidable combat emergency—because it would lead to a thrown track in short order unless extreme care was exercised. The lieutenant looked at me blankly. I ended the discussion before I lost my patience completely by telling him that the tank was deadlined; then I went off to find his troop commander. The idea that he had been content to bind up the wounded support roller with a cloth boggled my mind. It also showed the level of competence that we were beginning to encounter in our new lieutenants. Most of them were capable of learning once their errors were pointed out, but we could no longer assume that they all had some universal base of knowledge about their vehicles and responsibilities. The build up of troop strength in Vietnam was taking its toll in more ways than one when it came to qualified junior officers.

The Army transportation battalion, whose activities were the reason for the existence of our beach supply depot, was equipped with two sizes of amphibious cargo vehicles: large and larger. These vehicles were used to lighter supplies from the cargo ships anchored offshore to the beach storage sites. The larger type vehicle was called a BARC. When it was out of the water, its size was apparent: it was huge. Its tires were taller than a man, and the sides of the vehicles were another six or seven feet in height above the wheel wells; on top was a narrow, flat deck that surrounded the cavernous cargo hold. The narrow deck, about four feet across, covered a labyrinth of sealed flotation compartments, electrical connections, and mechanical equipment built into the walls to make the BARC work. All of that machinery came together at a very small cockpit that perched on the narrow deck at the aft end of the amphibious vehicle. The front of the BARC, of course, was a huge ramp that dropped down to give access to the cargo hold for loading or unloading on dry land.

About four hundred yards north of our supply depot perimeter, there was the abandoned hulk of one of these behemoths. It had become inoperable in a storm, we had been told, and had been washed ashore long before we arrived on the scene. For some reason the decision had been made not to try to recover and repair it, and it had simply squatted on the beach near the surf line, sinking a little farther into the sand with each changing tide. The transportation battalion maintenance people used it occasionally as a source of scarce parts, and they would travel out to salvage what they needed. We always provided a light escort for these salvage missions because we never knew when a band of North Vietnamese or local Viet Cong might be lurking out there looking for a likely target. It was just far enough away from the perimeter to make it prudent to provide a little protection.

One day in mid-July we were asked to provide such an escort for a salvage team from the transportation battalion, which wanted to get a couple of urgently needed parts from the hulk. We obliged by sending out three ACAVs from our headquarters security platoon. They formed a short column, the transportation battalion's maintenance crew sandwiched between the ACAVs. When they arrived at the inoperable BARC, the ACAVs formed a loose perimeter facing inland while the maintenance crew clambered up onto the BARC to go to work. Three of the salvage crew began to work on the shore side of the BARC, while the fourth went around the deck to the ocean side. There he lifted a hatch cover in the deck to gain access to the part that he wanted and was startled to see three people moving around in the semidarkness of the partially flooded compartment below him. He dropped the hatch cover back in place with a bang and quickly walked back to the rest of his crew to report what he had uncovered. They hurriedly abandoned their mission and the BARC, eyeing the still-closed hatch uneasily as they did so, and came running over to the nearest ACAV to report what they had found.

Our ACAVs quickly spun around to face the BARC and waited watchfully with their fully loaded heavy machine guns trained on the top of the BARC. The troopers yelled for the occupants to come out, using English and some broken Vietnamese phrases. Nothing happened. After a few minutes, it became apparent that whoever was inside was not coming out. Some of our security platoon troopers put on their gas masks, grabbed some tear-gas grenades, and climbed onto the BARC with drawn pistols at the ready. They opened the hatch that the mechanic had opened and dropped down several tear-gas grenades. Then they slammed the hatch cover shut, stepped back, and waited. In a few moments the hatch cover was pushed up, and eight gagging Vietnamese clawed their way out. They were quickly searched and placed under guard on the sand in back of our ACAVs. Under questioning by an interpreter, who had been sent out to join the group when the incident was reported to the command post over the radio, one of the detainees indicated that there were still some others hiding in the bowels of the BARC. Back went the troopers with their gas masks and pistols to search out the remaining people.

This time they lowered themselves through the hatch into the murky interior. Slowly they worked their way through the maze of fuel lines, electrical wiring, and machinery, but they could find no more Vietnamese. They found food, supplies, some ammunition, but no enemy soldiers. The waist-deep mix of oil and water and the tight space made it impossible to check all the nooks and crannies. Knowing this, the troopers pulled themselves and their confiscated gear back up through the hatch. They then moved back to the waiting ACAVs, which attempted to flush out the remaining enemy soldiers with their heavy machine guns. They peppered the sides of the BARC with their .50-caliber guns, but there was no response. They called back to squadron headquarters and requested a tank. One of B Troop's tanks was dispatched up the beach to join the small cluster of vehicles around the BARC. It fired four high-explosive rounds into the BARC, laying open great gashes in the light metal of its sides. Still no response. The troopers were sure now that nobody inside could have survived the shelling by the tank gun.

Again they climbed onto the BARC and again they lowered themselves into the hull. In a few minutes a voice called out that they had found some more Vietnamese. Slowly eleven more Vietnamese emerged from the open hatch under the watchful eyes of the troopers. They were all a bit dazed from the concussion of the exploding tank shells, but they had not a scratch on them. They had been hidden in the lowest part of the ocean-side corner of the BARC, and the shells had whizzed over without touching them. In all, we had now taken nineteen detainees from what we had thought was an empty, abandoned piece of equipment. We called for a large cargo helicopter and had them flown back to an interrogation center for questioning. We also loaded up the material we had confiscated: grenades, rifle ammunition, web gear, and parts of North Vietnamese uniforms. We did not find any weapons, and we never did hear why or for how long the Vietnamese had been living in that BARC. In the quiet that followed the departure of the helicopter, the transportation battalion mechanics went calmly back to work to salvage the parts that they needed, which had miraculously escaped harm from our shelling.

There was a sequel to this incident. Our new commander decided that he needed to be sure that there were no other bands lurking undetected in similar hiding places, so we spent a day searching our area for other abandoned hulks that might also conceal enemy soldiers. The only other likely hiding place that we were able to turn up was the hulk of an old coastal steamer that lay on its side in the surf several miles to the south of our beach depot. It had been lying there on its side since we had begun operating in the area, and it appeared to be pretty well filled with water when I flew over it to check it out. It also lay considerably farther out in the surf than the BARC had. I thought the chances were pretty slim that anybody could get out to it to hide, and I really doubted that there was enough dry space on her to make a very comfortable hiding place if someone could reach her.

Our commander, however, was eager for his first action and was not to be denied an expedition. He set off with three tanks from one of the troops to make sure that the partially submerged steamer was not being occupied. I flew column cover to point the way and to ensure that the little column did not stumble accidentally into more danger than it had bargained for. The march down was made without incident, however, and the tanks were soon lined up facing the hulk lying in the surf about three hundred yards out. I had the pilot hover us in back of the tanks to observe their fire and to generally keep an eye on the surrounding terrain. The squadron commander fired first. I felt the muzzle blast and watched for the impact, but there was none. Again the tank fired. The squadron commander reported on the radio that he could not spot his round. He fired a third round and still could not spot it, but this time I could. It splashed harmlessly into the water far past the derelict steamer. The other tanks took their turns, but with similar results.

It soon became apparent that our fire-control systems were so far out of alignment that our main tank guns were not able to hit a target at what normally would have been an easy range. We had not used our tank guns at ranges in excess of about two hundred yards since I had joined the squadron, so there had been little motivation to check their accuracy beyond that range despite the dictates of proper policy. Also, we had not really had the opportunity or place to do a thorough boresighting and zeroing exercise for our main guns. The squadron commander was not quite so accepting of this situation. He took it as another example of laxness that needed immediate attention. We quickly identified the worn parts that needed replacement in our tank fire-control systems, and that exercise made it clear that boresighting and zeroing was not going to do much good until we had those replacement parts for the worn systems and some new firing computers. Our busting through the jungle had taken a toll of the main gun linkage on all our tanks. In the month that remained of my tour, we did not receive the items that we needed to regain our long-range capability, and neither did we have a call for it.

One morning not long after our shooting expedition, I was startled to hear heavy machine-gun firing coming from the ocean. I drove down to the beach quickly, but I could see nothing. I then started to check with the Navy over the radio. Eventually we raised a Navy patrol boat and learned that it had been firing at a fishing junk in order to sink it. They had stopped the junk and asked the crew for identity papers because they had been fishing inside the three-mile forbidden zone. The crew did not have papers, and they were therefore taken aboard the patrol boat for delivery to the Vietnamese authorities, but the problem of the junk remained. The Navy solution had been to riddle the hull so that it would sink, and that was the firing we had heard. It was obviously none of our business, but the whole situation sounded a bit strange. We knew that the fishing villages sent their boats out fishing every day, and we doubted that they would want to go out beyond the three-mile zone in their motorless junks. In any event they obviously would have to go through it to get beyond it. It sounded like a case of "you can't get there from here" to us, and we rather doubted that the fishermen would carry their papers with them in an open boat or that the absence of papers warranted sinking their boat. But it was not our affair—we thought—and it was out of sight.

About noon I received a call on my radio from squadron headquarters telling me that there were some very excited Vietnamese men and women at the south edge of our perimeter, where it met the water. I had been checking our maintenance efforts in our vehicle park, but I quickly gathered up an interpreter and headed for the perimeter. I found about forty villagers trying to talk their way past our perimeter positions. They were very excited—angry, really—and they kept pointing out to sea in the direction of our beach operations. Through the interpreter I began to get the other side of the Navy patrol boat incident. The village, which had only one communal junk, was located a mile or so south of us, and the villagers had watched the encounter between their men and the patrol boat early in the morning. Though they did not know exactly what had transpired, they had seen the patrol boat fire at the wooden junk and then pull away. The extremely seaworthy junk did not sink; the bullet holes simply made it ride lower in the water. They did not know the fate of their men, but they could see their junk as it wallowed in the surf.

The villagers had gathered on the shore and followed the junk as the currents took it, hoping that it would be brought in close enough for them to go out and retrieve it—and probably feeling a great deal of fear as to what they would find in it. I had the interpreter explain that their men were safe and that they probably would be returning to the village by night. That helped, but they still wanted their junk, which they pointed to as it bobbed in the surf well within our perimeter. I could not take the chance of letting them come inside the perimeter, and the junk still looked to be too far out for them to hope to retrieve it without help. I supposed that they had thought to simply follow it up the coast until it drifted within reach, but here was our supply depot interfering. Somehow it all did not seem fair, and I told them that we would retrieve their fishing junk for them. They were suspicious; nevertheless, it seemed to mollify them, so I went off to fulfill my promise.

I drove along the beach to where the transportation battalion was busily going about its daily routine of lightering supplies from the cargo ships lying offshore to the beach and arranged with one of the battalion officers to borrow an amphibious supply vehicle for a while. I then had the vehicle follow me back to a point opposite the low-lying junk. I pointed it out to the driver of the amphibious vehicle and explained that I wanted to retrieve the junk so that I could return it to its owners. He looked at me a little strangely, but went at it with a will. After all, it beat making the boring runs back and forth between the shore and a cargo ship.

In short order he reached the junk, where he and his assistant driver managed to get a line on the junk and secure it. Then they headed in. All went well until they got close to shore; then the junk grounded. The amphibious vehicle started to drag it, and the strain on the wood frame of the junk was obvious even to me standing on the shore, so I signaled to the crew to stop. That did not work so well either! Once the slack went out of the line, every incoming swell slammed the junk into the back of the steel amphibious vehicle. I signaled the driver to try to keep the line taut without dragging the junk any farther and ran into the surf to cut the line. Where the junk was foundering, the water was almost waist deep. I used my sheath knife to cut the line, but it was such a thick piece of rope that even though my knife was sharp, it took time. Each incoming roller hit me at shoulder level and threatened to send the junk into me. The thought crossed my mind that it would really be ironic to be injured in the surf trying to rescue a wooden junk after eleven months in combat in Vietnam.

Fortunately that did not happen. The knife cut through the last strands, and my own driver and the assistant driver from the amphibious vehicle joined me in pulling the junk off the sand. We then got some more men to help float the junk south to the perimeter, where we turned it over to the grateful villagers. Their appreciation was a little lessened by the condition of the property I was returning to them. It was a lot the worse for wear. The heavy machine-gun rounds had torn holes in both sides of the boat in a dozen places, and the front had been bashed in by its foundering in the surf during my rescue attempt. In the end I was not sure whether I had made the problems worse by my inept rescue attempts, but I really did not know what else I could have done. Over the next few days the villagers repaired the boat; and then they sailed it off to their village. I wondered what they had done for a livelihood in the meantime, and I wondered if their men had gotten back in good order.

The more I thought about the situation, the angrier I became. Here we were, supposedly protecting the villagers from the enemy while busily destroying their means of making a living. As near as I could tell, they had not been guilty of any illegal activity, and they certainly had not attacked our patrol boat! After a little research, I found out that the three-mile prohibition was a Vietnamese rule imposed by the Vietnamese province chief. I asked why the U.S. Navy was so zealous about enforcing Vietnamese administrative policies, and I was told that it was part of their method of stopping infiltrators from coming ashore. That was not a very satisfactory explanation because it was fairly obvious that the fishermen were not infiltrators—at least a very minimum of checking would have disclosed that. In any event the suspicion should not have warranted the attempt to destroy the junk. In response the Navy told me that anything in that three-mile no-fishing zone was fair game.

It was clear that I was not going to get any satisfaction from the Navy on this one, so I took my complaint to the U.S. Military Assistance Command headquarters in our area. They listened politely to me but offered no solution. Finally, a lieutenant colonel told me that there was little that could be done to change the province chief's edicts and that I was wasting my time. I returned to my squadron unconvinced, but out of time and energy to pursue the subject, which didn't seem to be legitimately in my area of responsibility anyhow. Nevertheless, it surely seemed to go against all that we were trying to accomplish.

My squadron commander had not been terribly pleased with my diverting time to my little mission, and he was delighted when I returned my concentration to the administering of the squadron. I had found that his interest did not lie in the maintenance and supply aspects of the squadron, and, in fact, he had yet to make his way into the squadron maintenance area though it lay immediately across the sand track from our command post. His interest lay in the tactical action, and he was obviously disappointed with the quiet that he had found since his arrival. We, on the other hand, were delighted that the level of activity had slowed, having had our taste of action in the past seven months. We also knew that it was not likely to last, and we were content to enjoy it while it did.

Not so with our commander. He wanted action. In the course of the nightly briefings that we attended at the nearby air cavalry brigade headquarters, he had found that there was an area just to the south of us that had not been checked out in some time. There was a suspicion that there might be some North Vietnamese living there. The area, though just to our south, was separated from us by an unfordable river. As a result, we would have to make a march of some thirty miles in order to gain access with our armored vehicles. He pondered the problem for some days then devised a scheme whereby he would take two troops to sweep the area, leaving me in charge of the defense of the beach depot with only the borrowed infantry company on the perimeter and our own headquarters security platoon with which to do the job. I argued that we should wait until our third troop was released from its mission with the Marines up at Cua Viet, but my arguments were in vain. I pointed out that our primary mission was to protect Wunder Beach, but he did not want to listen. He wanted action, and the fact that he would be leaving the supply depot un-covered and that it would be impossible for him to come to our relief in a timely manner if we were hit during his operation made no dif-ference. Fortunately for me, conflicting requirements from brigade forced him to postpone the operation for the time being, but the in-cident took its toll of my confidence in his judgment.

Still another conflict had arisen between us in the course of plan-ning for that now-postponed operation, and that had to do with the swimming capability of our ACAVs. The armored personnel carriers, which had been turned into ACAVs by the addition of the extra ma-chine guns and gun shields, were capable of swimming. That capa-bility had been lessened somewhat by the addition of the extra weight of the added machine guns and forged steel shields that surrounded them. We had added still more weight with the extra boxes of ma-chine-gun ammunition, piled two deep, that covered the floor of each ACAV. Thus, the flotation capability had become marginal from a weight angle. Added to that marginal condition was the fact that every one of our ACAVs had been hit by some kind of enemy round, had been repaired numerous times, and had waterproof seals that had been dried out from their constant exposure to sand and salt air. Moreover, most of the rear ramp doors were warped to one degree or another from all of these abuses and no longer closed with a water-tight seal. For all these reasons the idea of swimming our ACAVs was an extremely bad idea. We had used them repeatedly for fording with no trouble, but we had not had to swim them in deep water, and we were not anxious to try. My arguments, however, appeared to our new commander to be just further evidence of our general laxness, and he was intent on changing that condition. The postponement of the operation, which had included a swimming phase, took the heat off the subject for the time being, but I was beginning to be very glad that I was getting close to leaving. It was time for a new order to go with the new commander, and it was apparent that my approaches were in conflict with his.

With that kind of conflict as background, I was more than ready when the time came for me to turn over my responsibilities to my replacement. Our operations officer, who had been promoted to that position from troop commander, was envious of my departure because he was even more uncomfortable with the new commander's ideas than I was. He had fought his troop through Tet and our other heavy actions and was not at all pleased to be working for a man who did not seem to appreciate the potential dangers of our operations and the very real limits to our capabilities. Unfortunately, there was nothing that I could do to help the situation.

In the last days of July, I wrote my final efficiency reports on the people who had been so supportive of me during my stint as the executive officer, took my replacement around to meet all my local contacts, and tried to avoid further conflicts with my new commander while still protecting the people who worked for me from some of his extreme ideas. Then I was standing at the helicopter pad for the last time. I had been farewelled at our little officers' mess the evening before, had been presented with a couple of awards at a suitable ceremony, and now I was leaving. The operations officer was there to see me off, and I realized that he and a couple of sergeants were the only ones left who had been with the squadron when I had joined it. Attrition and rotation had taken all the rest. It was obviously time for me to leave too so that the new order could get on with its business without the drag of the remnant of the old regime.

The helicopter made a stop at Camp Evans, which had first emerged out of the thick gray clouds back in March as we hovered straight down out of the overcast to its dirt landing pad on that first trip to

Dong Ha. Today we were making a standard approach to a properly marked blacktop strip under the direction of a control tower. The bustling airfield had cargo helicopters neatly parked along one side in revetments, and everything looked well cared for. What a change! When we lifted off again, we headed south along Highway 1, which was now an unbroken line of asphalt heavy with military and civilian traffic. As we skirted to the west of Hue, I could see our favorite highway bridge. It was completely repaired, and the infamous sunken span was bridged over with a newly decked replacement span. Then we were flying past the landmark radio towers south of Hue and overflying the road into the headquarters at Phu Bai. From there we headed out over the coast to fly around the Hai Van mountain mass before making our approach into Danang Air Base. There I made my way to the passenger terminal with my gear and signed up to hop my last flight south on a cargo plane headed to Bien Hoa. Luck was with me, and shortly I was flying south, sitting in lonely splendor on the crew bench at the back of the air-conditioned cockpit of a C130. At Bien Hoa I called our rear detachment and asked for a jeep to pick me up. After a short wait, I was once more driving along the dusty highway between Bien Hoa and Bear Cat.

I moved into a little wood hootch, which had been built back in December for our field grade officers, for my last few nights in Vietnam, but I spent most of my free time in one of the rear detachment buildings where there were people. At night it was strangely quiet as I lay on my cot, except for the distant sound of artillery, and I missed the background sound of the radio that had been my constant companion for so long. Even sleeping in my makeshift trailer in our command post area, I had been close enough to the command tracks to hear the background hum of the radios—and we had frequently had a small speaker wired in from the command tracks so that we could monitor the radios all the time right in our trailer. Now there was nothing. Along with the absence of radio sounds came the feeling that I no longer knew what was happening. A sudden burst of firing on the Bear Cat perimeter left me wondering what was going on, but they were no longer my troops that were involved out there, and I could no longer get an explanation by simply picking up my hand microphone. I felt helpless and not in control of my environment for the first time since I had joined the squadron seven months earlier. I did not like the feeling.

That feeling was intensified by the fact that the division had pretty well vacated Bear Cat by now. They had moved to their new home in the Delta, and only the administrative support elements remained to follow them. I would be gone before they moved south, but the defense of Bear Cat had passed out of the division's hands, and that did not improve my confidence in the security. Despite my feelings of insecurity, the nights did pass without incident. The days were filled with out-processing, turning in equipment, and purchasing the new accessories that went with my tan uniform as a result of my year in Vietnam. When I boarded the plane for home, I would be wearing for the first time the ribbons that represented the various awards and medals that I had accumulated during the past twelve months. I had given little thought to that change to my uniform during my tour because we lived in the jungle fatigue uniform, but now I realized that I would look like the soldiers in tan uniforms who had been waiting when I walked into the big shed at Bien Hoa a year ago. My uniform would now look as though it had spent a lot of time folded away, and it would now have on it the bits of color that represented service in a combat zone.

The final days went by very quickly. My major coup was obtaining, by pure luck, a seat on one of the charters that belonged to a major airline. These seats were prized because the service was a little better on them, they departed earlier in the day, there was an in-flight movie, and they stopped in Hawaii. Compared to going home, though, all those details were unimportant, but they made the preparations to leave much more exciting. As was the routine, I had to report to the 90th Replacement Company at Long Binh on the day before my flight. I said my goodbyes to D Troop and to our rear detachment and drove that road between Bear Cat and Long Binh in a squadron vehicle for the last time. As I unloaded my baggage at the 90th Replacement Company and thanked my jeep driver for his help, I realized that I was starting to shed my identity as the squadron executive officer. From here on I would be simply another major in the replacement system. I was assigned a small cubicle with a cot, and I spent the evening chatting with other anonymous officers who were either waiting to go home or waiting to start their tour in Vietnam. In the morning I put on my tan uniform for the first time in six months and threw out my last pair of jungle fatigues and jungle boots, which had been my second skin for a year. Shortly we were loading into a bus for the trip to that open-sided, tin-roofed shed that was the passenger terminal building at Bien Hoa Air Base.

In another half hour we were strapped in and taxiing down the runway, which had figured so largely in our action during Tet, and I was lifting off from Vietnam. Ahead of me lay the long flight home, a stop in Honolulu, where I was able to buy a huge bunch of "elephant ears" to take to my girls at home, and the landing at Travis Air Force Base in California. From there I took a taxi to the San Francisco airport and caught a regular commercial flight to New York. I knew that I was back in the United States, but it did not really feel like home yet. That feeling began to sink in when I stepped through the gate at LaGuardia Airport in New York to find my wife and my two daughters, both clad in the muumuus we had purchased for them seven months before in Hawaii. I sat in the back of the car with the two girls as we drove out of the city and up toward West Point. As we passed the familiar landmarks of the area where I had grown up and in which we had lived most recently, I began to believe that my tour in Vietnam had really ended.

# XIII
## Recall

The final struggle between North and South Vietnam began some four years after I left Quang Tri Province. I was in Heidelberg, by then, in the midst of a rainy, foggy autumn with low clouds rolling in and out of the river valley in which that city is located. Unlike the monsoons of four years earlier, this rain bothered me not at all in my clean, dry headquarters job. The newspaper headlines blared the latest North Vietnamese successes against the South Vietnamese, along with the latest bulletins on the peace negotiations that had been undertaken in Paris. I read that fire bases below the Demilitarized Zone were overrun, that the Cua Viet River was in enemy hands, that Quang Tri City was a desolate battleground, and that even Hue, fifty-five miles farther south, was threatened again from the traditional western approach.

Those place names were as familiar to me as my hometown, and I could still visualize the lay of the land and the turnings of the roads in Quang Tri Province as easily as I could recall the neighborhood in which I grew up. Recalling that Asian landscape brought me back sharply to that other rainy season halfway around the world when I had been neither clean nor dry. In the four years since I had left Quang Tri Province, I had learned that not all Army units had been as careful as mine had been about not firing heavy weapons into occupied villages without explicit permission, and I understood that not every Army unit had discriminated so well between armed enemy and apprehensive inhabitant. I had also come to understand the validity of many of the arguments against our involvement in Vietnam and had accepted our final disengagement as a rational course of action that might, in fact, be the only viable alternative left to us.

Notwithstanding all that, when I read that Charlie One had been abandoned (I lost a bunkmate just south of there); that the bridge at Dong Ha had been demolished (we lost nineteen men just north of there, and we could not identify our dead when our vehicles stopped burning); that fire base Bastogne, guarding the western approach to Hue, had been encircled (our detached cavalry troop lost a platoon sergeant each day for almost a week clearing the highway into that key outpost in the mountains overlooking the Ashau Valley); and that Quang Tri City had been overrun (I spent a night under an attack on its southern outskirts that cost us twelve killed and forty-seven wounded); it was hard to remain coolly rational. Those memories, and the memory of friends who were killed or maimed at Loc Ninh or west of Chon Thanh or near any of the other threatened outposts that were suddenly back in the banner headlines, made it very difficult to be objective about the high-level government officials and the largely self-serving protesters and the self-righteous wizards of morality who argued the pros and cons of the fighting in Vietnam for ten long years while men died and roads were built and areas were made secure for the local fishermen and farmers.

As the last American presence was lifted out of the embassy in Saigon some five months later, those memories caused the cavalry-man in me to overcome my intellectual pretensions and my logical thought processes. There welled up in me an insistent cry of frustration and bitterness directed at all the impotent talkers and planners and critics who claimed to know more about the war in Vietnam than the participants, while we in the U.S. Army were making our sacrifices, taking our wounds, and burying our dead.

As if those feelings of frustration and bitterness were not burden enough for those of us who served, there has followed the endless media mythology that the U.S. Army was defeated on the ground. As recently as October 1983, I came across an article in a major daily newspaper that characterized the final evacuation of the embassy in Saigon as "a dispirited American Army abandoning Saigon." The continued dissemination of such misinformation—the U.S. Army had turned over the fighting to the South Vietnamese months before Saigon fell, and only a few advisors and the State Department people remained when the final evacuation took place—continues to deprive our soldiers of the recognition for what they accomplished day in and day out on the ground.

The cruel epithet from the Civil War about "whoever saw a dead cavalryman"—the implication being that cavalry was always seen going to or coming from the battle, but never in it—was particularly appropriate to the media representatives who reported on Vietnam. Few of them were ever in the field until the major combat action was over. They congregated in great numbers at our major air bases and in Saigon, but they rarely lived with the troops in the field long enough to understand the context of what they were reporting. The television crews arrived after the major action, looking for sensational shots, but they never hung around long enough to record with any kind of sympathy what the troops faced day in and day out that brand of reporting apparently belonged to a previous generation of war correspondents. In fact, most of the media representatives who covered Vietnam were too young to have had the experience of World War II or Korea to draw on for comparison. By and large they had no experience of the military at all. They belonged to a generation that could easily escape military service entirely, and they were far more familiar with the college campus and the street protest than with the soldiers or the Army that they were writing about. To this lack of personal context, they added the antiestablishment bias of the era and a crusading fervor to find fault, even if they lacked the expertise to sort out perceived fault from real fault. Both kinds were reported daily, without any balancing accounts of our successes.

The most pernicious of all the media representatives were the television people. They had the same biases and fervors as their newsprint brethren, but it was intensified by their shorter deadlines and their greater need for sensationalism to earn prime time for their material. If we failed to provide a timely gaffe, they made one: they staged an ear cutting from an enemy corpse or edited footage for sensational impact—always out of context and usually with unfavorable implications for the U.S. Army.

During my subsequent year at the Command and General Staff College at Fort Leavenworth, a television network vice president came to talk to the officer student body about television journalism. Our questions centered on this apparent television quest for sensationalism. He defended it by telling us that "dog bites man" is just not news! Subsequently, I was to witness that same trite philosophy applied to race and drug problems in the U.S. Army in Europe after Vietnam. Support for a preconceived "man bites dog" story was somehow always wrenched out of the raw material to the disadvantage of the military establishment.

The coverage of Tet, 1968, is still the best example of that kind of selection process. Despite ardent disavowals, the attack on the embassy in Saigon, which was far more convenient to most journalists than the fighting in the countryside, received significantly more emphasis from the media than the very real American victory that ensued. The impression still retained by the general American public is that the embassy was the key action of Tet. That lasting impression testifies to the lasting effect of that particular piece of journalistic selectivity. The media's intentions were, in fact, irrelevant; what is relevant is the image that was conveyed. So well did the media do their work that even veterans of previous wars began to believe that Vietnam was somehow a less-worthy combat experience than their own.

If this account of my tour in Vietnam with combat units of the U.S. Army counters that image to some small degree and strikes a familiar chord with other ground combat veterans of other wars, then I have been successful. My goal has been to show that in combat only the names and the specific weapons change; the rest is timeless. What my generation of soldiers did in Vietnam is the same thing that other generations of soldiers did in World War II and Korea. We did no better, but we certainly did no worse. As for those from the concerned generations who did not serve during our years of involvement in Vietnam, I fall back on something that Oliver Wendell Holmes, Jr., said: "I think that, as life is action and passion, it is required of a man that he should share the passion and action of his time at peril of being judged not to have lived." Those of us who fought in Vietnam have lived in full measure; those who did not can never join our ranks. Recall has sounded!